UNSETTLED SUBJECTS

UNSETTLED SUBJECTS

Restoring Feminist Politics to

Poststructuralist Critique

S U S A N   L U R I E

Duke University Press   Durham and London   1997

© 1997 Duke University Press
All rights reserved
Printed in the United States of America
on acid-free paper ∞
Typeset in Sabon by Keystone Typesetting, Inc.
Library of Congress Cataloging-in-Publication Data appear
on the last printed page of this book.

To the memory of my mother
Odesse Ogul Lurie

CONTENTS

ACKNOWLEDGMENTS

Many friends and colleagues have contributed to this project. I would like to thank Elizabeth Abel for her support since the earliest moments of this study and for providing a model of critical excellence to which I continually aspire. Paula Sanders not only has made incisive comments on the manuscript but has been a constant source of emotional and intellectual sustenance. I am grateful, too, to Jane Dailey, Scott Derrick, Diane Dillon, Carla Kaplan, Chris Newfield, David Nirenberg, and Meredith Skura for their comments at various stages in the writing of this book. Among the readers of my manuscript, I owe a special debt of thanks to Helena Michie and Carol Quillen for their invaluable criticism and advice. I would also like to express my gratitude to the two anonymous readers for Duke University Press for their helpful responses. At Duke, too, it has been my good fortune to work with Ken Wissoker; I cannot imagine a more gracious and insightful editor.

Rice University provided research funding and leave time, for which I am very grateful. I also thank the Beatrice Bain Foundation at UC Berkeley, where I was a research associate early on in this project, for providing both full access to the university's facilities and an inspiring community of feminist scholars.

I appreciate very much the valuable research assistance of Chuck Jackson and Brinda Roy and the skillful proofreading of Terry Munisteri. I am particularly indebted to Louise Penner, who tirelessly assisted me in the final preparation of the manuscript.

INTRODUCTION

Theorizing Female Subjectivity

Academic feminist criticism is now over twenty years old, and its history has congealed into a familiar narrative: beginning with critiques of male (historical, legal, cultural) constructions of "woman," feminist criticism soon turned its primary attention to women's history and cultural productions. While initial efforts focused predominantly on white, middle-class women, subsequent criticism both exposed these limits and expanded them, emphasizing and elaborating differences between women in race, class, nation, ethnicity, and sexuality. Initiated by feminists who were excluded and/or misrepresented by mainstream feminist accounts of "women," the focus on women's differences was underwritten as well by poststructuralist feminism, which stressed not only the multiple referents for the category of "woman" but also the differences within particular female subjects. Concern with both kinds of difference has produced the most recent object of feminist theoretical inquiry: the self-different female subject, situated at diverse cultural locations, for whom gender intersects dynamically with numerous other social categories and discourses.

Working with this complex model of female subjectivity, feminists have pursued a range of important practices: the critique of the biases in white middle-class feminism; the description of feminist agency as an effect of instability in both subjects and terms; the investigation of interarticulations of gender with other cultural categories and discourses; and the effort to reformulate politicized referents for diverse women's subordination in the context of decentered subjectivity. However, these practices have developed unevenly and have generated various dynamics. While it is clearly possible and indeed necessary for each of these approaches to female subjectivity to enhance the others, tenacious impasses have also arisen between them. Specifically, the indispensable critique of feminist identity, along with the thematic link between unstable subjects and feminist agency, often functions to impede the poststructuralist analysis of female subordination.

Unsettled Subjects contributes to present efforts to displace such impasses and thus to expand feminism's capacity to use poststructuralist methodologies as much for the critique of patriarchal power as for the critique of feminism.[1] Recognizing that questions of female subjectivity are far from settled makes room for foregrounding descriptions of the relation between dominant gender ideology and its effects on "unsettled" female subjects — ones who negotiate multiple and unstable positions. Whereas poststructuralist feminism has encountered difficulties in formulating and pursuing descriptions of this kind, I will argue that a range of twentieth-century American women writers have prioritized such representations at diverse historical moments and in a variety of cultural settings. Indeed, historicizing such representations points to the urgent need for models that instigate feminist inquiry into the relation between dominant gender ideology and its effects on plural subjectivity. Moreover, I will further argue, illuminating such relations between female subjection and female self-difference is crucial both to apprehending the construction and to resisting the persistence of the impasses that have steered poststructuralist feminism theory away from feminist inquiry.

Numerous critics have noted the impasses that result when the critique of feminist identity produces "a persistently negative critique" that reduces difference between and within women to indifference regarding feminist aims (Chow 104). Paradoxically, feminist analyses of biases in white, middle-class feminism tend to produce a shift in critical attention from gender to other categories of analysis; the feminists under discussion emerge instead as agents of their race, class, and national positions. Furthermore, these critiques also frequently do not pursue the very contextualized accounts of different women that they forcefully recommend; thus the important emphasis on difference does not lead to inquiries into the shape of female subjection in diverse localities.[2]

Perhaps even more paradoxically, poststructuralist indifference to feminist aims informs specifically *feminist* claims about the shape of agency. Claims that the female subject constitutes "the permanent possibility of a certain resignifying process" (Butler, "Contingent Foundations" 13), that the continual reformulation of complex identities for the self-different female subject enables positive change, have more frequently underwritten a faith in future possibilities than the investigation of specific strategies for and shapes of such reconfigurations. Indeed, as theorists of third world women's agency have argued, mainstream theoretical feminism paradoxically has neglected to cite and to analyze existing material instances of the very kinds of resistance practices that it theorizes.[3]

While some critics have attributed this tendency to evacuate feminist politics from feminist theory to poststructuralism's insistence on the instability of political subjects and categories,[4] I locate the same impasse in the tenacity of paradigms that foreclose questions about how patriarchal power orchestrates female self-difference. Whereas such questions can be motivated only by a model that investigates the subject's interarticulated positions, the critique of feminist identity most often apprehends self-division as a matter of shifts between distinct positions.[5] And although poststructuralist theories of agency emphasize such interactive dynamics — transformations in gendered meanings rely on the continual (re)configuring of any one subject position with numerous others — the very association of such processes with resistance has blocked or marginalized their role in securing and maintaining subjection.

Increasingly, however, theorists are recognizing the need to investigate how power as well as resistance profits from self-different subjects and their participation in ongoing processes of resignification.[6] As Eve Sedgwick has argued in relation to queer theory, deconstructive approaches must begin to train attention on how discursive regulation can be enabled as well as undermined by the contradictions inherent to and supportive of complex configurations of meaning and identity (10). Instead of only staging a contest between juridical, exclusive meanings and the multiple, contradictory ones that can displace them, Sedgwick suggests that deconstructive analyses also consider "contests for discursive power . . . as competitions for the material or rhetorical leverage required to set the terms of, and to profit in some way from, the operations of . . . an incoherence of definition" (11). Following out Sedgwick's suggestion, Biddy Martin has noted the importance of interrogating how such "contests for discursive power" operate at the level of the self-different subject. She argues that an emphasis on the liberatory possibilities of the subject whose gender is continually articulated with numbers of other positions often forecloses an interrogation of how complex (re)signifying processes anchor and reify dominant configurations of gender (107).

As regards feminist practice, such an interrogation would seek to reveal

how dominant gender ideology secures the "material or rhetorical leverage" that sets the terms for intersections between gender and a female
subject's multiple (and often contradictory) other identifications (Sedgwick
11). On this model, moreover, differences between women can be cali-
brated not only in terms of membership in different social categories (e.g.,
race, class, nation, sexuality), but also in terms of how female subordination is cohered in various contexts with different women's multiple other
beliefs. Formulating difference between women in this way also can at one
time ground feminist alliances across social boundaries in a shared opposition to such structures of domination and keep visible their different consequences at discrete cultural sites.

However, even as critics begin to turn their attention to the relation
between gender ideology and female self-difference, it is important to recall
that poststructuralist feminism, in its long-standing privileging of the critique of feminist identity and the celebration of emancipatory instabilities,
has been notably resistant to such a reformulation. While the emergence of
new models and practices is cause for feminist optimism, there remains
reason to be wary of continued impediments to an inquiry into what are
arguably dominant gender ideology's most powerful and most covert operations. *Unsettled Subjects* begins, therefore, by interrogating such obstacles
themselves precisely in terms of the inquiry they stave off: how patriarchal
ideology profits from the female subject's negotiation of simultaneous
agendas.

Tenacious conceptual impasses in feminist theory, I suggest, are themselves products of how dominant gender ideology is capable of setting the
terms for the convergence of a critic's feminist and other beliefs, specifically
her subscription to other radical democratic discourses. A general symptom of this operation is that the very definition of "oppositional feminist
critique" has functioned to underwrite the impasse I have described as the
suspension of feminist practice between important critiques of feminist
identity and the analysis of patriarchal power. Indeed, in recent debates a
crucial tension has emerged between feminism's oppositional critique of
patriarchy and its status as radical democratic politics, with the troubling
result that feminism emerges as most oppositional when it is engaged in a
critique of feminism.

Chapter 1, "Poststructuralist Feminist Subjects," explores how the retreat from analyses of dominant gender ideology to other emancipatory
agendas affects the theorization of female subjectivity itself. Directing questions of subjection and self-difference to feminist theorists themselves, I

argue that poststructuralist theorists can be the very regulated subjects they fail to theorize adequately. We can understand the impasses that critics encounter to formulating a model of the subject that could explain how dominant gender ideology regulates female self-difference as symptoms precisely of such regulation at work. To the extent that patriarchal ideology succeeds in setting the terms for how their feminism is configured with their other radical democratic commitments, these critics neglect to consider and/or displace incipient attention to new models of the subject with a focus on prevailing "emancipatory" ones: the critique of feminist identity and the valorization of the unstable subject's capacity for resignification.

Yet if an analysis of these impasses reveals the relation between domination and self-difference that these critics fail to theorize fully, the three essays I discuss in chapter 1 also contest the poststructuralist retreat from feminist analysis. Some moments of such contestation point instructively toward the limits of the ability of dominant gender ideology to interpellate the feminist subject via her other oppositional commitments. When announced commitments to politicizing the unstable subject for feminism produce only critiques of female and feminist identity, the discrepancy comes to the fore. And when practices that are assumed to be emancipatory ones fail to enhance any oppositional politics and/or emerge as sustaining racist and classist ideologies, they come under scrutiny for their failures for feminism as well. At the same time, what promises to be a more consistently productive mode of intervention also emerges in these essays: the revision of prevailing theoretical models in light of the historicization of particular women's representations. Such contextualization not only disarms a priori theoretical agendas that can covertly reify patriarchal ideology, it also grounds new and more adequate theoretical models.

Throughout this study I contend that historicizing female and feminist subjects underscores the importance of a particular model for feminist analysis: the recognition that patriarchal power regulates as well as succumbs to the female subject's negotiation of multiple, interarticulated discourses. Furthermore, whereas poststructuralist feminism's difficulties in developing and/or pursuing such a model register in large part the regulation of the critic's multiple oppositional commitments, the outcome of this process has also prevented a feminist investigation of the coarticulation of gender subordination with discourses of domination. This latter inquiry has been all but unthinkable within poststructuralist analyses, in which the discussion of feminist alliances with dominant positions almost invariably produces a shift away from gender as a category of analysis for privileged women. Indeed, in this context, where the unsettling of prevailing models of subjectivity has proven most difficult, the historicization of women's writing is crucial to achieving unanticipated descriptions of the female subject. Thus *Unsettled Subjects* contextualizes female subordination in order to reveal it as the product of dynamic interarticulations of gender with both oppositional and dominant discourses. At the same time, this book charts feminist agency as the production of counter such interarticulations. In all instances the degree of success for feminist resignifications enabled by plural subjectivity and unstable terms relies upon the speaker's recognition of the dominant regulation of women's self-difference.

Historicizing the Feminist Subject in American Women Writers

Poststructuralist feminism's privileging of the critique of feminist identity and its emphasis on the possibilities of resignification have their analogues in new historicist interpretation. But while these two descriptions of the unstable feminist subject are usually opposed in poststructuralist feminism (feminist identity is exclusionary and feminist resignification is emancipatory), the two modes often collapse in new historicist accounts of white middle-class women writers. As Philip Fisher describes it, the new historicism demonstrates "the power of rhetorics, the incomplete dominance of representation and the borrowing or fusing of successful formulas of representation" (xv). However, new historical criticism of white women's writing tends to turn attention away from the feminist resistance to patriarchal representation, focusing rather on these women's participation in dominant discourses. In these accounts, feminist rhetorical interventions and borrowings often become indistinguishable from a manifestation only of class and/or race identity.[7] At the same time, investigations of women's efforts to enlist prevailing oppositional rhetorics for feminist aims, and of the difficulties they encounter in doing so, are strikingly absent. As a result, crucial considerations for a historicized feminist inquiry are neglected: questions of how certain subordinate subjects can be barred from access to existing emancipatory rhetorics; questions of how available liberatory discourses can help secure rather than displace female subordination; questions of the difference that gender subordination makes in an otherwise privileged female or feminist subject's negotiation of dominant positions; and inquiries into the negative consequences for feminism itself of its alliances with discourses of domination.[8]

Moreover, as in the case of poststructuralist feminism, new historical shifts from gender to other categories of analysis betray the critic's own vulnerability to pressures that deflect attention from feminist inquiry. As Judith Fetterly has recently claimed, how critics describe American women writers who are simultaneously disadvantaged and advantaged is a matter of political preference: "[W]hite and black women writers emerge from and represent in their works complex combinations of privilege and disadvantage.... [H]ow we construct these writers — as complicit, as resistant, or as some combination of these positions — is a *choice* we make on grounds essentially political" (608).

In this study, I make the choice that Fetterly argues is more often displaced by other constructions of the multiply positioned woman writer: to pursue a feminist analysis of American women's feminist writing, both theoretical and literary. In doing so, I seek to expand the critical choices available for the feminist interpretation of "complex combinations of privilege and disadvantage" by training attention on the way dominant gender ideology makes use of these combinations. As I have noted, chapter 1 analyzes the critical choices made by poststructuralist feminists in terms of the workings of this ideology. In the subsequent chapters I discuss three writers — Zora Neale Hurston, Ellen Glasgow, and Elizabeth Bishop — all of whom predicate effective feminist interventions on apprehending precisely the structure of subjectivity that has proven so difficult to formulate for poststructuralist feminism and the new historicism alike. Indeed, my contextualization of these writers' texts reveals their respective efforts to appropriate powerful political, psychological, sociological, and anthropological rhetorics in order to illuminate and politicize the complex construction of female subordination at diverse cultural sites.

As is the case with the theorists I discuss in the first chapter, Hurston, Glasgow, and Bishop write at historical junctures where, as a consequence of prominent political/cultural events and developments in theories of the subject, American feminism is poised to make signal inroads in revealing the operations of dominant gender ideology at the level of the subject. Whereas poststructuralist feminism has encountered obstacles to discerning and/or pursuing these operations, the literary writers foreground the role of self-difference in female subjection and predicate agency on reformulating the dynamics among multiple, intersecting positions. However, these writers also gloss the theoretical impasses by stressing the difficulties they face in making their analyses visible to their respective interpretive communities.

For both Hurston and Glasgow their novels are deliberate efforts to pursue and evaluate emerging opportunities for such illuminations. Hurston's indictment of how race and gender are coarticulated for the black female subject constitutes her contribution to contested and newly prominent Harlem Renaissance referents for "the black cultural experience." At the same time, she tries to appropriate antiracist analyses of intraracial power dynamics emerging from both African American folklore and the recent Scottsboro trials in order to denounce the silencing of black feminism by antiracism. Glasgow's novels invoke new theories of subjectivity as well as infamous political events of the period to illuminate and disrupt what she regards as the most important obstacle to white middle-class women's social evolutionary "development": the regulation of dynamics between their advantaged and disadvantaged positions that recruits consent to gendered subordination and threatens to recuperate feminist agency. Bishop's writing of the sixties and seventies similarly focuses on how feminism can be undermined by a subject's alliances with privileged positions. Her metacritique of her own efforts to authorize feminist resignifications with colonialist rhetorics links the female subject's early development to the adult feminist's quest for such authority. What Bishop comes to recognize about her own vexed strategies leads her to identify such self-destructive tactics as feminism's most urgent concern.

The Trajectory of the Text

In contrast to the theorists I consider in chapter 1, Zora Neale Hurston has no trouble discerning that her emancipatory commitments elsewhere can be mobilized to censure her feminist expression. Indeed this recognition is the focus of the texts I discuss, whose aims are both to expose and eliminate such censorship. Chapter 2, "Antiracist Rhetorics and the Female Subject: The Trials of Zora Neale Hurston," explores Hurston's strategies in *Their Eyes Were Watching God* (1937) and in her newspaper coverage of the trial of Ruby McCollum (1953) for indicting and displacing the intraracial codes of silence that prohibit black feminism in the name of antiracism. Hurston attempts to counter such codes by reformulating the intersection between antiracism and feminism for black women; to do this she forges antiracist rhetorics that support rather than proscribe black feminist analysis. Against the antiracism aligned with black male empowerment, Hurston invokes emerging discourses both from the rural folklore she herself had collected and from recent events at Scottsboro, discourses which illuminated and condemned intraracial deployments of antiracist and solidarity rhetorics for harmful ulterior motives. During the novel's trial scene, on which the chapter focuses, Hurston invokes these antiracist analyses in order to indict the misuse of black resistance rhetorics to enforce codes of silence.

In the end, however, Hurston emphasizes the continual contest between such reformulations of the relation between black feminism and antiracism and the reigning configuration of the two: the use of antiracism to silence feminism. This kind of contest is at issue when *Their Eyes* provides the intertext for her coverage of the trial of Ruby McCollum, a black woman who killed her white lover. Allusions to the novel in these articles, I argue, continue Hurston's efforts both to indict intraracial codes of silence with the antiracist rhetorics empowered by prominent, racist trials and to insist on the difficulties of recruiting these rhetorics for black feminism. While Hurston's texts display breathtaking alignments of black feminism with an array of black resistance discourses, they also stress that displacing reigning such configurations requires a community-wide recognition of how domination, in both sexism and racism, profits from the regulation of self-difference.

The desire for a similar public recognition of how power regulates self-difference also emerges as central to both Glasgow's and Bishop's notions of white middle-class feminist resistance. Whereas the first two chapters of *Unsettled Subjects* explore the capacity of dominant gender ideologies to profit from the coarticulation of a subject's feminism with other emancipatory discourses, the final two chapters investigate how female subordination is secured and feminism undermined by their respective articulations with discourses of domination. Chapter 3, "Women's Development and 'Composite' Subjectivity: Feminism and Social Evolution in Ellen Glasgow," first discusses Glasgow's efforts to bring to light an otherwise covert configuration of female subordination with race and class privilege by invoking both prominent political events and emerging notions of mental life. Her early novel *The Voice of the People* (1900) draws on both discourses to construct an analogy between the nonelite white politician, turned against his own class interests by an investment in empowered white masculinity, and the elite white woman compelled, despite her love for him, to reproduce within the "fittest class."

True to the aims of "eugenics" as Francis Galton described them in 1883, *The Voice*'s Eugenia Battle loses her battle against elite patriarchal controls over her reproductive choices. But this loss is also the occasion for Glasgow to resignify Darwin's "struggle for survival" as Eugenia's efforts to resist the dynamics that produce a self-policing of heretical desires. Such dynamics between a subject's advantaged and subordinate positions are already visible in the demise of the biracial Readjuster movement in late-nineteenth-century Virginia. Glasgow hopes to make this demise the model for the elite female subordination invisible within the terms of both class struggle and elite theories of social evolution. Like Hurston, however, Glasgow stresses the difficulty of constructing alliances, based on a shared recognition of how power works with self-difference, between the disenfranchised male and the woman whose subordination is desirable to him.

In *The Voice* Glasgow has recourse to another of Galton's concepts, that of composite mental imaging (modeled on his composite photographs of social types), to describe the mental processes whereby both nonelite white men and elite women consent to oppression. In her later and better known novel *Barren Ground* (1925), Glasgow links this kind of consent to Freud's oedipal male subject, against which she poses the feminist subject's resistance to such dynamics. This resistance, set in motion by an illegitimate pregnancy that produces identifications across social boundaries, foils the class and race distinctions that are the condition for elite women's misrecognition of gendered subordination as privilege.

However, the cross-class and cross-race identifications made possible by the effort in Virginia to sterilize Carrie Buck, a poor white woman deemed "unfit" on the basis solely of her illegitimate reproduction, are also the occasion to revitalize the distinctions that recruit consent to gendered oppression. At the same time that such identifications liberate *Barren Ground*'s protagonist from her fantasies of a privileged but subordinate femininity, they lead to change only for the white woman. A continued inscription in vexed distinctions shows up as well in her tendency to authorize unpopular feminist interventions with the racist rhetoric that, Glasgow stresses, nullifies feminist aims. It is a temptation, moreover, that at times the narration itself does not escape. Yet, by measuring such multiple effects of cross-cultural identification in terms of their assets and liabilities for feminist change, Glasgow stresses the need to guard against the slippage between emancipatory identifications and exploitative ones. Ultimately, she predicates her vision of a feminist social evolution on transmitting culture to specifically "nonoedipal" subjects who are capable of resisting, with the help of productive identifications with disadvantaged others, the dominant regulation of self-division.

As is the case with Glasgow's novels, Elizabeth Bishop's poetry and travel writing represent female subjectivity as a site of contestations over the effects of intersecting disadvantaged and advantaged positions. And, like Glasgow in *Barren Ground,* Bishop emphasizes the similarity between the mechanisms that exploit subordinate female subjects' self-difference and the dynamics that undermine feminist agency. Also influenced by psychoanalysis, Bishop constructs female subjects who are, unlike Glasgow's, as vulnerable to oedipal dynamics as males. Specifically, the child's identification with competing maternal and cultural voices is the precursor of an adult feminist subjectivity torn between resistance and the terror of the losses that it will mean. Such speakers' strategies are poetic in a way that implicates poetic multivalence in the preservation rather than the disruption of dominant ideology: they pursue a simultaneous "calling . . . and retreating" (Bishop, "Brazil, January 1, 1502") that embeds resisting representation in the very discourses that proscribe it.

Chapter 4, " 'Caught in a Skein of Voices': Feminism and Colonialism in Elizabeth Bishop," focuses on the shape these strategies take in Bishop's writing about Brazil: the use of American colonialist rhetoric to authorize figurations of feminist and homoerotic representation. The figurations at stake throughout this writing, I argue, are resignifications of Melanie Klein's notions of "good" and "bad" mothers, ones meant to extricate Klein's paradigms of female development from their patriarchal thematics. However, my foregrounding of this vexed fusing of colonialist and feminist discourses is also the occasion to trace Bishop's metacritiques of her own strategies in the Brazil poems and in the travel book *Brazil* (1962). Even as these texts appeal to colonialist rhetorics for authorization, they also register Bishop's awareness that her feminism is both urged toward and undermined by such "empowering" rhetorics. What the Brazil writing offers, I argue, is Bishop's persistent meditation on the complex psychic and social pressures that inform her productions of feminist resignifications, including those she initially presents as simply the happy effects of linguistic instability. Like Glasgow, she shows that emancipatory rearticulations can also provide the occasion for dominant ideology to reassert itself.

Bishop's final feminist project elevates producing a vigilance about strategies for resignification over an uncritical pursuit of resignifying unstable terms. I conclude this chapter with a discussion of the later poem, "In the Waiting Room" (1971), which imagines a revisionary psychoanalytic antidote to the orchestration of women's advantaged and disadvantaged positions that recuperates feminist resistance for dominant gender ideology. Here a revised Kleinian "good mother," supported not by colonialist rhetorics but by a feminist reformulation of Klein's terms, makes the condition for good mothering and its corollary, community membership, a vigilance against mediating resistance with dominant discourses.

A recognition of how power profits from self-difference, preferably one that is public knowledge in the respective interpretive communities addressed, emerges from all three of these writers as a central condition for feminist change. Indeed, each one tries to resignify a pivotal concept in the influential discourses of their time to produce a vigilance against this mode of domination: for Hurston this concept is the "black antiracist subject," for Glasgow it is the Darwinian "struggle for survival," and for Bishop it is the Kleinian "good mother." At the same time, these writers attribute the difficulty of displacing hegemonic configurations not only to the tenacity of entrenched meanings but also to continual contests between power and resistance for leverage over the feminist subject's multiple agendas, contests that appear to heat up especially as she pursues emancipatory resignifications.

For poststructuralist feminist theory these contests have been staged largely over the coarticulation of the critic's feminist aims with her other oppositional commitments. But the institutional support enjoyed by that feminist theory which favors the critique of feminism over feminist critique may register the role of the critic's privileged investments as well. Pressuring feminism simultaneously from radical democratic and conservative directions, then, dominant gender ideology has worked to block the descriptions of the subject that can enable the most effective feminist analysis. *Unsettled Subjects* pursues these descriptions; but as the following chapters illuminate the unstable subject as the site for complex regulation, they also chart the successful modes of contestation, in both the theoretical and literary texts, that can guide more adequate formulations of feminist agency.

Chapter 1

POSTSTRUCTURALIST FEMINIST SUBJECTS

Even as feminists increasingly investigate the relation between unstable female subjects and dominant gender ideology, I have argued, it is important to interrogate the impasses that have impeded and continue to compete with such promising developments. These impasses occur when the preoccupation with the critique of feminist identity, a critique that importantly destabilizes the category of "woman," also functions to deflect attention from the analysis of patriarchal power. And the complementary approach to the critique of identity, the celebration of a female subject's capacity for resignification, most often theorizes future possibilities that remain unformulated. Together these modes of analysis have led poststructuralist feminism away from feminist analysis, a trajectory that has been authorized in radical democratic terms; for feminism is frequently deemed most oppositional when it performs or advocates self-critique. When such oppositional insistence on differences between women functions primarily to shift categories of analysis from gender to other ones (e.g., race, class, nation), however, patriarchal power is granted an immunity to interrogation.

In this chapter I discuss three essays that respond to this impasse by attempting to reformulate politicized referents for the female and/or feminist subject. What all three demonstrate is why models of subjectivity that direct attention to how gendered domination relies on as well as succumbs to a subject's self-difference have been difficult both to formulate and to pursue. At issue is a competition between possible new oppositional formulations of subjectivity and reigning ones, which often retain their predominance. On the occasions when new models succeed in emerging, they remain vulnerable to displacement by the prevailing models that privilege for feminist politics the critique of identity and the valorization of multiple reference as emancipatory.

These difficulties in formulating a countermodel of the subject register, I will argue, precisely the operation of the regulatory mechanisms that cannot be fully illuminated without such a model. That is, the impasses in these essays emerge as themselves the product of how dominant gender ideology governs the critic's negotiation of multiple political and institutional commitments. In the case of these poststructuralist feminists, then, we can see how the regulation of female self-difference succeeds in preventing the emergence of the very formulations that could expose it. Yet to varying degrees and as a consequence of their commitment to feminist politics, the three essays also contest this prohibition. As we shall see, such contestation emerges from the capacity of oppositional politics to undermine the patriarchal agendas for which they can be appropriated and from historicizing female and feminist subjectivity.[1]

I begin with a discussion of Judith Butler's "Contingent Foundations: Feminism and the Question of 'Postmodernism'" (1992), which prioritizes for poststructuralist feminism, and in the name of radical democratic politics, a polemic against stable referents for feminist terms. However, the very feminist issues she raises to support this polemic reveal its limits, including the fact that its a priori oppositional status blocks the emergence of crucial alternative descriptions of unstable subjectivity. From here I turn to the practice of white poststructuralist feminism as it interprets black women's culture and texts. It is in this context that the critique of white feminist identity is both indispensable and vulnerable to appropriations by dominant gender ideology. Christine Stansell's "White Feminists and Black Realities: The Politics of Authenticity" (1992) makes a conceptual leap for feminist theory, as it distinguishes between productive and conservative modes of the critique of white feminist identity. In another important move, Stansell calls for replacing a model of the subject that shifts people between categories with one that examines the effects of interarticulated positions. Nonetheless, despite a productive application of this model to black women's subordination, she continues to explain the coarticulation of race and gender for white women only in terms of an exclusionary white identity. If, in the course of this essay, a new oppositional formulation of unstable subjectivity emerges for black women, its application to white women is intercepted by privileging the critique of white identity.

Barbara Johnson's "Thresholds of Difference: Structures of Address in Zora Neale Hurston" (1987) explicitly links the possibility of rethinking

deconstruction's models of difference to the multiple agendas a critic negotiates. That is, she overtly thematizes the process that, I am arguing, governs covertly the projects of all three of these essays. Moreover, she discerns
in such structures of problematic address a similarity between the pressures
on her own writing and those that Hurston negotiates. Despite these insights, however, her rethinking of the relation between self-difference and
race representation is inhibited precisely by the multiple political and theoretical agendas she initially notes. These produce a prohibition against
feminist reading in the name of antiracism whose hallmark, for both Hurston and herself, is the inability to distinguish a regulatory from an emancipatory self-critique.

I conclude my discussion on the note of recuperation, not in deference to
a monolithic, implacable mode of regulation but in order to foreground the
importance of continually interrogating how power makes use of self-
difference. At the same time, as I have noted, these essays also register the
possibilities for resignification that poststructuralist feminists have been
prone to celebrate. Such celebrations, present here in both Butler and
Johnson, however, must be qualified by the difficulty of resignification dramatized by all the essays; for all three document a competition in which the
self-difference that is the condition for challenging received meanings and
identities is at the same time the condition for a reassertion of them.

Framing the Subject of Feminism

Judith Butler's article, "Contingent Foundations," responds to feminist
concerns that postmodernism, by destabilizing terms for female subjects
and female bodies, disempowers feminist politics. However, her laudable
effort to make such instabilities the very condition for a radical democratic
feminism is limited by a singular preoccupation with persuading feminists
to destabilize their terms. As a result of this tenacious focus, an argument
for a destabilization of terms that enables multiple (but unexplored) future
meanings blocks a consideration of how dominant gender ideology also
profits from self-difference and unstable terms.

By thinking of politicized categories as efficacious but contingent and
mutable, Butler usefully claims, deconstructing feminism's terms widens
the scope of rather than prohibits a "political necessity to speak as and for
women" (15): "To deconstruct the subject of feminism is not, then, to
censure its usage, but, on the contrary, to release the term into a future of

multiple significations, to emancipate it from the maternal or racialist ontologies to which it has been restricted, and to give it play as a site where unanticipated meanings might come to bear" (16).

The virtue of this formulation is, as Butler phrases it in a later text, that "the sense of futurity opened up by the [political] signifier as a site of rearticulations . . . is the discursive occasion for hope" (*Bodies That Matter* 219). By "politicizing *dis*identification" (219), women excluded by certain formulations of "woman" can resignify the term. And different female subjects, even as they deploy their respective articulations of "women," can keep the term under continual suspicion, not only for its potential exclusions but for its possible recuperation by patriarchal meanings.

But although such a deconstruction of the feminist subject promises hope for, rather than aims to censure, the political usage of feminist terms, here it does not lead to an exploration of what such a usage might look like for particular women. Instead of discussing possible articulations of feminist subjectivity, Butler proceeds to keep the feminist "question of postmodernism" focused on a polemic about the need to deconstruct feminist categories. If this polemic can be seen as leaving to others the politicized articulations it also advocates, a crucial "unanticipated" description of feminist subjectivity is foreclosed altogether: the subject whose potential for rearticulation, enabled by her self-difference, is the condition for producing and maintaining patriarchal meanings. This description of the subject cannot emerge, I will argue, on account of the referents Butler attributes to "restricting" and "emancipatory" discursive strategies, respectively: restriction is a function of exclusionary identifications and "the release [of stable terms] into a future of multiple significations" ("Contingent Foundations" 16) is the condition for emancipation. This opposition between restrictive identity and a liberating production of different significations precludes questions of how patriarchal power can regulate, as well as succumb to, multiple referents for and continual renegotiations of what "woman" means. And prime among such elided questions is that of how such regulation works by articulating female identity with a subject's other positions (in race, class, nation, institutional affiliation, and so on).[2]

Butler's theoretical preferences for the meanings of "restricting" and "emancipating" strategies also have an analog in her descriptions of what constitutes the feminism bound up both with dominant ontologies and with the institutional power that supports them. Addressing what she perceives as an academic feminist establishment reluctant to scrutinize both its terms and its affiliations, Butler cautions her readers to recognize that questioning "the implication of the terms of criticism in the field of power is . . . the very precondition of a politically engaged critique" (7). What feminists must realize is that power operates in advance to establish "who will be the subject who speaks in the name of feminism," and, as a result, critics must be wary of "who . . . gets constituted as the feminist theorist whose framing of the debate will get publicity" (8).

While it is easy to endorse such vigilance about the inscription of feminist critics in institutional power, we must notice that Butler's admonition is directed only toward those critics whom she feels are reluctant to examine their politicized terms. As a result, she leaves uninterrogated the power that authorizes the "subject of feminism" whose singular project is the critique of feminist identity. For Butler, feminist entanglements with suspect institutional power have their symptoms only in the assertion of feminist terms; conversely, the critique of those terms signals only resistance to institutional power. Following out her own prescriptions for scrutinizing successful academic discourses, however, we should ask: What kinds of power might underwrite a feminism presented as most oppositional not when it analyzes patriarchal power (although it recommends future such analyses) but when it practices or advocates only self-critique?

Certainly patriarchal ideology benefits when feminist analysis itself is displaced rather than materially engaged by the critique of feminist identity and/or the polemic in favor of such critique. That such a displacement occurs in the name of a more democratic feminism registers the fact that patriarchal prohibitions can be interarticulated with otherwise oppositional interpretive strategies. And the status currently enjoyed by a singular feminist focus on the critique of feminist identity marks how such interarticulations can attract the support of institutional power. Thus, I am arguing, we need to consider how Butler's influential framing of feminist debate is implicated, however unwittingly, in a complex "field of power," one where institutional and patriarchal power can converge with otherwise oppositional politics and epistemologies. For her prioritizing of a polemic about the need to deconstruct feminist identity, advanced in the name of a more radically democratic feminism, here effectively limits feminist deconstruction to the insistence that feminists must destabilize their terms.

Nevertheless, her interest in making the deconstruction of the feminist subject enrich rather than delimit feminist politics helps expose the way her own framing of this project undermines it. If this kind of framing is symptomatic of how patriarchal ideology can regulate a critic's multiple oppositional commitments, Butler's feminist politics also pose a challenge to this regulation. Although the deconstruction of the feminist subject insistently means for Butler a return to the polemic against feminist identity, she does not eliminate, as such polemics usually do, specific references to the effects of patriarchal power. Indeed she raises feminist issues that can be fully explored only by considering how gender ideology requires unstable female subjectivity. As a result, avoiding such an inquiry becomes visible as a repeated displacement of feminist issues with a polemic against feminist foundational terms.

Rather than only enumerating feminism's exclusions, Butler predicates the essay's initial argument against feminist identity on an analogy with the way other emancipatory rhetorics can exclude "women." When she notes that "otherwise compelling call[s] for radical enfranchisement" can erase women as the subjects of oppression, and when she asks, "How do we theorize the exclusion of women from the category of the oppressed" (14), Butler introduces into her argument a crucial issue for contemporary feminism: the tendency for women's oppression to disappear in or even bolster other oppositional discourses. But her answer to the question of how this exclusion is accomplished — that oppression can operate through "the very *erasure* that grounds the articulation of the emancipatory subject" (14) — tells us only what can be theorized by describing the identity formation of diverse emancipatory subjects. And it does so because her question is framed by an a priori theoretical agenda: to use a feminist recognition that other emancipatory subjects can exclude women to spark a recognition that feminist subjects can be grounded by similar erasures. Indeed, her agenda guarantees from the outset a predetermined shift in critical attention from the critique of patriarchal ideology (which benefits from the exclusion of women from categories of the oppressed) to the critique of feminist practices.

What remains untheorized, as a result, are perhaps the most urgent questions for contemporary feminism about the erasure of women's oppression in the name of other oppositional categories: How can critiques of feminism's exclusionary identity themselves contribute to the elimination of women from the category of the oppressed? How do a woman's self-divisions generate her commitment to a critique (often a self-critique) of feminist identity that omits women from the category of the oppressed? What we cannot illuminate with the model of discrete exclusionary subjects, nor even with a model of one subject who shifts between exclusionary positions, is how women can come to articulate a *feminist* position that eschews the practice of feminist politics itself. How can we explain a feminism that insists on, without investigating, differently located women while it effectively shifts certain "women" from the category of "oppressed" to that of "privileged" (in race, class, nation)? For these inquiries we need a model that links discursive regulation not only to a subject's stable, exclusionary identity but to the way identity itself is inherently unstable, constituted as an interarticulation of a subject's multiple positions and investments. Indeed only such a model can illuminate the dynamics by which the question of the exclusion of "women" from the category of the oppressed, once it is brought under discussion, continues to have for this poststructuralist feminist critic its "anticipated" and most politically effective feminist referent in the question of feminism's oppressive exclusions. Moreover, that this question is Butler's main concern in an academic feminist climate that overwhelmingly takes differences between and within women as a point of departure for criticism and theory would seem to indicate a critical impasse. Butler's difficulty in rearticulating the possibilities for poststructuralist feminist analysis, I am suggesting, may be symptomatic of a process that prevents her from theorizing its effects: the regulation of intersections between feminism, radical democratic politics, and theoretical commitments that shifts attention away from "women" as a category of oppression.

In a subsequent passage Butler similarly effaces a feminist question she raises about the workings of patriarchal discursive power with a polemic about the importance of interrogating feminism's politicized terms. Against a debate that opposes the discursivity of women's bodies to their material reality, Butler persuasively argues that "th[e] discursive ordering and production of bodies in accord with the category of sex is itself a material violence" (17). Accordingly, she proposes to articulate how, because discourse produces material effects, sexual violence against women is "more pervasive, more constitutive, and more insidious than prior models have allowed us to see" (18). In this vein she reminds us of "the legal restrictions that regulate what does and does not count as rape" (18) and brilliantly demonstrates how patriarchal "antirape" rhetoric is capable of defining "the sex of a woman" so that "the very terms by which the violation is explained *enact* the violation" (19). But her insistence on the violence of patriarchal discursive productions leads only to the admonition that feminists who take for granted their own terms (like the "sex of a woman") risk "keeping in their place the very premises that have tried to secure our subordination from the start" (19). True enough, but this argument shifts critical attention away from the complexity of how a "pervasive, insidious" patriarchal violence is constituted by discursive regulation and back to the fact that feminists must eschew foundational terms.

By again prioritizing this admonition, one that reactivates the opposition between a regulatory referentiality and a resisting destabilization of terms, Butler misses an opportunity to pursue unanticipated referents for how discursive regulation works with unstable reference and with a female subject's self-difference. Because she continues to privilege the critique of foundational terms as the most important issue that poststructuralism can raise for feminist politics, she does not pursue the implications of her own insights for describing the patriarchal construction of subordinate female subjects. Feminists are now familiar with Butler's first example of discursive materiality — the fact that "rape" is arbitrarily recognized or not according to the social categorization of diverse female bodies. But it is more difficult to recognize how patriarchal "antirape" rhetoric can describe sexual violence against the same female body in contradictory ways. What material regulatory effects are achieved when "rape" describes both the violation of a woman's body and the violation of her husband's right to violate that same body? How does this contradictory definition produce a confusion for certain women between protection against dangerous offenders and violation by legitimate ones (husbands)? What is the relation between this kind of paradoxical definition, a female subject's self-difference, and her consent to gendered subordination? What role, for one example, do the dynamics between the privileges and oppressions of middle-class white women play in securing this confusion and this consent?

Such questions might well follow from Butler's analysis of the terms that can at one time explain and enact violation. But her point about these terms is rather that they seek to establish irreducible referents for categories like "sex" and, therefore, should be a lesson for the feminists who also deploy foundational terms. As a result of prioritizing the analogy between patriarchal foundations and feminist ones, she shifts critical attention from potentially new questions of how patriarchal power can regulate unstable reference to canonical ones about destabilizing feminist terms. An academic feminist who is unaware of the discursivity of terms like "sex," "woman," and "rape" would be, I hopefully submit, a rare specimen in the 1990s. More urgent inquiries for poststructuralist feminist analysis, taking the discursivity of terms and the instability of subjects as points of departure, would theorize how dominant gendered regulation requires as well as succumbs to interarticulations of multiple discourses and the resignifications they enable.

Butler's instruction to feminists that the "[feminist] subject, its gender, its sex [and] its materiality" (19) must be understood and deployed as unstable categories, of course, need not foreclose these investigations. However, her return to the argument against stable referents for feminist terms effectively does; the insistence that feminists must realize that their categories are discursive becomes the destination of her argument rather than the launching site she seems to want it to be. While the singular focus on the critique of feminism's terms can remind feminists to be wary of "keeping in place" patriarchal premises about irreducible foundational meanings, it also keeps in place a concern with feminist foundations at the expense of theorizing how the unstable female subject is the site for patriarchal discursive regulation.

Butler returns to this sticking place for poststructuralist feminism precisely because of the kind of operations from which this impasse deflects attention: the way the dynamics between multiple, contradictory motivations can silence or dilute feminist analysis in other agendas. As a result of prioritizing the critique of feminist identity in the name of a more democratized practice, the project of politicizing the deconstructed feminist subject slips repeatedly from training attention on modes of patriarchal domination to instructing feminists in the need to destabilize their categories. The result is a trajectory away from feminist analysis itself, reenforced by retaining the premise of an establishment feminist identity politics, in large part, it seems, so that she can pursue a "radical democratic" polemic against it. In the interests of establishing the urgency of this polemic, Butler ignores a more prevalent body of feminist criticism, practiced both by white, middle-class women and by women of color, that contextualizes its claims for "woman." She also does not acknowledge the poststructuralist feminist theory that attempts to reconcile unstable categories not only with the articulation of local feminist terms but with political alliances between differently located women.[3]

As she repeatedly limits her announced desire to articulate a postmodern feminist politics, Butler's earlier call to interrogate whose framing of the feminist subject is institutionally successful raises important questions for her own very influential framing of feminist debate. If as a result of such interrogation we begin to discern "unanticipated" complexities in the oppositional critic's "implication . . . in the field of power" (6–7), if we can see in this case how a commitment to the oppositional potential of a theoretical discourse limits feminist deconstruction to a critique of feminism, we may see as well in this essay the limits of the mechanisms that can use one emancipatory discourse to intercept or silence another. We can see, that is, both the dominant regulation of self-difference (when patriarchal ideology helps to set the terms for the most progressive mode of feminism) and the role of self-difference in contesting that regulation (when introducing crucial feminist issues challenges this regulation). For if the former operation here succeeds in stalling the feminist analysis Butler also wants to pursue, it is her commitment to feminist politics that brings this paradox to critical light, that unintentionally makes visible unanticipated ways in which patriarchal ideology, bent on recruiting the oppositional as well as the conservative critic, does its work.

Feminist Subjects in the Context of "Race"

How much more sharply and intelligently feminists black and white need to think about "race," not solely as an issue of the racist proclivities of white identity but as a paramount issue for women of our time. —Christine Stansell, "White Feminists and Black Realities: The Politics of Authenticity"

Thus far I have argued that the impasse poststructuralist feminism encounters in applying theories of the unstable subject to an analysis of dominant gender ideology arises when the critique of its own terms is regarded as feminism's most oppositional mode. While the interrogation of feminist identity is clearly indispensable to feminist politics, a fully politicized feminism must not fail to train its attention on the patriarchal policing of female self-difference. Indeed, I have argued, the poststructuralist impasse for feminism, constituted when patriarchal ideology governs coarticulations of a critic's feminist and other oppositional commitments, itself represents an instance of this kind of regulation.

One of the most prominent contexts for productive critiques of feminist identity is the analysis of white women's reading of black women's texts and culture.[4] Black feminists have importantly foregrounded the inadequacy of white women's categories for black women, the academy's marginalization of black women's own analyses of oppression, and the need to question the multiple critical agendas that white women may bring to the critique of black patriarchy.[5] White feminists' own deployments of such critiques have been most effective when, following the lead of black feminists, the critique of white identity has taken as its necessary goal the enhancement of black feminism.

At the same time, certain white feminist critiques of cross-race interpretation, those whose concern with white identity displaces the feminist analysis of both black and white women, have functioned to perpetuate the impasse for poststructuralist feminism. These critiques function, as I have argued, not only to preclude a feminist analysis of such practices. They also intercept and prevent a (potentially reciprocal) cross-race feminism capable of strengthening local feminist politics, of helping to formulate what may be unspeakable for black and white women respectively, and of illuminating by cross-race analogy otherwise invisible structures of male domination within a particular feminist critic's own cultural context. But discerning how a singular attention to white identity can also serve patriarchal ideology has been difficult, precisely because critiques of white identity are indispensable to cross-race reading. How might we illuminate and redress the patriarchal effects of such critiques without diminishing their oppositional power? Indeed, how might cross-race feminist reading become the occasion for constructing a bridge rather than an impasse between the critique of white feminism and the critique of dominant gender ideology in both black and white contexts?

Christine Stansell's article "White Feminists and Black Realities: The Politics of Authenticity" (1992) offers an instructive version of such a bridge. As she brings an important critique of white feminism to bear on cross-race reading, Stansell also cites instances of problematic critiques of feminist identity. And in both cases, her goal is to increase white feminism's capacity to support black feminism at a crucial political juncture: the black feminist critique of Clarence Thomas's nomination to the Supreme Court. In addition, as she elaborates black feminists' analyses of how gender is articulated with race and class for black women, Stansell stresses the limits of white feminism's multiple-identity models that shift subjects from one position to another. As a result, she calls for a model capable of theorizing how a subject's multiple positionings can be coarticulated for patriarchal and other dominant interests.

Nevertheless, the essay ultimately dramatizes the ongoing difficulty faced by radical democratic feminists in discerning the counterproductive aspects of their own and others' critiques of white feminist identity. In the end, and in the wake of Hill/Thomas, Stansell is much more comfortable in describing how race, gender, and class are configured in the production of black women's gendered subordination than in articulating how such inter-articulations contribute to white women's inscription in patriarchal ideology. To the extent that she retains for white women the identity model she reveals as inadequate to the description of black women's negotiation of feminism and antiracism, I will argue, Stansell succumbs to the kind of patriarchal regulation in white contexts whose effects she is able to expose in black ones.

Stansell's essay examines white feminists' limited comprehension of black women's subordination in the context of Anita Hill's allegations against Clarence Thomas. As they discerned recognizable modes of patriarchal oppression in Hill's testimony about sexual harassment, she argues, white feminists were unable to interpret or unwilling to learn about modes of subordination specific to black women. Although Thomas had launched his conservative career in 1980 with a politically expedient, "unabashedly racist and misogynist" misrepresentation of his sister as a "welfare queen" (262), and despite newspaper coverage of and black feminist commentary on this history, white feminists recognized his sexism only in the context of Hill's sexual harassment allegations (260–63).

Importantly, Stansell also makes a point of distinguishing her critique of white feminism's blindspots from more prevalent modes of critiquing white feminist identity, ones that neglect rather than further the analysis of black women's subordination. Whereas she aims to underscore black feminists' analyses of gendered subordination, "present modes of [white] feminist antiracism," Stansell notes, demonstrate a singular preoccupation with confrontational or self-critical scrutiny of feminism's white identity (253). Such a preoccupation, every bit as much as the feminist misreading of black women, "allow[s] a lack of interest in and active ignorance about the complexity of current Afro-American politics" (254). Recognizing the liabilities of this practice for black feminist analysis, Stansell points out the conservative effects of a methodology characterized more often as white feminism's most oppositional mode. Instead of being the corrective to feminist deployments of exclusionary categories of "woman," as Stansell emphasizes, such a singular focus on white identity can perpetuate these exclusions.

Thus a commitment to black feminist politics motivates Stansell to discern erasures that have been difficult to describe precisely because they are perpetrated in the name of an antiracist, antiexclusionary feminism. At this moment, then, recognizing the failure of an announced oppositional strategy to materially engage either feminist or antiracist politics marks the limits of dominant gender ideology's capacity to function in the name of oppositionality. We see, then, how this ideology can succumb to the very radical democratic politics it can also appropriate.

Just as encouraging is the fact that when Stansell's own critique of white identity leads directly to black feminist interpretation, this focus produces a call for revising multiple-identity models of female and feminist subjectivity. Because her critique of identity ushers in rather than cancels out contextualized feminist analysis, it also has the potential to produce rather than block new formulations of female and feminist subjectivity. That is, as Stansell succeeds in replacing the impasse between the scrutiny of feminism's assumptions and the pursuit of feminist analysis with a necessary connection between the two, she also succeeds in displacing an identity model of the unstable female subject with one that focuses on interarticulations of race, class, and gender.

In her concluding comments Stansell attributes both white feminism's deployment of limited categories of "woman" and its compensatory preoccupation with white identity to an inadequate concept of the unstable, multiply positioned subject:

The interventions of [black feminist theorists] remind us how much more sharply and intelligently feminists black and white need to think about "race," not solely as an issue of the racist proclivities of white identity but as a paramount issue for women in our time. The shell game of identity politics — moving people from the "black" box to the "woman" one, and from the "woman" box to the "white" one — may protect white feminists from the uncomfortable business of learning and thinking aloud about male privilege in black politics. But unless we grow more skillful in our thinking and our tactics, as we learned, we have little to counter the conservatives' sleight-of-hand. (266–67)

Black feminist theorists reveal that white feminists' "shell game of identity politics," including the feminist antiracism that focuses only on "the proclivities of white [feminist] identity," is inadequate for understanding either how race and gender intersect for black women or how conservative sleights of hand can build on the misrepresentations that serve black patriarchal power. Directly preceding these remarks, Stansell has shown how Hill/Thomas dramatized both these operations. First, Thomas's disguising of sexism as antiracism succeeded in garnering black support for the former in the name of the latter: "[His] contempt for Anita Hill came clothed as a black man's brave stand against racism; veiled by the symbols of race and masculinity, his misogyny went uncontested among many black people" (266). Such veiling of misogyny in antiracist rhetoric, as black feminists have emphasized, is a forceful strategy for constructing and perpetuating black women's subordination, most notably by enforcing the code of silence against black feminism that Hill made so visible in her violation of it. At the same time, Stansell points out, the Republicans were able to bolster their nomination with a strategic rhetoric in which "a black woman who speaks of sexual oppression by a black man come[s] to be seen as a [racist] white man's pawn" (266).

Thus as Thomas condemns black feminism for being complicit with racist attacks on black men, and as conservative interests exploit this vexed mode of antiracism in order to disarm Hill's threat to the nomination, we see very clearly the need to consider how "race" and female subordination are coarticulated for black women. We also see clearly that when white feminists move black women from the "black" box to the "woman" one, they are handicapped both by their ignorance of black women's specificity and by a model of subjectivity that simply shifts people between what are in fact interarticulated positions.

But while the essay sharpens our thinking about how black female subordination is constituted as a coarticulation of gender, race, and class positions, it retreats from a similar way of thinking about the white women whose antiracist feminism does not include feminist analysis. The need to replace a feminist analysis that shifts subjects between categories like "race" and "gender" with one that examines the interarticulations of such categories does not extend to a consideration of the antiracist feminists who think about "race" only as an issue of feminists' white identity. Indeed when Stansell attributes this preoccupation with the critique of whiteness *to* white identity, she herself describes white women only in terms of "the proclivities of white identity" (266).

We will recall that "a lack of interest in and active ignorance about" black politics, one "disguised as reverence toward an undifferentiated Afro-American experience," are, according to Stansell, the motivations for such a restricted critical approach (254). With this interpretation, however, Stansell also shifts people from the "woman" box to the "white" one and thus perpetuates for her analysis of white feminists the very identity model whose limitations she brings to light for black feminists. As a result, questions of how radical antiracist politics can veil the masculinist elimination of feminist ones, so important to the understanding of how black feminism is silenced in antiracism, do not emerge as pertinent to a white feminist antiracism in which feminist analysis disappears.

The beginnings of such questions may lurk in Stansell's ambiguous explanation of why models of plural subjectivity that describe shifts between discrete identities have proven so tenacious for white feminism: "[T]he shell game of identity politics," she claims, functions to "protect white feminists from the uncomfortable business of learning *and* thinking aloud about male privilege in black politics" (267; emphasis added). But what does Stansell mean by "uncomfortable business"? To the extent that this phrase refers to "learning about male privilege in black politics," she invokes her earlier indictment of an indifference to such knowledge, covered over by a racist reverence for "undifferentiated categories" of "race." "Uncomfortable business" in this sense means the discomfort involved in relinquishing an inadequate category of "race" by pursuing the hard work of research.[6]

But while this analysis of white identity is indispensable, it is also limited by its singular concern with shifting people from "women" to "white." How might thinking "more sharply" about the dynamics between antiracism and feminism further illuminate why "present modes of feminist antiracism encourage confrontations and self-castigation" among white feminists more (or even rather) than contextualized black feminist analysis (253–54)? How does patriarchal power benefit when feminist reading becomes an "uncomfortable business" for white feminist antiracism, producing a practice that both ignores black feminism and shifts white feminists from oppositional to only dominant subjects? How is this power articulated with the race and class politics that white feminists may prioritize over feminist analyses of patriarchal power?

Stansell herself seems to gesture (if obliquely) toward such questions when the "uncomfortable business" of cross-race feminist reading involves not only "learning about . . . male privilege in black politics" but also "thinking aloud" about it (267). Discomfort in "thinking aloud" is not simply a matter of difficulties in displacing "active ignorance" but rather one of difficulties in resisting prohibitions, including those authorized by antiracism, against discussions of "male privilege in black politics." Such discomfort, that is, could be the effect of convergences between white feminism and antiracist politics that are regulated in part by patriarchal ideologies. As the result of masculinist "sleights of hand" that conflate feminist analysis with dominant race and class politics, it can become difficult for radical democratic feminists, black and white, to pursue feminist inquiry across as well as within race boundaries. As a result, it also can become more comfortable to turn "feminists" into "whites" than to pursue a feminist analysis of such prevalent transformations. In both cases, patriarchal power benefits.

In light of Stansell's condemnation of the discomfort that stops white feminists from pursuing discussions of black women's subordination by black men, it is surprising that she has so little to say about an important source of it. Indeed she herself seems to experience discomfort in "thinking aloud" about the relation between patriarchal ideology and the "uncomfortable business" of contextualized cross-race feminist reading. While she does emphasize that, before Hill's allegations, "among feminists . . . Thomas's invocation of racial oppression virtually immunized him to public interrogation" of his misogyny (260), Stansell does not specifically consider how this kind of immunity may be indebted to the patriarchal regulation of white feminists' simultaneous commitments to antiracism and feminism. Like the white feminists who choose an antiracist castigation of white feminism over the contextualized inquiry into black women's subordination, the white feminist reluctance to oppose Thomas's nomination is a matter only of ignorance and a misguided reverence for African American race solidarity, a reverence that has class and race, but not masculinist, motivations.[7]

Ultimately, in fact, even Stansell's hints of an intersection between masculinist and antiracist taboos against white feminist cross-race reading are elided when the kind of rhetorical disguises that allow feminism to be assimilated to racism are attributed only to conservative politics. Stansell concludes the essay by remarking that "unless we grow more skillful in our thinking . . . , as we learned, we have little to counter the conservatives' sleight-of-hand" (267). When in the end the disguising of dominant aims as antiracist ones emerges primarily as a "conservative" strategy, she not only diminishes her analysis of Thomas's patriarchal uses of oppositional rhetorics in intraracial contexts. She also effaces entirely the barely glimpsed question of how, in the name of an antiracism that can be appropriated for masculinist agendas, radical democratic white feminists can choose to avoid both black and white feminist analysis.

Thus at the very moment when Stansell calls for feminists to develop a model of subjectivity that can illuminate how gender is articulated with race, and specifically with antiracism, she effectively limits the feminist application of that model—the scrutiny of how patriarchal gendering can intersect with antiracism—to black women and the manipulation of this mode of domination to conservative political interests. Such a conclusion seems to suggest that her own critical practice is affected by the very dynamics that her "more skillful thinking" cannot illuminate fully when it comes to describing white feminist subjectivity: a coarticulation of white feminist, antiracist, and class politics that, by effacing feminist analysis in other oppositional discourses, benefits dominant gender ideology.

After Hill/Thomas, at least for the present political moment, it has become easier for both black and white feminists to "think aloud" about vexed intersections of black feminist and radical discourses without the "uncomfortable business" of violating the parameters either of a radical category of "race" or the category of "radical politics" itself. But white feminists should be wary of letting Hill/Thomas make it possible to locate these modes of patriarchal domination solely in black contexts and to characterize them ultimately as the tool of "conservative" political interests. Stratifying poststructuralist feminist analysis in this way clearly serves both racist and white patriarchal agendas: the regulation of female self-difference, when it serves patriarchal aims, becomes a strategy deployed only by black men and suffered only by black women, and white feminist politics are eliminated in a singular focus on whiteness.

Stansell's central and important point is that if white feminists are to be of use to black feminism, they must overcome their reluctance to analyze how black antiracist politics can be appropriated to silence and subordinate black women. But we must also notice that in the wake of Hill/Thomas she herself has no difficulty in "thinking aloud" about such "male privilege in black politics" (267). In contrast she does not implicate dominant gender ideology in the fact that white feminist inquiry, in both black and white contexts, is frequently effaced by a white feminist's antiracist commitments. Indeed that she does not make such an observation may well be a symptom of the role of gender ideology in silencing white feminism.

Nonetheless, the essay ultimately dramatizes how the convergence of white poststructuralist feminism with other oppositional politics can begin to break free of its prevailing mode, the construction of white feminism as most oppositional when it is involved only in the critique of its own dominant affiliations. In the course of "White Feminists and Black Realities," Stansell challenges this mode on its own oppositional terms, demonstrating that dominant gender ideology can succumb to the very resistance discourses it also mobilizes on its own behalf. If she goes on to practice a version of this mode, her interest in the "uncomfortable" aspects of white feminist antiracism begins to challenge it as well, playing out an ongoing contest between the mechanisms of patriarchal ideology and a resistance to them. At this juncture, then, where the unstable subject as the site for complex patriarchal domination begins to grow more visible for both black and white women, white poststructuralist feminism may be poised to displace the impasse between the (continually necessary) critique of feminist identity and the critique of patriarchy's regulation of female and feminist self-difference.

Retreating from Feminist Subjects at the Threshold of Racial Difference

If I initially approached Hurston out of a desire to re-referentialize differ-
ence, what Hurston gives me back seems to be difference as a suspension of
reference. —Barbara Johnson, "Thresholds of Difference"

Stansell's essay both maps the direction for a more effective poststructuralist feminist criticism and demonstrates how this progress can be impeded at certain junctures. In play at several crucial moments in Stansell's argument is a competition for what politics will set the terms by which her feminism is coarticulated with her other oppositional commitments. Keeping in mind the strategies that, as the essay shows us, will help win this contest for both feminist and radical democratic politics (the questioning of announced "oppositional" strategies that impede oppositional aims; the necessity of making the feminist critique of patriarchal ideology follow from rather than disappear in the feminist critique of feminist identity; the historicization of female subjectivity), I want to continue my focus on the contest itself. For it is this contest, more than an unfettered trajectory toward enlarging the scope of feminist politics, that continues to characterize poststructuralist feminism. Turning now to an instance of literary and textual criticism, I will explore how the kinds of progress Stansell's essay achieves for feminism, specifically the insistence on new models of unstable subjectivity derived from contextualized interpretation, can be foiled by the tenacious prohibiting of feminist interpretation in the name of antiracism.

As regards white feminism's capacity to formulate how power can regulate the dynamics between simultaneously held positions for white as well as black women, Barbara Johnson's influential essay "Thresholds of Difference: Structures of Address in Zora Neale Hurston" (1987) seems to begin at the conceptual site where Stansell's essay leaves off. Here a white feminist, whose previous reading of Hurston has illuminated the relation between black women's self-divisions and the prohibition of black feminism in the name of antiracism,[8] begins a new essay by attributing her present difficulties in reading Hurston's texts to the effects of her own self-divisions.

Her approach to Hurston on this occasion, Johnson claims, has been "repeatedly stopped" because it is framed by multiple "structures of address":

In preparing to write this paper, I found myself repeatedly stopped by conflicting conceptions of the structure of address into which I was inserting myself. It was not clear to me what I, a white deconstructor, was doing talking about Zora Neale Hurston, a black novelist and anthropologist, or to *whom* I was talking. Was I trying to convince white establishment scholars . . . that the study of the Harlem Renaissance is not a trivialization of their humanistic pursuits? Was I trying to contribute to the attempt to adapt the textual strategies of literary theory to the analysis of Afro-American literature? Was I trying to rethink my own previous work and to re-referentialize the notion of difference so as to move the conceptual operations of deconstruction out of the realm of abstract linguistic universality? Was I talking to white critics, black critics, or myself?

Well, all of the above. (317)

Thus a "white deconstructor's" important scrutiny of her motivations for "talking about Zora Neale Hurston" intersects with a consideration of "to *whom* [she] was talking," the multiple interlocutors for whom the representation of "race" is a central factor. However, having described the multiple agendas that have produced this impasse, Johnson immediately reveals a resolution to it and proceeds with an extended reading of a number of Hurston's texts. Nevertheless, I will argue, breaking the impasse to reading Hurston still leaves a crucial, unacknowledged obstacle to the scope of this reading in place: the interdiction against describing Hurston's feminist representation of "race." That is, while the concern with white identity in the context of multiple critical agendas "repeatedly stops" but does not finally prevent Johnson's focus on Hurston's texts, a prohibition against a *feminist* illumination of these texts remains in place.

If Johnson's initial impasse recalls Stansell's claim that a focus on white identity can displace and prevent white women's attention to black women's specificity, the absence of feminist reading from Johnson's subsequent account of Hurston registers what Stansell cannot quite talk about: a slippage between the antiracist critique of white identity and prohibitions against both supporting black women's feminist analyses and describing white feminist impasses. The problem, of course, is not that a vigilance about white identity informs Johnson's cross-race reading; indeed, critics have persuasively argued that the essay requires more such vigilance.[9] Rather the problem occurs when feminist criticism per se becomes indistinguishable from the manifestation of white identity, producing not a necessary attention to contextualized interpretation but a prohibition against "talking about" black women's representation of intraracial male domination.

As a result of this prohibition, moreover, Johnson's initial desire to "rethink [her] own previous work and . . . to re-referentialize the notion of difference" does not produce the recognition of how power works with self-difference that, for example, follows directly from Stansell's black feminist interpretations and, as we shall see, from Johnson's own previous work on Hurston. Although the essay makes room for rethinking her previous theoretical preference for linking the suspension of reference to agency, she ultimately retreats from considering the relation between domination and unstable reference. Indeed, I will argue, the essay demonstrates how interdictions against feminist analysis contribute to the ease with which incipient questions of this kind can be eliminated by prevailing questions of whether or not to referentialize politicized terms.

Certainly, Johnson begins as she will eventually conclude with the latter question; her interest in "rethinking" the notion of difference refers to the possibility of referentializing rather than suspending terms for "race." At the same time, Johnson's foregrounding of how her own dilemma of multiple address brings pressures to bear on this "rethinking" introduces another possible trajectory for it. With the very description of her own impasse in reading Hurston, she trains attention on how unstable referents for the self, produced by simultaneous, contradictory "structures of address," are the condition for producing prohibitions against pursuing certain descriptions of "race." Furthermore, this relation between self-difference and "race" representation turns out to be precisely what distinguishes Hurston's notion of racial difference. Indeed Johnson's own interpretive impasse turns out to dovetail with Hurston's referent for "race" when Johnson claims that Hurston articulates racial difference *as* the dealing with intersecting demands of multiple address: "What finally struck me was the fact that what I was analyzing in Hurston's writings was precisely . . . her strategies and structures of problematic address. It was as though I were asking her for answers to questions I did not even know I was unable to formulate. I had a lot to learn, then, from Hurston's way of dealing with multiple agendas and heterogeneous implied readers" (317). Thus the example of Hurston promises help in articulating the relation between "problematic structures of address" and the kind of impasse Johnson confronts in writing about Hurston. What first authorizes this white critic's cross-race reading is the sense of sharing with Hurston "structures of problematic address" that involve the expectations of powerful "implied readers." At this point, that is, Hurston's strategies are announced as the model for thinking "race" precisely in terms of how a black female subject deals with such multiple agendas.

It is surprising, then, that instead of "learning from Hurston" how self-difference can ground interdictions, Johnson abandons such impasses as a subject of investigation once she has overcome her own inability to write about Hurston. In the course of the essay, Hurston's representation of dealing with multiple agendas turns out only to reiterate deconstruction's familiar narratives of self-difference. Most prominently, "Thresholds" depicts Hurston as celebrating the subject's resignifying agency; she takes charge of "problematic address" by appropriating discursive identities and their respective agendas for her own strategic uses. And on the rarer occasions when such discursive appropriations reify dominant meanings for "race," Hurston performs an emancipatory self-critique of her entanglement with dominant identity. As Elizabeth Abel has noted, Hurston becomes for Johnson "a deconstructive critic's dream" (481).[10]

Yet if this discovery in Hurston of deconstruction's reigning paradigms marks a white feminist's appropriation of a black woman's text for an a priori critical agenda (Abel 489), that agenda is a distinctly *nonfeminist* one. Although, as Abel persuasively argues, constructing "race" as a discursive position helps resolve Johnson's impasse by authorizing her own cross-race reading (482), this authorization comes with a condition: that "race," however subject to resignification, will be in this essay a category uninflected by gender conflict. This limit on the referent for "race" means that Johnson's reading of Hurston's negotiation of multiple address cannot yield an account of how Hurston understands the relation between such negotiations and the prohibition of feminist representation. While the initial justification for "talking about" Hurston comes from Johnson's sense that her impasse is the effect of a "problematic multiple address" she shares with Hurston, the interdiction of feminist reading allows the analysis of impasses to give way to a celebration of the unstable subject's agency.

Because Johnson avoids feminist interpretation at a crucial moment in the essay, I will argue, she misreads the very Hurston passage she selects as a mirror of her own dealing with "heterogeneous implied readers" (317). And this misreading, in turn, blocks Johnson's ability to rethink, as she has in a previous essay, the uses of unstable subjectivity in the production of subordinate black female identity. When the misread Hurston becomes the support for returning incipient questions of how power works with self-difference to questions of whether or not to destabilize referents for racial difference, Johnson fails to illuminate the mechanisms that prohibit feminist representation, both as they are registered in Hurston's text and as they operate in Johnson's own cross-race reading.

Significantly, at the very moment when Johnson finds Hurston rethinking her own deconstructive strategies in the context of addressing "heterogeneous implied readers," she forgets her initial interest in how such problematic address creates impasses. By way of concluding her essay, Johnson discusses the original "folktale" with which Hurston concludes her collection of African American folktales, *Mules and Men* (1935). In the tradition of these folktales, Hurston's story of how cats developed their signature habit of "washing after eating" becomes the occasion to represent a trickster manipulating the protocols that threaten her survival:

> Once Sis Cat got hongry and caught herself a rat and set herself down to eat 'im. . . . So jus' as de cat started to eat 'im he says, "Hol' on dere, Sis Cat! Ain't you got no manners atall? You going set up to de table and eat 'thout washing yo' face and hands?"
>
> Sis Cat was mighty hongry but she hate for de rat to think she ain't got no manners, so she went to de water and washed her face and hands and when she got back de rat was gone.
>
> So de cat caught herself a rat again and set down to eat. So de Rat said, "Where's yo' manners at, Sis Cat? You going to eat 'thout washing yo' face and hands?"
>
> "Oh, Ah got plenty manners," de cat told 'im. "But Ah eats mah dinner . . . and uses mah manners afterwards." So she et right on 'im and washed her face and hands. And cat's been washin' after eatin' ever since.
>
> I'm sitting here like Sis Cat, washing my face and usin' my manners. (245–46)

Johnson responds: "So ends the book. But what manners is she using? Upon reading this strange, unglossed final story, one cannot help wondering *who, in the final analysis, has swallowed what.* The reader? Mrs. Mason? Franz Boas? *Hurston herself?*" ("Thresholds" 327–28; emphasis added). Thus Johnson discovers that Hurston's representation of Sis Cat's "dealing with . . . heterogeneous implied readers" quite precisely mirrors the structure of her own initial dilemma (317): as Hurston manipulates the expectations of the patrons who exerted financial and intellectual control over the writing of *Mules and Men,* she, like Johnson, engages in a self-critical address that rethinks her trademark strategies. For, Johnson claims, in addition to announcing her successful dealing with her patrons' agendas (the "manners" they expect her to observe), the tale registers Hurston's recognition, in the form of an address to "Hurston herself," that she can be the dupe of her own trick (328). Whereas tricks on the patrons involve "conforming a narrative to existing structures of address while gaining the upper hand" (328), the self-address critiques the potential dangers of such strategic conformity.

Thus Hurston emerges from this passage as the black resisting subject whose agency involves both manipulating the demands of numerous addressees and critiquing the "manners" she may unwittingly reify in the process. Despite her deliberate invocation of the similarity to her own initial dilemma of multiple address, however, Johnson does not indicate that the tale raises questions of how a subject's dealing with multiple agendas can produce impasses as well as opportunities. If Johnson's self-address is fettered by the agendas of powerful interlocutors, Hurston's is an emancipatory one that furthers her escape from such agendas. It is not surprising, then, that, when Johnson's reading of this passage explicitly provides the resolution to the rethinking of difference that is at stake in her own self-address, this rethinking is now posed as an emancipatory moment. Freed (by her account of Hurston) of critical pressures to referentialize racial difference, Johnson's self-address now is at one time emancipatory for her critical practice and the vehicle for reaffirming deconstruction's paradigm of difference as agency: "If I initially approached Hurston out of a desire to re-referentialize difference, what Hurston gives me back seems to be difference as suspension of reference" (328).

However, precisely to the extent that Johnson keeps her interpretation of Hurston as well as her own self-critical rethinking within the bounds of deconstruction's canonical debate about reference versus the suspension of reference, she avoids theorizing the relation between self-difference and prohibition that so centrally concerns her at the outset. Significantly, Johnson's investment in the canonical debate is also inextricably bound up with her observance of an interdiction against talking about Hurston's representation of intraracial gender conflict. Indeed the most dramatic symptom of this interdiction is her assertion that the "Sis Cat" tale even includes an address to "Hurston herself." In fact the tale provides no evidence whatsoever for an address to "Hurston herself" in which the author rethinks her strategies for manipulating race representation for white patrons. Rather, projecting the address to "Hurston herself" onto the tale betrays Johnson's desire to reproduce her own self-critical address in Hurston's text, where self-critique becomes only an emancipatory mode. As Johnson does so, however, she writes over Hurston's representation of how Sis Cat is coerced into a self-critique that produces, rather than undermines, the adherence to oppressive manners.

Certainly it is plausible to suggest Mrs. Mason and Franz Boas as implied actors in this enigmatic tale that marks the completion of a project over which they exerted control. However, Johnson's suggestion of the self-address is more arbitrary. In the context of Hurston's identification with Sis Cat, the discovery of a self-address is motivated only by the pun Johnson makes on "swallowed," a term *she* introduces: "But what manners is she using? . . . [W]ho, in the final analysis has swallowed what?" Only by using "swallowed" to mean "tricked into believing" is Johnson able to include Sis Cat/Hurston among the possible dupes of Sis Cat's own trick on the rat. Only with Johnson's pun can Sis Cat's notably unambiguous "et right on 'im" become the occasion for Hurston to notice that she can be duped into reifying racist protocols at the moment when she thinks she is "using manners" on her own terms.

Thus the pun on "swallowed," clearly meant to call celebratory attention to the role of suspended reference in the interpretive process itself, produces a reading of Hurston that finds her valorizing, in interracial contexts, deconstruction's location of agency in the subject's exploitation of suspended reference. However, as we shall see, rather than mirroring Hurston's notion of agency, Johnson's multiplication of the referents for Hurston's "et right on 'im" effaces Hurston's representation of both domination and agency in *intraracial* contexts. That is, it is precisely Johnson's desire to apprehend (both her own and Hurston's) agency as the capacity to suspend reference that leads her to misread Hurston's very different characterization of the relation between agency, discursive instability, and self-critique.

Johnson's second path to producing Hurston's self-address is the suggestion that she varies her identification with the two black tricksters in the tale; if we read Hurston also as the "rat" that tricks the patron, Sis Cat becomes the patron whose countertrick reveals the danger of antiracist tricks that attempt to exploit the patrons' own racist protocols ("manners"). Yet this reading glosses over the most literally represented advocate of "manners" in the tale: the black male trickster "rat." As a result, Johnson also ignores the intraracial dimension of the trickster contest at the center of the tale. Without a doubt, the trickster rat's initial besting of a stronger predator on her own terms marks him as the traditional figure of black resistance to white racist power. But it is precisely this classic subject of black resistance that Hurston complicates by making him a "rat" concerned with imposing "manners" that Sis Cat hastens to observe. With this representation she invokes a tenacious intraracial, gendered conflict: the use of antiracist self-criticism to silence black feminist resistance. By projecting onto Hurston an oppositional self-critique in interracial contexts, Johnson effaces Hurston's representation of a regulatory self-critique in intraracial ones. Indeed, Johnson's failure to recognize both the intraracial context and the gendered distinction between the trickster rats results in a reading that reproduces the assimilation of black female intraracial subjectivity to the classic subject of black male interracial resistance — the very process that "Sis Cat" protests.

When Sis Cat is tricked into letting the "rat" get away by observing the "manners" he easily persuades her to use, the tale alludes to a drama Hurston will explore in subsequent works: the masculinist "trick" that eliminates black female resistance to male domination by appealing to protocols of race solidarity black women also want to observe.[11] Significantly, *Mules and Men* observes these protocols at precisely the juncture where *Their Eyes Were Watching God*, her next work, will flout them. In her report that a Polk County black woman has not been prosecuted by white law for shooting and killing her husband, Hurston does not entertain the possible feminist dimensions to the act; indeed, she represents it as a symptom only of a murderous complicity with white racism that she extends to black women generally: "Negro women *are* punished in these parts for killing men, but only if they exceed the quota. I don't remember what the quota is. . . . One woman had killed five when I left that turpentine still where she lived. The sheriff was thinking of calling on her and scolding her severely" (*Mules and Men* 60). This kind of hyperbole, in which black women are assimilated to the aims of white racist law, will be presented in *Their Eyes* as a black male strategy for silencing black feminism. Here, however, it is articulated in Hurston's own narrative voice and for reasons that emerge when, in the very next passage, she describes her strategies for being accepted by the rural community she wants to document. Because the folk suspect her of being an agent of white law, she describes herself as a fugitive from white justice and as a result is accepted (60–61). Taken together these passages dramatize Hurston's anxieties about her authority to represent black culture. Demonstrating that she can be trusted to do so means posing herself against white law; but she secures these antiracist credentials at a high price — the hyperbolic representation of black women as complicit with the aims of white racism. At the same time, however, Hurston prefigures her subsequent challenges to the pressures that govern her discourse here by registering that the self-presentation required by the community is fabricated. Already, then, Hurston marks her use of such intraracial "manners" as a strategic one.

Once she is released from the constraints imposed on *Mules and Men* — a release she may well anticipate in this "unglossed final story" that occurs "after a break but without preamble" (Johnson, "Thresholds" 327) — Hurston uses the folk material she has collected to represent both "black culture" *and* black feminism, including the codes of silence that are enforced against black women by equating their feminist resistance with white racism. In this vein, Sis Cat's concern with "using manners" without succumbing to their detrimental effects (i.e., letting the "rat" go) gestures towards a strategic use of intraracial protocols that authorizes rather than requires an indictment of black feminism. When the cat manages both to "et right on [the rat]" and to adhere to the "manners" that previously stopped her from doing so, the tale anticipates Hurston's strategies for authorizing her feminist representation in *Their Eyes* and other texts: using the analytic powers of antiracist discourse (the "manners" at issue in the tale's intraracial context) to expose and resist the appropriations that can make antiracism the alibi for prohibiting black feminism.

As in "Sis Cat," *Their Eyes* registers the intensity of black feminist anger in the deliberately provocative elimination of the offending black male. Yet when the point of the trick is both to outwit the "rat" and retain the "manners" that initially allowed him to outwit Sis Cat, Hurston foreshadows the novel's strategies for making antiracist discourses authorize rather than prohibit black feminist representation. "Sis Cat" itself offers a version of this strategy when the implied analogy between white racist manners and intraracial codes of silence recruits a powerful discourse on resisting white racist manners to inspire support for an unspeakable feminist indictment of intraracial codes of silence.[12] If Sis Cat's initial encounter with the trickster rat represents her observance of these codes in *Mules and Men* (and in a number of other texts that precede it), the second one prefigures her subsequent efforts to appropriate antiracism to authorize the very feminist representation antiracist rhetorics historically have prohibited.

Indeed, as we shall see in chapter 2, the final, enigmatic passage in *Mules and Men* constitutes a link between other intraracial trickster contests Hurston developed from the folk material — the story "The Bone of Contention" (unpublished until 1991) and the play *Mule Bone* (1931; 1991) — and the trial scene in *Their Eyes*. All of these texts, moreover, invoke an important version of this genre in which a "badman trickster," who turns traditionally interracial strategies against other blacks, can be foiled by a better, more community-minded trick.[13] At the heart of both the story and the play is a trial in the black community where a "bad" trickster who uses race solidarity rhetoric to support his intraracial crime is outwitted by a countertrick that invokes black rhetorics for the aims of justice. "Sis Cat" 's intraracial scene of conflict is a transitional representation between the story's and the play's concern with besting such a badman trickster and the novel's appropriation of this authorized mode of representing intraracial conflict for a feminist indictment of codes of silence. In *Their Eyes*, as I will argue in chapter 2, a trickster contest over what agendas are served in the name of black solidarity reappears in the scene of Janie's trial before a white court; there Hurston's narration competes with black misogynistic narratives for the authorization conferred by antiracist rhetorics.

Thus the assumption only of an interracial context for the tale leads Johnson to miss a central referent for the "manners" Hurston is concerned with: intraracial gendered protocols that enable black male "tricksters," precisely because they articulate a classical mode of black antiracist resistance, to disarm black female resistance. From this vantage point the first encounter between Sis Cat and the trickster rat formulates the effects of the self's multiple agendas not as increasing the speaker's ability to escape any particular identity but as the ability for a coarticulation of agendas to prohibit the pursuit of one agenda in the name of another. Most importantly, instead of presenting self-critique as the unencumbered vehicle of agency, "Sis Cat" shows how a willingly embraced self-critique can function to turn a black female subject against her survival interests. "Hol' on dere, Sis Cat! Ain't you got no manners atall?" says the trickster rat, and Sis Cat, who would "hate for de rat to think she ain't got no manners," lets the rat escape (245). In addition, Hurston's concept of agency responds specifically to the way domination benefits from self-difference; agency consists in reconfiguring the intersection between antiracism and black feminism so that it supports rather than censures black feminist critique.

The tale's representation of dealing with multiple agendas, then, offers a formulation of unstable subjectivity that surpasses the explanatory power of deconstruction's reigning models for the relation between self-difference, domination, and agency. By foregrounding how a black female subject's dealing with multiple agendas (her desire to "eat" the "rat" and her desire to observe the "manners" that the rat invokes) can be regulated by a black male trickster's appeal to intraracial "manners," Hurston implicates the instability of the referents for antiracist manners as well as the differences within subjects themselves in conservative processes of resignification.

While the multiple referents for antiracist "manners" underwrites slippages between the misogynist silencing of black female resistance and antiracist protocols (so that such manners refer to self-censoring), black women's self-difference, the dynamics between their positions in race and gender, leads to a policing of their own feminist resistance in antiracist terms.

How, then, do these formulations disappear in Johnson's inquiry, which begins by seeking in Hurston a model for explaining the kind of problematic address that produces impasses to representation? This disappearance is all the more puzzling in light of Johnson's previous strategies for reading Hurston's representation of black female subjectivity. In an earlier article, "Metaphor, Metonymy, and Voice in *Their Eyes Were Watching God*" (1984), Johnson balances her claim that Hurston represents "the incompatible forces involved in her own . . . [self-]division" as the vehicle of agency with a demonstration that Hurston links domination to the regulation of the subject's divisions (212). The black woman's situation, Johnson argues, constitutes an "impossible position between two oppositions [black versus white; male versus female]," because the four poles of this structure "are constantly being collapsed into two" (215). As a result, the black woman's resistance to white racism makes her resistance to intraracial male domination impossible: "If the black woman voices opposition to male domination, she is often seen as a traitor to the cause of racial justice" (215). And when Hurston "represents Janie as acquitted of the murder of Tea Cake by an all-white jury but condemned by fellow blacks," her aim is to demonstrate this impossible position of the black woman (215). At this point in the essay, then, the unstable reference for self-different subjects that under certain circumstances can enable black female resistance is revealed also as being the condition under these classic circumstances for prohibiting black feminism.

In "Metaphor," Hurston's representation of black female and feminist subjectivity inspires Johnson to reformulate questions of self-difference and resignification, to interrogate how domination works by collapsing in order to resignify the simultaneous agendas a subject negotiates. Why, then, does "Thresholds," which explicitly looks to Hurston's example in order to reformulate questions of "dealing with multiple agendas" (317), efface Hurston's representation in "Sis Cat" of how this regulation works in intraracial, gendered contexts? And why is this effacement, which also obscures Hurston's analysis of how self-critique can inhibit agency and resistance, achieved by projecting onto Sis Cat an emancipatory self-critical address, unfettered by the pressures of multiple agendas?

The answers, as I have suggested, lie in the converging agendas that inform Johnson's own self-critical address, ones whose constraining influences she thematizes at the outset of the essay but does not avoid. Johnson's refashioning of her own self-critique, itself pressured by powerful interlocutors, as the emancipatory self-critique she projects onto Hurston is motivated at another early moment in "Thresholds." Here the terms for what will emerge as Hurston's address to herself are set by a shift in what guides Johnson's interpretation of how "Sis Cat" represents Hurston's strategies for "dealing with multiple agendas": a shift from reading Hurston as caught up, like Johnson, in the problems created by "dealing with multiple agendas" to reading Hurston in light of Langston Hughes's critique of her.

Directly following Johnson's initial celebrations of Hurston's strategies for reversing and undermining received oppositions, including reversals of interracial theatrical space, Johnson also cites Hughes's critique of Hurston's "performances." According to Hughes, Hurston enacted "race" in troubling ways; in his view, white people "paid her just to sit around and represent the Negro race for them, [as] she did it in such a racy fashion." Moreover, he claims, "to many of her white friends, no doubt, she was a perfect 'darkie'" (Hughes, *The Big Sea* 238–39, qtd. in "Thresholds" 319).[14] While Johnson responds with a defense of Hurston here, nonetheless it is Hughes's critique that shows up in Johnson's subsequent claim that in "Sis Cat" Hurston registers a self-critique of her strategic performance of racist manners.

Turning Hurston into Hughes at the point when "Sis Cat" provides the ultimate terms for Johnson's rethinking "difference" in the context of "race" is symptomatic of how this rethinking is governed by particular agendas for the meaning of "race." Although Johnson does not cite at the outset the imperative to avoid a description of "race" that involves gender conflict,[15] her ventriloquizing of Hurston with Hughes's critique plays out this prohibition. Projecting onto "Sis Cat" a self-critique that reveals Hurston as theoretically in agreement with Hughes's (belligerent) concerns about her performance of "race" registers an imperative to erase intraracial conflict between genders with an alliance around shared antiracist discourses. Johnson's achievement of this alliance, however, makes her an unwitting participant in dynamics that historically have been used to eliminate black feminist representation.

While a vigilance against reifying racist representation in interracial contexts clearly can have oppositional aims shared by all African Americans, here Johnson's privileging of Hughes's discourse compels Hurston's text to inscribe this vigilance at the cost of revealing Hurston's own feminist project: her representation of the *misuses* of appeals to such vigilance and the self-critiques they are meant to inspire in the context of intraracial gendered conflict. When Hurston emerges not as a critic of these misuses but as critic of her own potentially racist representation, Johnson's interpretation is complicit with the very regulation of black women's resistance that "Sis Cat" tries to bring under scrutiny. But if Johnson turns out to enforce the masculinist "trick" that the folktale exposes and outwits, it is because she herself succumbs to a version of it: in an antiracist effort to eliminate gender conflict from the category of "race," the white critic compels Hurston's text to observe the very "manners" it indicts.

Furthermore, the process comes full circle. Precisely because she takes her final reading of Hurston as the model for her own problematic "dealing with multiple agendas," Johnson retreats from theorizing how intersecting agendas pressure her account of Hurston and thus from the rethinking of "difference" she bases on it. Because Johnson effaces "Sis Cat" 's revelation of disciplinary uses of self-critique, she similarly effaces how multiple agendas regulate her own self-address. Whereas she initially presents her self-address, in which she rethinks reigning ways of characterizing "difference," as vulnerable to the prohibitive agendas of her several "implied readers," in the end self-address is the site only of vigilance against such pressures. What she misses, as a result, is the way a potentially emancipatory self-critique of her allegiance to deconstruction's paradigms for understanding difference — one that might produce an unanticipated focus on how domination profits from unstable reference and self-difference — quickly yields to the influence of a regulatory self-critique that prohibits her recognition of Hurston's feminist representation. And the effect of this prohibition on her rethinking a theory of "difference" in the context of "race" is to replace incipient questions of how "dealing with multiple agendas" can produce impasses with the familiar assertion that unstable reference, as regards both subjects and terms, is a condition for agency. Indeed with this assertion Johnson equates her agency as a critic with the authorization, derived from her (mis)reading of Hurston, *not* to rethink deconstruction's emphasis on the relation between suspended reference and a politics of resistance. As a result, she ultimately misapprehends a self-address that blocks her rethinking of an oppositional theoretical discourse as one that enables her to avoid constraints on such rethinking. In so doing she enacts what I have argued is the central dilemma of white poststructuralist feminism: an inability to distinguish a regulatory self-critique, para-doxically sponsored by a prevailing oppositional theory of the subject, from an emancipatory one.[16]

Nevertheless, "Thresholds" importantly thematizes, in the description of Johnson's dilemma of address, how rethinking reigning concepts of dis-cursive and subjective difference can be blocked by the multiple agendas, political and theoretical, that guide the self-criticism of white antiracist feminists. As significantly, Johnson's brief overview of her own dilemma of address, as she notes, points to questions she is as yet unable to formulate. Among the obstacles to formulating new questions about the relation be-tween power, agency, and difference that come into focus in the course of the essay is the capacity of entrenched debates about the wisdom of referen-tializing politicized terms to block interrogations of the dominant uses of "difference as suspension of reference" (328). However, while Johnson ultimately keeps her thinking within the bounds of the former debate, she also approaches the threshold of reformulating the relation between domi-nation and self-difference, and she does so because she perceives a similar-ity between her problematic "dealing with multiple agendas" and Hurs-ton's. That is, the essay identifies, if it fails to pursue, a crucial common denominator that poststructuralist feminism can offer differently located women: the recognition that patriarchal power regulates self-difference at discrete cultural sites. In Johnson's very inability to elaborate this insight in ways that continue a reciprocal illumination both of Hurston's text and of her own dilemma of interpretation, we can discern the forceful operation of such regulation.

Like the other essays I have discussed, then, "Thresholds" plays out an ongoing contest between dominant gender ideology and a radical demo-cratic feminism for leverage over a critic's multiple oppositional agendas. However, even as these critics remain vulnerable to regulations they can-not, as a consequence, adequately theorize, they usefully represent both this vulnerability and modes of contesting it. Thus an interrogation of the post-structuralist impasse between the oppositional critique of feminist identity and the critique of dominant gender ideology can itself contribute to new feminist formulations of the unstable subject as well as to revised concepts of domination and agency, respectively.

Chapter 2

ANTIRACIST RHETORICS
AND THE FEMALE SUBJECT

The Trials of Zora Neale Hurston

Whereas poststructuralist feminism has found it difficult to recognize how its coarticulation with other oppositional discourses can impede feminist analysis, Zora Neale Hurston is acutely aware of how black feminism can be silenced by masculinist appropriations of antiracist discourses. As a result she takes as her most urgent feminist projects the critical representation of and the construction of counterstrategies to such operations. Both projects are central to *Their Eyes Were Watching God,* where she elaborates strategies for breaking the hold of dominant gender ideology on the antiracist discourses that black feminists also embrace.

Agency as Hurston conceives it in black feminist and antiracist terms is not simply, as poststructuralist critics have claimed, a matter of celebrating the suspension of reference for racial difference (Johnson, "Thresholds" 318), of demonstrating "the continuous possibility of rupturing cultural identity rather than proposing an alternative" (Wald 91). Rather, for Hurston agency is an urgent matter of constructing alternative coarticulations of the multiple positions that subordinate subjects traverse. In this chapter I will explore her prime strategy for resisting the black masculinist regulation of black women's multiple interests: a reformulation of antiracist discourses themselves with the goal of reconfiguring the coarticulation of gender and race for black men and women alike.

Their Eyes pursues the formulation of antiracist discourses that support rather than undermine black feminist politics. Some of these reconfigurations rely on the processes that, as we have seen in chapter 1, have proven effective for white feminists' rethinking of certain modes of white feminist antiracism: the capacity of oppositional discourses to eventually undermine the masculinist ideology for which they have been appropriated. For

Hurston, however, such transformations can only be sustained when they are underwritten by deliberate reformulations of antiracist discourses that forge alliances between black feminists and black men. Against the discourses that collapse antiracist aims with black masculinist ones, Hurston poses ones, appropriated from folklore and contemporary political events, that illuminate and indict both the *misuse* of antiracist discourses to support other agendas and the way such misuses serve racist interests. It is these discourses that Hurston hopes will authorize in antiracist terms the critique of the masculinist appropriation of antiracism. Thus the novel points to a crucial mode of intervention in the capacity for dominant gender ideology to benefit from the other resistance discourses that feminists espouse: the necessity for both feminism and other oppositional rhetorics to analyze and foreground how subordination can be secured by exploiting a subject's pursuit of simultaneous agendas. It is this referent for antiracist politics that Hurston prioritizes in *Their Eyes* in order to authorize the novel's own feminist critique and violation of intraracial codes of silence.

At stake is Hurston's ability to represent black feminism in the context of Harlem Renaissance debates about the representation of authentically black cultural experience. While debates about authenticity included contests between the vernacular and "standard" English, between representations of rural southerners and urban northerners, Hurston appropriates rhetorics from all these genres.[1] Although both recent critics and her contemporary ones position the novel on the side of the southern vernacular, I argue that *Their Eyes* aims to counter black male misogyny by mobilizing antiracist analyses of power emerging in both rural and urban representation in the 1930s. In the course of Janie's trial for the killing of Tea Cake, the central focus of this chapter, Hurston invokes both the intraracial trickster contest from rural folklore and the urban rhetorics forged in the context of the prominent Scottsboro trials to indict the codes of silence that Janie obeys and that Hurston's narration breaks. Rather than presenting a competition between genres and regions, the trial scene stages an intraracial contest between competing antiracist rhetorics that traverse these categories: on the one hand those that equate antiracism with black male empowerment and involve the silencing of black feminism; on the other, emerging ones that analyze intraracial misuses of antiracist discourses and the complicity of these misappropriations with racist interests.

Thus Hurston hopes the novel will function to develop and disseminate emerging antiracist rhetorics that could authorize black feminist analyses of codes of silence as a misuse of antiracist rhetorics. Indeed, she hopes that her black feminist novel, in the context of an emerging African American literature and with the help of Scottsboro's rhetorics, can do the cultural work for black feminism that Scottsboro did for black men in interracial contexts. That she wants her novel to produce the kind of powerful interventions Scottsboro achieved is evident also from her subsequent coverage in the *Pittsburgh Courier* of the trial of Ruby McCollum for killing her abusive white lover. In these articles key passages from the novel help make the story of the racist court's cover-up of white male miscegenation inextricable from the intraracial silencing of black feminism. But if Ruby McCollum's trial is the occasion to directly authorize the novel's feminist project with a trial whose antiracist impact Hurston represents as like that of the Scottsboro trials, invoking *Their Eyes* as the intertext for the trial invokes as well the specific mode of authorization the novel privileges: making the black feminist subject the model for the subject of black antiracist resistance.

Constructing the "Woman" Subject of Black Resistance

It cannot be that I shall live and die as a slave. . . . Besides, I am but a boy, and all boys are bound to some one. . . . There is a better day coming. . . .
You have seen how a man was made a slave; you shall see how a slave was made a man. —Frederick Douglass

Now, women forget all those things they don't want to remember, and remember everything they don't want to forget. —Zora Neale Hurston

Hurston's allusions to Douglass's slave narrative in the opening paragraphs of *Their Eyes Were Watching God,* as Henry Louis Gates Jr. has argued, clearly locate her novel in a tradition of black resistance writing (*Signifying Monkey* 172). But the more "enigmatic" aspects (172) of Hurston's revisionary chiasmus can be explained, I will argue, in terms of her effort to reveal and redress the opposition between black resistance discourses and the novel's black feminist representation. The rewriting of Douglass inaugurates the novel's extended and difficult project of authorizing black feminism with the very resistance rhetorics that excluded women and, in twentieth-century contexts, prohibited black women's critiques of black male domination. As we have seen, in *Mules and Men* Hurston's access to antiracist rhetorics that both confer community membership and enable her authorship of a book representing "authentic" black culture means participating in rhetorics that link rebellious black women to white racism. Here, however, Hurston begins her feminist contribution to Harlem Renaissance literature by highlighting the exclusion of women from antiracist subjectivity in a prominent resistance text.

When Hurston rewrites Douglass's "You have seen how a man was made a slave, you shall see how a slave was made a man" (107) as "women forget all those things they don't want to remember, and remember everything they don't want to forget" (9), she introduces into a classic figuration of black resisting subjectivity the women excluded by it. In doing so she immediately calls attention to the fact that Douglass's generic "man" more accurately refers to gendered "man."[2] Participating in what Richard Yarborough has described as a discourse in which "[both black and white] Afro-American spokespersons . . . saw the crucial test of black fitness to be whether or not black men were . . . 'manly'" (167–68), Douglass imagines that "a slave [is] made a man" when a boy grows into one. His "I am but a boy, and all boys are bound to someone" translates a hoped-for escape from slavery into a narrative of male development (107), and thus when he is grown, as Valerie Smith has noted, Douglass links this escape to overpowering an abusive slaveholder with manly physical strength ("Loopholes" 216).

But along with foregrounding and reversing Douglass's exclusion of "woman," Hurston's revision of the chiasmus also shifts the oppression at issue to black women's intraracial subordination. As Ann du Cille points out, when "women forget all those things they don't want to remember" it is a symptom of their subjection to "the power of illusion and ideology" (101). Accordingly, the novel goes on to explore how such forgetting contributes to Janie's subordination, culminating with the focus in the trial scene on intraracial "codes of silence." In requiring the forgetting of one set of oppositional interests (feminism) in another (antiracist solidarity with black men), such codes applied as well to literary representation. Thus *Their Eyes* thematizes and attempts to authorize its own representation of black male violence against and domination of black women.

Allusions to Douglass can initiate the novel's project of forging alliances between black feminism and black male antiracism, however, only when Hurston gestures toward covert racist strategies to which Douglass is both subject and oblivious. Whereas the famous chiasmus describes the trajectory from "slave" to "man" as a straightforward reversal of circumstances, Hurston's links emancipation to reversing processes of selective remembering and forgetting by which power recruits consent to oppression — processes that she might well have discerned in the gendering that informs Douglass's vision of emancipatory reversal.

That is, the reformulation of Douglass that illuminates the structure of intraracial gendered oppression (where black women forget their oppression in race solidarity) is, as *Their Eyes* will strive to demonstrate, equally indispensable for enhancing the scope of antiracist analysis. Douglass's construction of a slippage between freedom and manhood, for example, clearly could profit from an inquiry into how black men are at risk by collapsing the liberated black subject with a universalized masculinity. Indeed at the very moment Hurston emphasizes that the famous chiasmus excludes black women, her counterformulation is also meant to *include* Douglass by implicating him in forgettings that compromise black male agency. As the articulation of women's difference in the opening passages genders the "man" in Douglass's chiasmus, it also genders and racializes the "every man" Hurston invokes in the passage that precedes her definition of "women": "Ships at a distance have every man's wish on board. For some they come in with the tide. For others they sail forever on the horizon, never out of sight, never landing until the Watcher turns his eyes away in resignation, his dreams mocked to death by Time. That is the life of men. Now, women forget all those things they don't want to remember, and remember everything they don't want to forget" (9). Hurston's meditator on the ships invokes, of course, Douglass's own meditation that precedes his formulation of the chiasmus. In contrast to Douglass's concept of "man," however, Hurston's "Watcher," who shares "every man's wish," is at best a passive recipient of a bounty attributed arbitrarily to different men and at worst the less lucky subject of delusions who blindly expects the powerful ships to deliver.[3] Hurston calls attention, then, to the disadvantages in black masculinity that Douglass effaces both in the chiasmus and in the meditation on the ships that leads up to it.

For Douglass's meditation charts a striking oscillation between an awareness of his "wretched condition" and a forgetting of it in an apprehension of interwoven concepts of freedom, whiteness, and masculinity (106). Initially he perceives that "[t]hose beautiful vessels, robed in purest white, so delightful to the eye of freemen, were to me so many shrouded ghosts, to terrify and torment me with thoughts of my wretched condition" (106). Within the space of a paragraph, however, the terror and torment of whiteness disappears, leaving only the reverence for an almost heavenly whiteness. In an apostrophe whose addressee is also "no audience but the Almighty," Douglass praises and longs for the protection of the white ships: "You are freedom's swift-winged angels. . . . O that I were free! O, that I were on one of your gallant decks, and under your protecting wing!" (106). From here he resolves that with God's help ("O God, save me! God, deliver me! [106]) he will flee on the bay, previously troped as the "broad bosom . . . ever white with sails" (106) that "shall bear [him] into freedom" (107). Thus "whiteness," initially a signifier of terror, transforms into the overdetermined mark of freedom, divine power, and a white maternal function that "bears" him into freedom. When these images lead in the same paragraph to the chiasmus that links freedom to attaining the "manhood" all (and only) males grow into, Douglass "forgets" not only black women (an elision also registered in the fantasy of being "born" by a white maternal agency into freedom) but also the gendering of black men, free as well as slave, in white racist patriarchal terms.

Hurston's revision of the meditation on the ships, then, critiques Douglass's dream of a masculinity that eliminates racist distinctions between men and benefits from white power. And the revisionary chiasmus that illuminates how black women embrace subordination by forgetting gender in race turns out also to be a model for how a black male subject can unwittingly reify racist categories when his concept of freedom involves forgetting race in (male) gender. Accordingly, *Their Eyes* thematizes not only Janie's selective memory but also that of the black men whose strategies for forgetting racist oppression include both the unwise pursuit of white male support and the reproduction of white patriarchal strategies that could be fatal to black men in interracial contexts. Moreover, for these twentieth-century men the slippage between antiracist agency and masculinity that can play into white racist agendas takes a destructive form in intraracial contexts: the forgetting of and/or reaction against white racist humiliations through the domination of black women.

However, if describing the shape of intraracial black female subordination provides a model for discerning the liabilities in black men's vexed formulations of agency, Hurston's prescription for black women's resistance to intraracial male domination also proposes an alternative model for black antiracist resistance. As she locates her trope for feminist agency ("remember[ing] everything they don't want to forget" [9]) at the rhetorical site where Douglass links antiracist agency to manhood ("you shall see how a slave was made a man" [107]), Hurston suggests that remembering the subordination effaced by simultaneously held beliefs, dominant as well as oppositional, should inform antiracist notions of agency, especially those that link black emancipation to achieving manhood.

With this reformulation of classic categories for both oppression and agency, the black female subject, traditionally excluded from and/or silenced by modes of black resistance subjectivity, becomes the model for them. Black male agency, if structured like black feminist agency, would involve a vigilance about how racism profits when black liberation is apprehended as "manliness." If Douglass's chiasmus can be seen as "the central trope of slave narration, in which a slave-object writes himself or herself into a human-subject" (Gates, *Signifying Monkey* 172), Hurston's version strikes a cautionary note about the capacity of racist ideology to regulate that writing through the rhetorical slippages and transformations that can produce the vexed notions of "humanity" to which subordinate subjects aspire.

Accordingly, crucial to the model of black resistance subjectivity that Hurston's narration develops in Janie's trial scene is a vigilance about authorizing black feminist representation with the "white" discourses that can also undermine it and/or exclude the interests of black men. Instead of aligning her critique of black masculinist strategies with the racist discourses available to her in the white court, she invokes black folk "trials" that judge contending tricksters and, most emphatically, the new antilynching rhetorics that had emerged from the recent and prominent Scottsboro trials. Whereas she must rewrite Douglass to suggest important parallels between the aims of black feminism and those of antiracism, the antiracist rhetorics that emerged in the 1930s themselves were capable of constructing such analogies. In both the folk and the urban rhetorics, which directed attention to the harmfulness of intraracial misappropriations of antiracist rhetorics for ulterior motives, Hurston finds lexicons with which to condemn codes of silence in antiracist terms.

Especially with Scottsboro comes the possibility of replacing the slippage between antiracist agency and empowered masculinity with a formulation that could resist such a slippage: black agency conceived as a persistent critique of how power works, whether it be white racism or black sexism, by generating a forgetfulness of oppressed positions in more compelling identifications. It is a possibility, however, that must contend with the tenacity of the very ideological operations it exposes. Indeed Hurston's project in the trial scene is to represent both strategies for and the difficulty of actually accomplishing what the novel's initial revision of Douglass's chiasmus suggests: transforming powerful concepts of black resistance as "becoming a man" to ones that prioritize the foiling of power's manipulation of the black subject's self-divisions by "remember[ing] everything [you] don't want to forget." Such a concept of agency is arguably the contribution Hurston wanted to make to Harlem Renaissance competitions over the referent for the wisdom that "black culture" had to offer as it emerged into the American mainstream. As the novel strives to authorize black feminist literary representation at this crucial juncture, it reflects what du Cille has termed Hurston's "political activism that recognize[s] and attempt[s] to both define and disrupt [the] intersection between racism, sexism, and classism" (99).[4]

Forgetting All Those Things They Don't Want to Remember: Janie's Subordination and Tea Cake's Agency

Directly after defining "women" in terms of the revisionary chiasmus, Hurston introduces Janie as the subject who "forgets everything she doesn't want to remember": "So the beginning of this was a woman and she had come back from burying the dead" (9). The "dead" in question is Tea Cake, and "burying" him refers not only to his funeral but also to the repression of Tea Cake's violent possessiveness that informs Janie's loving memory of their relationship.

By far the best of her husbands, Tea Cake is also a problem.[5] Despite her eventual resistance to two previous and unloved husbands, Janie tolerates in a "self-crushing love" the physical abuse (192), possessive jealousy, and displacement of anger toward whites that Tea Cake (even if only on occasion) is capable of doling out. In response to unfounded fears of Janie's interest in a lighter-skinned man, Tea Cake, like the abusive Joe Starks, "slapped her around a bit to show he was boss"; for, "[b]eing able to whip her reassured him in possession" (218). Nonetheless, the next day Janie makes "men dream dreams" by "the helpless way she hung on him," and Sop-de-Bottom, Tea Cake's friend, thinks him a particularly lucky man because Janie's light skin makes it possible for "[u]h person [to] see every place you hit her" (218). Selective remembering informs both partners' participation in this relationship: Janie's forgetting of abuse for love; Tea Cake's forgetting of both Janie's welfare and his own powerlessness to express rage toward whites by exerting power over the light-skinned black woman. If Janie's dream of love obscures Tea Cake's abuse of her, black "*men* dream dreams" (emphasis added) in which their vulnerability to white racism is repressed in their power over black women.

A ferocious storm provides the occasion to make what both lovers "forget" dangerous for the black male who ostensibly benefits. In the case of Tea Cake, when white men compel him to bury the storm's dead and to privilege white bodies over black ones (251–54), Hurston literalizes Tea Cake's strategies for forgetting white power as "burials" of whites instigated by and beneficial to racist power. In Janie's case, her repressed feminist rage emerges, albeit in disguise, as her lethal warding-off of Tea Cake's mad attack. Bitten by a rabid dog in the course of saving Janie from the storm, Tea Cake eventually falls sick, goes mad, and attacks Janie in a fit of jealousy, spurred on by Sop-de-Bottom's suggestion that Janie has poisoned him in order to pursue a lighter-skinned man (266). While Janie shoots Tea Cake in self-defense against a rabid attack, this attack resonates with the earlier race-inflected jealous violence that here escalates into a life-threatening situation (273).[6] And although her mournful response is to hold her dead lover and "than[k] him wordlessly for giving her the chance for loving service" (273), her actions have already spoken louder than words, giving substance to an earlier formulation of her "self-crushing" devotion to Tea Cake as a "lov[ing] him fit tuh kill" (262).

Yet the disguising of Janie's feminist resistance to Tea Cake, her struggle against a rabid man instead of a possessively violent lover, contrasts with previous direct representations of Janie's feminist anger, especially, as we shall see, with the diatribe that breaks her silence about misogynistic uses of "signifying" in Eatonville. Why, then, would Hurston return her heroine to advocating a "wordless loving service," albeit one inflected by a lethal self-defense, in her final love affair? She does so, I will argue, in order to address a metanarrative to the novel's central concern with representing black male abuse of black women, a concern that violates codes of silence for black feminism. By strategically (but also transparently) adhering to such a code in the case of Tea Cake, Hurston generates a trial that thematizes such codes for Janie's interracial speech. In the wake of Tea Cake's death, the forgetting that secures Janie's gendered subordination becomes a matter of adhering to codes of silence for what can be said about black men in white contexts, codes that prohibit black feminist complaints in the name of race solidarity. As she demonstrates the adverse effects for black men of the code Janie obeys, Hurston makes dangerous her own narrative disguise of Tea Cake's abuse and implicitly defends the novel's substantial representation of black male domination.[7]

Earlier, in the all-black context of Eatonville, Janie has dramatically claimed the right to appropriate black cultural idioms — in the form of the "signifying" that creates community — for a feminist representation posed against black men's misogyny. If that appropriation alludes to a gendered contest over the content of "black culture" in the literature of the Harlem Renaissance, Janie's killing of Tea Cake and her subsequent trial put codes of silence, and thus the authorization of black feminist representation, at the center of this competition. But even as she indicts these codes Hurston attempts to replace a gendered contest over the meaning of "black culture" with a consensus. In the course of Janie's trial, Hurston predicates black feminist representation in white "courts" on an appropriation of black rhetorics that not only counters their masculinist (mis)uses but also links feminist resistance to the antiracism that unites the whole community before white racist law.

Tricksters and Trials

Janie's trial has precursors in other Hurston works where trials represent the complex relations between intraracial conflicts, including but not limited to gendered ones, and white law. In *Jonah's Gourd Vine* (1934), a black couple's divorce hearing in a white court is the occasion for Hurston to support codes of silence that prohibit negative representations of black male sexual behavior by black women. Although John Pearson's second wife, Hattie, has legitimate complaints against an unfaithful and physically abusive husband, her willingness to voice them to white authorities makes John, who neither refutes the charges nor brings any of his own, the hero of the day. John sees "the smirking anticipation on the faces of the lawyers, the Court attendants, the white spectators" (167) and refuses to counter with Hattie's infidelities, which he feels the white assembly would read through their racist understanding of black women as sexually licentious (169).

While Hurston gives the code of silence priority over Hattie's complaints, she does so in terms that insist the code must work to protect black women as well as black men from racist stereotyping. Moreover, as is the case with *Their Eyes*, by the time of its trial *Vine* has already portrayed John's cruelty toward his exemplary first wife for white as well as black readers. Thus Hurston constructs a paradoxical distinction between her solidarity with the antiracist aims of the code of silence and her literary authority, nonetheless, to represent black male abuse of black women.

This paradox finds a potential resolution in the trial before a black "court" that Hurston records in "The Bone of Contention" (written in the early 1930s but published for the first time in 1991) in which an intraracial trick that divides the black community is foiled by a better one that serves the community's best interests. By taking this trial as a model for Janie's trial scene Hurston attempts to replace the antagonism between black feminism and black antiracism with a shared opposition to codes of silence, revealed as intraracial tricks. Not only do such codes deploy solidarity and antiracist rhetorics in the interests of black male domination, they will emerge in the trial scene as being harmful to black men and women alike.

An elaboration of the folktale material Hurston collected for *Mules and Men* (1935), "The Bone" stages its trial as the scene of exposing bad intraracial "tricks" and valorizing the redemptive countertricks that foil them. The plot pivots around the intraracial trial of Jim Weston who injures Dave Carter with a mule bone in order to steal the latter's turkey. In true trickster fashion Jim's defender, Reverend Simms, tries to beat white law on its own terms: he claims that a "mule bone" does not qualify as a weapon within the terms of white law ("The Bone" 36). The problem, of course, is that this kind of trick tries to legitimize intracommunity crime; Jim and his defender emerge as the "badman" tricksters that John Roberts describes in his study of black folk traditions, *From Trickster to Badman,* figures who deploy an attractive resistance to white law but do so in ways that divide and/or do injury to the community (171–220). Even when the "prosecuting" Elder Long foils the initial "trick" by interpreting white law to include mule bones, the defending Reverend Simms continues his effort to recruit antiracist sentiments for his client by appealing to the supremacy of black culture: "Never mind bout dem white folks laws. . . . Dis is a colored town. . . . Dem white folks laws dont go befo' whuts in dis sacred book" (37–38). Thus the story emphasizes that black resistance rhetoric, here an appealing elevation of "colored" laws over white ones, can be appropriated for ulterior motives that endanger the community. In the end, however, Reverend Simms's new trick is foiled by a better one when Elder Long claims that mule bones *are* weapons in the Bible as well; interpreting the implications of biblical passages to support the aims of justice in the black community, Elder Long is triumphant, and Jim Weston is banished.

It is this kind of intraracial trickster contest over the solidarity discourses that unite the black community that Hurston uses as a model for the conflict between her own narrative strategies in the trial scene and those deployed by "Sop and his friends," a conflict in which both parties invoke solidarity and antilynching rhetorics to authorize their respective but not equally just causes. Reiterating the lessons of "The Bone" 's intraracial trial, Hurston characterizes the code of silence as a bad trick, a misappropriation of black resistance discourses for the interests of male domination.

However, before she appropriates "The Bone" 's folk wisdom for the novel's trial scene, the story provides the plot for the text of the play *Mule Bone*. Originally written in collaboration with Langston Hughes as a dramatic version of the short story, *Mule Bone* became the site for a now notorious struggle in which Hurston ultimately claimed sole authorship. As a result the play, ultimately in various versions, remained unpublished until recently. While we will never have a full accounting of what motivated this struggle over authorship,[8] textual evidence points to the probability that a gendered competition over the content of black cultural representation played a part. Plot changes, between the story and the play, between successive versions of the play, and between the play and *Their Eyes,* indicate Hurston's desire to disentangle "authentic race representation" from misogynistic representation.

As Henry Louis Gates has claimed, while *Mule Bone,* written in the vernacular, had the potential to "revers[e] the racist stereotypes of the ignorant dialect-speaking darkey . . . of the minstrel and vaudeville traditions," it also "reinscribe[d] the explicit sexism of [the vernacular] tradition" ("Tragedy" 22). However, the play's sexism was not a function primarily of its representation of vernacular traditions; *Mule Bone* departs from the vernacular story "The Bone of Contention," precisely in its sexism. The story foregrounds a conflict between a bad intraracial trick, motivated by a fight over who has killed a turkey, and a reverse one that saves the day for justice. But the collaborative version of *Mule Bone* both makes a woman the cause for the initial conflict and rehabilitates the badman trickster in a male bonding based on the repudiation of the woman. Whereas in the story a selfish trickster, one who misuses solidarity rhetorics, threatens black community, in the play a selfish black woman does so; the "play centers on Jim and Dave, a two-man song-and-dance team, and Daisy, the woman who comes between their singing and dancing."[9] And while Hughes has falsely claimed authorship of elements that occur in the original Hurston story, there seems little doubt that, as he has claimed, he was responsible for framing the trickster contest with the gendered one ("Letter" 230).

Although the evidence for what motivated Hurston's claims to sole authorship is inconclusive and points to personal as well as political motivations, we do know that, subsequent to the collaborative efforts and before there was any contest over authorship, Hurston rewrote parts of the play, reinstalling the story's turkey as the source of the instigation for the bad trick (Hemenway 167). But perhaps a greater clue to Hurston's discomfort with Daisy's ultimate role in *Mule Bone* is the rewriting of that role in *Their Eyes*. Like the play, the novel presents as delightful a contest of "signifying" between Jim and Dave in their efforts to win Daisy's affections. However, Janie's enjoyment of the scene is "ruined" when her husband orders her back to work (108). Although she "wanted to hear the rest of the play-acting and how it ended" (109), Janie never does. If this "play-acting," presented in the novel as well as in *Mule Bone* as an indigenous vernacular art form, centers on a delightful courting practice, there remains a question about the "ending" of the play. Having raised the question of where this entertaining "signifying" might lead, the chapter answers it in terms that echo the ending of *Mule Bone;* the courting of Daisy ushers in a narration of Joe's physical violence against Janie, and the chapter ends with black men disparaging a black woman for the trouble she causes the man who loves her. That is, this chapter reproduces the play's trajectory from celebrating indigenous black culture in the context of playful relations between genders to linking that cultural form to the denigration of black women.

While Janie "wallows" in the "big blow-out laughs" generated by Jim and Dave's courting of Daisy, she has a markedly different response to the men who claim their right to beat troublesome black women. She does "what she had never done before, that is thrust[s] herself into the conversation" (116–17). Doing so means appropriating the hyperbolic storytelling that characterizes the community's "play-acting" to point out that the black male domination of black women can compensate for racist oppression: "Sometimes God gits familiar wid us womenfolks too and talks His inside Business. He told me how surprised He was 'bout y'all turning out so smart after Him makin' yuh different. . . . It's so easy to make yo'self out God Almighty when you ain't got nothin' tuh strain against but women and chickens" (117). Thus the reproduction of *Mule Bone*'s vexed gender relations leads in the novel to a black feminist appropriation of the discourse presented in the play as the signal artistic achievement of the vernacular tradition. If the intraracial trickster contest at the heart of the play has the potential to link this cultural tradition to feminist analyses of intraracial masculinist tricks, the play displaces this possibility by shifting attention from the badman trickster to a bad black woman. In this passage of *Their Eyes*, however, Hurston redresses that outcome by producing another ending to the "play-acting," one that claims the community's traditional artistic mode for black feminism precisely because that mode has been mobilized against women.

Not surprisingly, then, Janie's "thrust[ing] herself into the conversation" is followed by Hurston's narrative resurrection of the intraracial trickster contest for the express aim of authorizing the novel's black feminist representation (117). "The Bone" 's focus on how bad tricks can divide the black community, displaced in *Mule Bone* to a focus on how a bad woman comes between male comrades, returns in Janie's trial with the feminist mission of exposing just such displacements as bad tricks. Indeed the very structuring of the trial scene as an intraracial trickster contest constitutes the first move of Hurston's "countertrick" that poses solidarity rhetorics against Sop de Bottom's "antiracist" but false charges against Janie. From here the other authorizing rhetorics Hurston invokes are the narratives and analyses that emerged from the most highly visible courtroom dramas of the early 1930s: the Scottsboro trials. For like "The Bone," Scottsboro foregrounded the harmful effects of compromising antiracist aims with ulterior motives, and, like the ultimate feminist project of *Their Eyes,* the peculiar dramas of these prominent trials gestured toward the wisdom of alliance, rather than antagonism, between feminist aims and antilynching politics.

Black Feminist Representation and the Scottsboro Trials

With its focus on trumped-up charges against Janie, its foregrounding of "law over mob rule" rhetoric as denying rather than extending legal process to blacks, its representation of intraracial misuses of antilynching rhetoric for ulterior motives, and its allusion to imperatives that dictate women's narratives about black men, Janie's trial enlists the high visibility of these issues in the context of the Scottsboro trials. Famous for demonstrating to white America that false charges of rape against black men were likely to be upheld by racist juries, Scottsboro provided a significant challenge to stereotypes of black men. If, as black feminists recently have argued, the Hill/Thomas exchange reveals that black women have not had their "Scottsboro," that they have had no equivalent symbolic "corrective to stereotypes" in intraracial as well as interracial contexts (Painter 211–12), Hurston's representation of Janie's trial offers, I will argue, an early effort to marshal the corrective force Scottsboro generated for black men in the interests of critiquing, on Scottsboro's antilynching terms, intraracial codes of silence for black women.

In March 1931, nine young black men (ranging in age from thirteen to twenty years old) were falsely accused of raping two white women, Ruby Bates and Victoria Price, aboard a train the men had hopped at Stevenson, Alabama; and after a speedy trial, pressured by threats of mob violence, all but the youngest were sentenced to death (Carter 3–10). Because of the number of defendants, their youth, and the harshness of their sentences, the trial, in contrast to many similar cases, generated outrage across America and made Scottsboro "synonymous with Southern racism, repression, and injustice" (Carter 50). Also pushing the issue of "legal lynching" to the forefront of the struggle for black rights, the Scottsboro trials dramatized the inadequacy of antilynching efforts, prioritized in the thirties by the NAACP, that focused on guaranteeing legal process to black prisoners (Hall 197). Intraracial critiques that already had linked the NAACP platform to limitations imposed by white supporters gained momentum with the blatant failure of legal process for the Scottsboro defendants.

Even more emphatically, the fact that intraracial antilynching rhetoric and strategies could be compromised by even mobilized only for ulterior motives underwrote the allegations made by both sides when the Communist Party's International Labor Defense (ILD) struggled with the NAACP for control of the appeals trials. On the one hand, the ILD garnered black support for its accusations that the NAACP's funding and image concerns, which made them slow to take up the initial Scottsboro defense, made them "traitors to the Negro masses" and "secret allies of lynchers" (Carter 61–62). On the other, the ILD's own subsequent defense of the youths was compromised by efforts to appropriate the national scandal of Scottsboro to support the aims of class struggle in America. This agenda, as NAACP spokesmen and other critics charged, contributed to legal lynching when the prosecution capitalized on the jury's hatred both of Communists and of the intervention of northerners in their affairs (Carter 167–69, 240).[10] That is, each side claimed that the other's antilynching rhetoric and strategies, because they were compromised if not overridden by ulterior motives, were complicit with legal lynching. Moreover, at the same time each side regarded such charges, when leveled by the other "complicit" side, as a strategy that itself abetted legal lynching. As Scottsboro made the sham of due process visible to white America and prioritized it for black politics, black discourses also revealed both that legal lynching was facilitated when intraracial ulterior agendas compromised antilynching aims and that allegations of such complicity could serve these ulterior agendas. The latter discourses, I will argue, provide the lexicon for Hurston's indictment, in the trial scene, of the use of antilynching rhetoric to coerce codes of silence against black feminism.

But in order to make tenacious deployments of antiracism for masculinist ulterior motives undesirable for black men as well as black women, Hurston has recourse to other Scottsboro rhetorics, ones that foregrounded the relation of white patriarchal power to the aims of lynching. For the trials both generated contradictory narratives for the relation between white women's sexual propriety and their participation in legal lynching and implicated white male domination of white women in the conviction of the defendants. After the initial trials the Communist press, NAACP pamphlets, and black newspapers emphasized Ruby's and Victoria's "bad" sexual characters: both were poor whites with histories of prostitution, and their immorality showed up in their willingness to make false allegations against innocent men (Goodman 189–90).[11] However, when Ruby Bates recanted during Haywood Patterson's appeal, it became clear that charges of white women's sexual immorality could work as easily for the prosecution as for the defense. Just as the defense and black critics earlier had linked Ruby's sexual promiscuity to her false testimony, so now did the prosecution invoke her sexual immorality against her efforts to tell the truth.

In order to discredit her recantation the prosecution and the white racist press painted Ruby as an immoral woman willing not only to sell her body but also to sell out her culture by siding with the northern, Jewish, Communist interests that, they argued, had bought her false recantation. So powerful was this argument that the jury refused to consider the validity of her testimony and again convicted Haywood Patterson. If the defense and the black press initially had pinned their hopes for acquittal on constructing a link between the women's sexual immorality and their betrayal of black men, the prosecution's similar attacks on Ruby's promiscuity showed how such charges, especially when linked to allegations of race betrayal, could help nullify a white woman's truthful defense of black men.

Moreover, the reaction to Ruby's truthful testimony had the potential to reveal how white women's subjugation to white men was integral to the logic of lynching. While it was likely that Ruby's initial fabrication of black male rape was motivated by a desire to accede to the respectable white femininity the allegations earned her in racist circles (Goodman 21–22), the consequences of her recantation revealed that such respectability depended on, indeed was synonymous with, adherence to the racist scripts that perpetuated white male domination of both black men and white women.[12] The very white people who advanced the physical protection of white women as their alibi for lynching threatened to lynch Ruby for her recantation; indeed, these threats were so palpable that the National Guard was called in to hide and protect her (Carter 234–35). When this white woman refused to stick to the false charges whose effects shored up white male supremacy over black men and white women, protection was replaced by vengeful retaliation.

After the second conviction of Haywood Patterson, Ruby made a number of widely attended public appearances on behalf of the defendants, claiming in nationally publicized speeches that she had been forced to lie at the initial trials and that she had feared she would be lynched if she had not adhered to the story (Goodman 198; Carter 249). Indeed fears for her life functioned to keep Ruby from testifying in person at the subsequent appeals. As a result of these events, antilynching explanations of why the women lied in the first place shifted from their "immoral" sexual behavior to the fact that the initial testimony had been coerced by strong powers. While Ruby, coached by the ILD, identified these powers primarily in class terms (Goodman 198), her drama also vividly implicated white women's subjugation to racist patriarchal imperatives in the practice of legal lynching.

Indeed Scottsboro coincided historically with the emergence of an organization that would go on to make white feminist analysis central to antilynching activism in the 1930s: the Association of Southern Women for the Prevention of Lynching (1930–42). Insisting on crucial links between false allegations of black male rape, white women's belief and/or participation in such charges, and the subordination of white women, the ASWPL argued that white women's vulnerability to black men was the alibi not only for heinous racist crimes but also for insuring white women's desire for a protective subjugation to white men and their consent to refrain from participation in the public sphere. Bearing out their own theories that lynching often had more to do with intimidating white women than with protecting them, the ASWPL women discovered that, like Ruby, they became targets of lynching threats when they challenged prevailing racist scripts about black men (Hall 152–53).

Especially if glossed by the ASWPL analysis, which was prominent and extremely effective in combatting lynching by the mid-thirties, the nullification of Ruby Bates's recantation had the potential to connect the black defendants' convictions to a white woman's incapacity to counter intersecting racist and patriarchal imperatives for what she could say about black men. Hurston very likely seeks to invoke this connection when she constructs in Janie's trial a connection between *black* masculinist imperatives for black female speech and white racist distortions of Janie's testimony. In doing so Hurston attempts to recruit black outrage over the silencing of Ruby Bates's recantation to support her own resistance to intraracial codes of silence for black feminism. Indeed the chronological shift in Scottsboro's antilynching rhetorics, the move from allegations of the women's sexual immorality to allegations that racist men first coerced and later distorted Ruby's testimony, underwrites the difference between Sop's "antiracist" efforts to coerce Janie's testimony and Hurston's feminist deployment of antilynching rhetoric.

Remembering Everything They Don't Want to Forget: Janie's Trial as an Intraracial Trickster Contest

Hurston sets the scene of Janie's trial by locating her as vulnerable not only to the alien white court but also to the members of the black community.[13] On the one hand, "twelve strange men who didn't know a thing about people like Tea Cake and her were going to sit on the thing" (274); but on the other, those who know them well have turned against her: "[S]he saw all of the colored people standing up in the back of the courtroom. Packed tight like a case of celery, only much darker than that. They were all against her, she could see. So many were there against her that a light slap from each one of them would have beat her to death. She felt them pelting her with dirty thoughts" (275).

Janie's initial perception of "the colored people" emphasizes their weakness in the white courtroom; nonetheless, as the novel has already emphasized, racist oppression can fuel intraracial domination, and Janie feels powerfully threatened by the crowd. Invoking Scottsboro's prominent exposé of the falseness of rape charges against black men, Janie perceives the black crowd as a kind of "lynch mob" from whose trumped-up charges *she* is physically in danger. At the outset of the trial, then, Hurston constructs a link between antilynching rhetoric and resistance to what will soon be revealed as strategies that coerce codes of silence by opposing black feminism to antiracism.

Indeed while such codes work by compelling black women to "forget" their subordination in an allegiance to race solidarity, here Janie begins to reverse this process, to remember the domination previously effaced in loving solidarity. Importantly, Hurston predicates this remembering on an appropriation of the antiracist rhetorics that at this point cohere the black community against her. As Janie watches the false allegations gaining momentum, the crowd appears to talk "all together like a choir" (276); accordingly, Janie will do her best to restore her place in the community by demonstrating her adherence to the antiracist principles in which the charges are figured forth. At the same time, Janie's capacity to remember the sexist domination that masculinist antiracism suppresses also relies on the effects of the antiracist discourses she embraces. Tea Cake's possessive "light slap," previously understood as an indication of love, surfaces in the passage on the black crowd as Janie's trope for intraracial male domination precisely *because* that domination takes the form of a "mob's" false charges.

Importantly, such an awareness arises "automatically" for Janie as she reacts against the threatening "mob"; black feminist awareness, Hurston implies, can emerge from its suppression by masculinist uses of antiracist discourses when analyses of racist domination shed light on intraracial male domination. What she imagines, that is, is a process whereby black masculinist strategies succumb to the very oppositionality of the resistance discourses they appropriate. Such processes, however, also require the support of deliberate formulations of intersections between black feminism and antiracism. Thus the opening passages initiate the trial scene's overall calculated effort to rearticulate the intersection between black feminism and antilynching rhetorics.

These efforts are posed against the narrative the community would like to present, which, in the context of the novel's previous events, emerges as one that mobilizes black masculinist antiracism: "[The black spectators] sent word by the bailiff to Mr. Prescott they wanted to testify in the case. Tea Cake was a good boy. No nigger woman ain't never been treated no better. Naw suh! He worked like a dog for her and nearly killed himself saving her in the storm, then soon as he got a little fever from the water, she had took up with another man. Sent for him to come from way off. Hanging was too good" (276). This story attributes an act that Hurston, if not Janie, has implicated in feminist resistance to Janie's willingness to kill Tea Cake in the interests of "another man" who, we know from Sop's previous race-inflected suspicions, is the light-skinned Mr. Turner. We also know that Sop, who will soon emerge as the spokesman for the crowd, is capable of displacing whiteness onto light-skinned blacks; he has done so earlier in his projection of whiteness mastered onto the bruised, submissive Janie.

Thus Janie's (feminist) self-defense is transformed into an act of intersecting sexual transgression and race betrayal that is congruent with the aims of lynching: she joins the light-skinned man from outside the community in his desire to get rid of the darker Tea Cake. And, of course, her pursuit of an acquittal from the racist court for the killing of a black man is easily assimilated to Sop's false interpretation. Such a translation of black feminist resistance into betrayals of the race are symptomatic of the strategies used to enforce codes of silence against black feminism. As Kimberle Crenshaw has noted, although many black women, recognizing the potential for racist appropriations, voluntarily refrain from critiques of black men, "the maintenance of silence also has coercive dimensions" manifest as transformations of feminist resistance into race betrayal (420).

But while these trumped-up charges will be successful in coercing Janie's adherence to codes of silence, they inspire a very different response from Hurston's narration of the trial scene. Here she both stresses the harmful effects of Janie's capitulation to these codes and vindicates her own breaking of them earlier in the novel, using black cultural and antilynching rhetorics to authorize her critique. Invoking "The Bone" 's intraracial trickster contest between bad and good deployments of black solidarity rhetorics, Hurston reveals the crowd's charges against Janie as a misappropriation of antilynching rhetoric by alluding to the lessons of Scottsboro. First she implicates these false charges in those leveled against Ruby's recantation by the prosecution and echoed by an angry mob. When the charges against Janie link an implied race betrayal to a woman's sexual immorality and describe her complicity with a man "from far off" that should be punished by hanging, Hurston attempts to liken black strategies for intraracial male domination to the white ones Scottsboro revealed as bound up with the legal lynching of black men.

This intersection of black patriarchal rhetorics with antiracism, on the one hand, and with racist patriarchal strategies, on the other, betrays a confusion between black resisting subjectivity and a universalized masculinity empowered locally by the domination of women. Such forgetting of raced masculinity, of course, effaces the disastrous consequences of white patriarchal aims for black men as it here also exacerbates a lack of concern about black women's vulnerability to racist stereotypes. In their doomed effort to recruit white male support for the condemnation of Janie's resistance to a black man, Sop and his backers, in contrast to John Pearson's vigilance in *Jonah's Gourd Vine*, invoke racist stereotypes of black female promiscuity and desire for "white" men. But as the trial scene proceeds, Hurston again recruits Scottsboro's lessons to help Sop and his friends remember what they forget by collapsing male empowerment with antiracism. Although he is oblivious to the implication of his rhetoric in the white patriarchal discourses that so recently have put black men at risk, Sop is reminded rudely of the difference race makes in masculinity when he tries to testify:

"Mistah Prescott, Ah got somethin' tuh say," Sop-de-Bottom spoke out anonymously from the anonymous herd. . . .

"If you know what's good for you, you better shut your mouth up until somebody calls you," Mr. Prescott told him coldly.

"Yassuh, Mr. Prescott."

"We are handling this case. Another word out of *you*; out of any of you niggers back there, and I'll bind you over to the big court."

"Yassuh." (277)

Emphasizing the power of the white court to transform intraracial black masculinist discourse into deferential interracial speech, this passage serves to remind Sop of the racist differentials between men he can try to ignore in the black township of Eatonville. Moreover, when this racist reprimand involves the silencing of an unruly mob, it immediately invokes Scottsboro's most prominent antilynching analysis: that the elimination of mob rule in favor of granting black men due process often simply produces "legal lynching." With the silencing of the *black* mob, Hurston vividly underscores this analysis, making the prohibition of "mob rule" inextricable from the denial of black participation in due process. Yet this strong critique of "legal lynching," constructed as it is in the context of Sop's efforts to shore up intraracial male domination, is troubled by the way it positions Janie as the benefactor of racist law and Sop as the victim of that law. By making this gendered relation to antiracism the outcome of indicting the reprimand to the black "mob," Hurston registers her recognition that Scottsboro's most influential discourses could be more easily mobilized in intraracial contexts against rather than for black feminism.

However, if the passage that portrays the racist silencing of the black "mob" seems to put the indictment of legal lynching on Sop's side, it also announces the biggest stakes for the "trickster contest" between Sop's masculinist deployment of black resistance rhetorics and Hurston's counter, feminist one: the competition over whose aims will be authorized by Scottsboro's powerful condemnation of racist legal systems. For, we will recall, Scottsboro's hallmark critique generated a number of rhetorics about the functioning of racist due process, including ones that had the potential to link the denial of black male civil rights not to the interference with intraracial masculinist goals but to critiques of them. Accordingly, for the remainder of the trial scene, Hurston will link the racism in the legal process that acquits Janie not (as Sop wants to) to the articulation of black feminist resistance but, as with the virulent exchange of charges between the NAACP and the ILD, to the effects of what, she has implied, are the ulterior motives in Sop's use of antiracist themes: the desire to enforce a code of silence against black feminist representation. And these effects, in turn, become recognizably dangerous in the context of the coercion of Ruby Bates's initial testimony and the subsequent discrediting of her recantation, both of which could take on feminist dimensions in light of the ASWPL's successful emphasis on the relation between lynching and the oppression of white women.[14]

Demonstrating the effectiveness of the "trick" that silences black feminism by transforming it into a violation of race solidarity, Janie observes a code of silence about black male abuse — and she does so precisely by adhering to Hurston's own strategic coding of feminist anger. However, Hurston makes Janie's story, delivered against a background of perceived lynching threats from a hostile "mob," as potentially dangerous for black men as was Ruby Bates's inability to displace white male prescriptions for what could be said about black men. On the one hand, Janie's story produces "unconscious" slippages between the terms that adhere to the code and those that reify hateful allegations against black men. On the other, it articulates a narrative of wifely devotion on the occasion of black male death that, as it crosses racial boundaries, too easily translates into the racist scripts the jury wants to hear.

About to begin her testimony, Janie's most urgent concern is to counter the community's false charges: "First thing she had to remember was she was not at home. She was in the courthouse fighting something and it wasn't death. It was worse than that. It was lying thoughts. She had to go way back to let them know how she and Tea Cake had been with one another so they could see she could never shoot Tea Cake out of malice" (278). The priority Janie gives to "remember[ing] she was not at home" but before the white court, coupled with the imperative to replace the black spectators' "lying thoughts" with a story that proves her loving commitment to Tea Cake's welfare, registers how the charges of race betrayal have succeeded in making Janie adhere to a code of silence about Tea Cake's abuse. Because she remembers the protocol she must observe in white racist contexts, Janie reiterates the cover story that originates, of course, in Hurston's own strategic capitulation to the code: "She tried to make them see how terrible it was that things were fixed so that Tea Cake couldn't come back to himself until he had got rid of that mad dog that was in him and he couldn't get rid of the dog and live. He had to die to get rid of the dog. But she hadn't wanted to kill him. A man is up against a hard game when he must die to beat it. She made them see how she couldn't ever want to be rid of him" (278).

In the very language that adheres to the code Hurston also both embeds a critique of her own strategic conformity to it and sets the stage for Janie's coded testimony to have dire effects on the racist court.[15] It is, of course, only because of Hurston's coded narration that "things were fixed so" that Tea Cake turns into a mad dog and must be shot. Along with the sexist/rabid "madness" that inhabits Tea Cake, what is so "terrible" is the way the code of silence requires black women to disguise male violence. But if such a "fixing" of what can be said of black men is terrible for the women whose feminist resistance it prohibits, such dictates here prove equally terrible for black men. When she invokes a folk saying that refers to the tenacious horrors of racism — "a man is up against a hard game when he must die to beat it" — Hurston attempts to reveal the code of silence and the narratives that enforce it as elements of a willing rather than a coerced black male participation in the games by which racism perpetuates its power.

First, the terms of the code emerge as jarringly compatible with lynching rhetoric: references to a black man as a "mad dog" are, of course, blatantly resonant with racist epithets. But Hurston's point is that these epithets coincide *not* with Janie's articulation of a feminist complaint but with the story that veils it, one that originates with Hurston's own narrative coding of Janie's defense against Tea Cake. That Janie is unaware of this intersection of referents for "mad dog" seems to be symptomatic of an unconscious eruption of unspeakable and potentially vengeful rage. The consequence not only of the abuse she is forbidden to represent but also of the false charges that both reify racist stereotypes of black women and endanger her life, this rage proves more certainly dangerous for black men than a critique of intraracial male domination.[16] Only this rage, Hurston implies, interferes with (and unwittingly so) Janie's vigilance against reproducing racist stereotypes in white contexts.[17]

Secondly, Hurston adds to this warning about generating black female rage a more forceful and elaborate reminder, one that counts on recalling the plight of Ruby Bates, that racist judges and juries can distort women's testimony about black men to fit racist scripts. While this distortion may be facilitated by Janie's vexed terminology that erupts despite (and because) of her silence about Tea Cake's abuse, the jury's racist interpretation benefits more directly from the part of Janie's story that obediently sticks to a narrative of wifely devotion. Hurston implicates black masculinist prescriptions for black female speech in the ease with which Janie's coded testimony can be assimilated to racist patriarchal agendas. As the judge gives directions to the jury, he leaves room to translate her story of a loving wife's self-defense in circumstances beyond her control into a celebrated shooting of a black man: "Gentlemen of the jury, it is for you to decide whether the defendant has committed a cold blooded murder or whether she is a poor broken creature, a devoted wife trapped by unfortunate circumstances who really in firing a rifle bullet into the heart of her late husband did a great act of mercy. If you find her a wanton killer you must bring in a verdict of first degree murder. If the evidence does not justify that then you must set her free" (279). By stressing the relation of "evidence" to "justification," the judge's remarks invoke how racist summations to juries, like the one that famously misrepresented Ruby's recantation, can make a woman's testimony justify the very a priori scripts about black men that she wants to counter. Accordingly, the judge's discourse exhibits symptoms of such an effort. Rather than instructing the jury to consider whether the killing was done in self-defence, he poses a "wanton killer" against a "devoted wife," caught in significantly vague "unfortunate circumstances," whose attentions to the heart of her black husband are mercifully lethal. As it seems to play out (and play to) a fantasy that *all* female powerlessness and all wifely devotion (perhaps especially that of the light-skinned black woman) serve white male supremacy, the judge's discourse constructs a relation between the concept of devoted wives and the "great act" of killing a black man. Thus Hurston seems to warn against intraracial "fixings" of black female speech in ways that dovetail with racist patriarchal meanings for obedient, devoted women.

If it takes some rhetorical maneuvering to make a black woman's adherence to black masculinist dictates intersect with white racist narratives of appropriate femininity, Hurston concludes the trial scene by again alluding to the *easy* fit between Sop's allegations, meant to coerce codes of silence, and the racist narratives white men demand of and/or arbitrarily attribute to (here, black as well as white) women's speech about black men. Earlier the similarity between Sop's trumped-up charges and the racist ones that disallowed Ruby's recantation may be undetectable to many readers because black patriarchal rhetoric, silenced with racist threats, is collapsed with a resistance to racist due process. Now, however, when the context for revealing similarities between black masculinist strategies and white racist ones is the evaluation of Janie's testimony by the racist court, Hurston is able to remind her readers that Scottsboro's racist due process relied heavily on both the coercion and the distortion of a woman's testimony about black men. Black masculinist coercion, which leads to the court's distortion of Janie's coded testimony, Hurston implies, fuels the racist verdict.

At the same time, the narrative that has coerced Janie's coded speech dovetails precisely with the racist one that distorts her testimony. That is, Hurston shows that the discourses about black women that serve male domination in black contests, ones that exploit antiracist rhetoric for ulterior motives, can in themselves underscore those that vindicate the legal lynching of black men in white contexts. As she awaits the verdict, Janie fears that the jury will base its decision on a "misunderstanding" similar to the one circulated by Sop: "It was not death she feared. It was misunderstanding. If they made a verdict that she didn't want Tea Cake and wanted him dead, then that was a real sin and a shame. It was worse than murder. Then the jury was back again. Out five minutes by the courthouse clock" (279).

Now Janie's fear of the community's "misunderstanding" of her is indistinguishable from her fear that the jury similarly will conclude "she didn't want Tea Cake and wanted him dead." Of course, such a conclusion by a racist jury would not reflect a sympathy with Sop's perspective, nor would it produce a guilty verdict. "A verdict that she didn't want Tea Cake and wanted him dead," even as it would give credence to the charges that coerce codes of silence, would coincide as well with racist narratives that insisted "white" women found black men abhorrent and black women preferred white men. That the light-skinned Janie could trigger one or both scenarios is assumed even by the black spectators; as one man remarks after the trial, "[Y]ou know dem white mens wuzn't gointuh do nothin' tuh no woman dat look lak her" (280).

Thus Hurston suggests that like the jury that misinterpreted Ruby Bates's testimony to sustain racist narratives, this jury hears what it wants to hear. Significantly, what it hears in Janie's coded testimony is exactly the narrative Sop would have liked to present. The narrative meant to control what black women can say about black men is indistinguishable from the racist narratives that white men coerce from and/or attribute to "white" women in order to construct alibis for legal lynching. Black readers outraged over the coercion and distortion of Ruby's respective testimonies might now reevaluate the wisdom of pursuing in intraracial contexts the coercions of female speech that are so costly for black men in white racist ones.

For Hurston leaves no doubt that this court, despite its "just" verdict, is a racist one. "Out five minutes by the courthouse clock," the jury clearly invokes those other juries that quickly returned racist verdicts for falsely accused black men: Haywood Patterson's first conviction took a mere twenty-five minutes, and his second, the occasion of Ruby's recantation, took only moments (Goodman 145). Finding Tea Cake's death "to be entirely accidental and justifiable" (279), the verdict both serves justice and resonates with racist justifications. Racism, however, here intersects not with Janie's articulation of feminist resistance, as Sop's narrative alleges, but with the effects of the ulterior motives in Sop's use of antilynching rhetorics: the code of silence Janie obeys, on the one hand, and the jury's consequent ability to bend her testimony to "fixed" racist narratives for what can be said about black men, on the other.

As the trickster contest between masculinist and feminist deployments of antiracist rhetorics draws to a close, then, Sop's condemnation of black feminist resistance is revealed as a misappropriation of antiracist rhetoric that is also harmful to black men, and black feminism emerges as congruent with a number of Scottsboro's analyses of racist due process. Nonetheless, the competition between just and unjust solidarity rhetorics remains alive and well. Indeed, at the end of the trial scene Hurston gives the last interpretive word to a black man's invocation of a tenacious folk saying: "[U]h white man and uh nigger woman is de freest thing on earth" (280).[18] Although they recognize the racism in the verdict, including the likelihood that the jury makes Janie's story reflect its own racist desires, the black men who discuss the trial are oblivious to the way the verdict both distorts Janie's coded testimony and dovetails with their own collapsing of black feminism with white racism. Instead of recognizing, via the Scottsboro lexicons invoked in the trial scene, the liabilities in such strategies for agency, these men respond to the failure of their coercive false charges in white courts by renewing them in black conversations.

Echoing Sop's earlier assimilation of Janie's self-defensive act to the aims of white racist men, these concluding comments participate in the rhetoric meant to coerce black women's forgetting of and/or silence about male domination. But, as the novel has tried to demonstrate, these comments are themselves symptomatic of black male efforts to forget race oppression in intraracial male dominance, a forgetting that in interracial contexts has

disastrous effects. Black men's forgetting of race in gender is not only structured like black women's forgetting of gender in race; the former manifests
itself as the silencing of black feminism on antiracist terms. While Hurston's model for agency—a "remember[ing] [of] everything [you] don't
want to forget" that is vigilant about how domination can regulate the
dynamics between a subject's multiple investments (9)—could intervene in
these dynamics, her male characters continue their efforts to forget racism
in intraracial masculinity by compelling black women's forgetfulness of
gendered oppression. Just as the tenacious sayings that link black women to
white racism survive the trial's critique of such strategies, what "Sop and his
friends" want after the trial is, alas, Janie's "quick forgetfulness" (281).

Nevertheless, the trial scene's ingenious rearticulation of antiracism and
black feminism points to the antilynching rhetorics (on the injurious effects
of pursuing ulterior motives in the name of antiracism; on the possible
racist consequences of black patriarchal strategies) that have the potential
to forge sustained democratic alliances between black men and black
women. If Sop and his friends remain caught in the first term of Hurston's
revisionary chiasmus—a forgetting of one set of interests in another—
when they link agency to sexist manliness, the novel constitutes an effort to
inspire in its readers the remembering that exposes and reverses such forgetting. Hurston's project, we will recall, is to make the black female subject who forgets gendered oppression in race solidarity emerge as the model
for the male subject whose resistance is compromised by forgetting race
in gender (in ways that both play into white racism and oppress black
women). Success would mean that black male resistance to racist strategies
could prioritize resistance to how domination orchestrates self-difference;
this analysis, in turn, could produce an antiracist alliance with black feminism and, as a result, a repudiation of injurious masculinist strategies. It is
this vision, of an antiracism that not only authorizes (rather than prohibits)
black feminism but also becomes the grounds for eliminating intraracial
sexism, that Hurston offers in her major contribution to Harlem Renaissance representations of the African American cultural experience.

The Antiracist Heroine as Black Feminist: The Trial of Ruby
McCollum and *Their Eyes Were Watching God*

That Hurston hoped her novel would accomplish the kind of vindication
of black feminism in African American contexts that Scottsboro accom-

plished for black resistance to racist due process in white contexts is borne out in her coverage, fifteen years later, of the trial of Ruby McCollum in Live Oak, Florida. Like the novel, the articles seek, through the antiracist rhetorics generated by a racist trial, to equate racist restrictions on a black woman's testimony with intraracial prohibitions against black feminist speech. Central to the drama of this trial were the racist prohibitions on Ruby's testimony about what motivated her to kill her white lover, the prominent Dr. Adams. Although Ruby was allowed to report her affair with Adams, she was not permitted to link her crime to the physical and emotional abuse in the relationship, including threats and actions taken against her life. Such testimony surely would have meant a conviction of manslaughter rather than of first-degree murder; but it also would have meant that the fact of white male miscegenation would have taken center stage at the trial. The official story, and the one for which Ruby was convicted, claimed that an "irate Negress, enraged over a bill for medical charges," had slain the kindly white doctor.[19]

If Ruby is silenced, however, Hurston's articles for the *Pittsburgh Courier,* a black newspaper, give voice to the accused woman's side of the story. Significantly, they do so in terms that, as they reveal the racist cover-up of white male miscegenation, invoke in precise phrases from *Their Eyes* the story of a black woman's subjection to black male domination and physical abuse. By making her feminist novel an intertext for representing what racism makes unspeakable for a black woman on trial, Hurston's objective with the novel's address to black readers is underscored: to recruit the potential for a publicized trial to authorize in antiracist terms the feminist violation of intraracial codes of silence.

Here, however, the task is greatly facilitated by the fact that the black woman on trial, rather than being regarded as complicit with white law, is understood as clearly threatened by a racist legal process. In contrast to the community's attitude toward Janie, Ruby (as Hurston presents her) is seen as an antiracist heroine both because she was willing to resist a powerful white man and because she is caught up in a racist legal process. Hurston promotes this view throughout her several articles, but nowhere more forcefully than in the opening sentences of her first installment. Posing Ruby's act against one of Stephen C. Foster's "world-famous songs" that claims "the head must bow, and the back will have to bend . . . wherever the darky may go," Hurston concludes: "It is obvious that he did not contemplate a Negro woman on trial for her *life* for shooting to death a prominent white physician" ("1st Day" 1 and 4).

Thus Hurston begins her inventive coverage of the trial by representing it as, like the Scottsboro trials, an occasion to challenge racist stereotypes about blacks. Indeed despite the fact that the trial was being largely ignored in the white press (McCarthy 180),[20] Hurston presented Ruby, the challenger of "world-famous" images of blacks, as "the tragic star of a world-shaking drama" whose story was having a profound impact on America: "In a blindingly brutal light, America has discovered that the separation of the races is a fiction" ("Folds of Fate" 2). If Scottsboro revealed that stereotypes of black men as rapists were often trumped up to serve white male interests, the McCollum trial could reveal not only that blacks were defiant but also that antimiscegenation rhetoric, used to vindicate lynching, coexisted with the toleration of white male sexual access to black women. Having presented Ruby's case as continuing Scottsboro's challenges to trumped-up charges against and racial stereotypes of black men, however, Hurston then tries to appropriate this corrective antiracist power, and the black support of it, for lifting intraracial prohibitions on black feminist representation. Throughout the articles, Hurston makes the antiracist violation of white strictures on Ruby McCollum's speech inextricable from the feminist violation of intraracial codes of silence.

For readers of *Their Eyes,* Hurston's first installment on the trial makes it clear that the narration of Ruby's trial attempts to resolve the competition over antiracist rhetoric that structures Janie's trial scene. Here, in a description that explicitly recalls the novel's introduction of the intraracial trickster contest, Hurston instead announces the unity of her newspaper narration with the community's antiracist sentiments:

> The Negro spectators, all seated in the gallery, leaned forward and all looked in the same direction like cows in a pasture. Their eyes were fixed hopefully on [defense attorney] P. Guy Crews. . . .
>
> "That lawyer is no good" a man in the second row murmured in deep disappointment. "Why don't he let her talk?"
>
> "That's what I say" a woman's voice grumbled. "He ain't let her say a word since the mess started. Shucks! You can learn more from the newspapers than you can from her." ("1st Day" 4)

Instead of wanting to counter her testimony, the black spectators have come, Hurston tells us, "to hear what Ruby McCollum was going to tell" (4). Whereas in the famous novel the narrator competes with the black crowd for antiracist rhetorics, here "our reporter" herself is part of the gallery of spectators. And while these spectators are similarly characterized as dehumanized by the white court (in the novel, "packed in like celery"; here, "cowlike" in their dependence on that law), this disenfranchisement produces not an antagonism to the black woman's testimony but anger over the restrictions on her speech.

Moreover, if Ruby's story is silenced by the white court, it is, as one of the female spectators notes, also available — but only in the newspaper articles on the trial. Importantly, and as Hurston knows very well, the only such articles are her own. In an effort to keep the story of white male miscegenation from circulating, local authorities not only had arranged for Ruby to suffer a barbaric and near fatal forced abortion but also had barred all contact between Ruby and the press, white as well as black.[21] Thus the community's call to "let Ruby talk" leads directly and only to Hurston's coverage of the trial; and the reader who followed the *Courier* articles would discover that when Hurston speaks for Ruby she links the violation of white racist rules for what can be revealed about this black woman to the violation of black male "antiracist" ones.

What both sets of rules have in common is that they serve the patriarchal domination of black women in white and black contexts respectively. Thus this reporter, announced in most of the installments as a "famous novelist," endows Ruby McCollum, the antiracist heroine, with the black feminist struggles of Janie Killicks Starks Woods. Like Janie's, Ruby's sexual and emotional desires are presented in a positive light; and, like Janie's, the continual disappointments Ruby encounters on these scores are the drama of suffering that takes central stage. Although Ruby dreams of a "bee for her blossom" ("Life Story/3rd Installment" 2), a phrase that tropes Janie's sexual desire and Tea Cake as object of that desire, she marries a physically abusive, unfaithful black man, and this abuse makes "something sacred and precious [fall] off the shelf in [her] heart" ("Life Story/6th Installment" 4), the exact effect produced by Joe Starks's abuse of Janie (*Their Eyes* 112). Furthermore, the white man's domination exacerbates that of the black man's. While Ruby feels desire for the white doctor (a representation, as Hurston will emphasize in a subsequent text, as prohibited within black contexts as within white ones),[22] especially as his initial courting compensates for Sam's abuse, coercion and physical violence mark the later stages of their relationship as well. Only when she agrees to do as the doctor desires, for example, does he change a medication that is making her very sick ("Life Story/6th Installment" 4).

In addition, Ruby's husband, Sam, was aware of Adams's abuse of his wife but permitted it because the doctor, who was politically connected, "let him run numbers for [Ruby's] sake" (Huie 76). Nonetheless, Sam was furious about the second pregnancy, and Ruby feared his reaction to the birth of another light-skinned child. According to Hurston, in the end Ruby understands her crime as motivated by fear of both the black husband and the white lover: "I was between two guns that morning . . . the gun of my husband and the gun of Adams" ("Life Story/9th Installment" 3). In fact, when Sam McCollum has a heart attack and dies upon hearing of his wife's act, Hurston implies that Sam's untimely end is a product of the same justifiable resistance Ruby directs against Dr. Adams. For "as much as she regretted the deaths of Dr. Adams, and her husband," like Janie, "she had only acted instinctively, to — in a way — protect her own life" (3).

In Hurston's description of Ruby McCollum's trial, then, the black spectators' call "to let Ruby talk" is imagined as extending the community's desire to break racist strictures on the black woman's speech to an authorization for a feminist breaking of intraracial codes of silence. Because in this instance racist strictures are also white patriarchal ones, and because Ruby suffers abuse from a black man as well, Hurston is able to construct an equation between antiracist and black feminist representation. However, when the resulting united front of the feminist reporter and the antiracist spectators supports the story of a woman named "Ruby," a story silenced by a racist court but resurrected in the language of *Their Eyes,* Hurston registers the need to fortify the articles' feminist strategies with those of the novel. Without the allusion to Ruby Bates in the context of *Their Eyes,* Ruby McCollum's largely unremarked trial could not, despite Hurston's hyperbolic claims, be associated with highly visible antiracist interventions that, in turn, could be logically linked to the authorization of black feminism.

Achieving an effective, rather than merely a rhetorical, feminist slippage between the famous white antiracist heroine and the largely invisible black one depends on invoking for the story of Ruby McCollum the novel's analogy between Ruby Bates and Janie Woods. Of the two texts, the novel and the newspaper coverage of the trial, only the novel makes the intraracial silencing of black women harmful, as was the silencing of Ruby Bates, to black men; only the novel makes analogies between the black male subject of racism and the black female subject of intraracial gendered subordination. Only by ventriloquizing Ruby McCollum with Janie Woods could the "famous novelist" remind her readers of a link between the antiracist analyses of the processes that harm black men and the intraracial ones that harm black women.

On the one hand, Hurston's story of Ruby McCollum eliminates the intraracial struggle at the heart of Janie's trial and thus appears to achieve the novel's aims. But on the other, her strategy for achieving this resolution yields precarious results, relying as it does on the arbitrary transformation of an antiracist narrative the community calls for into a feminist one that might incense her black readers. Despite the appreciation expressed (significantly) by a black female spectator, we know from the novel to which she so pointedly alludes that Hurston's black feminist narrative is *not* the story many of the spectators want Ruby to tell. Indeed, by articulating the moment of her narrative's unity with the community in the very rhetoric with which the novel sets up a contest between masculinist and feminist deployments of antiracism, Hurston also reminds us of the tenacity of the competition she here presents as finally won.

It is this reminder, I believe, that the novel's intertextual presence in the story of the antiracist heroine as black feminist is meant to instigate. By invoking the novel's trial Hurston reactivates the recognition both of an ongoing competition for how race and gender will be coarticulated for black women and of the necessity for the kinds of resolutions to the "contest" that the novel envisions. Without these considerations, the transformation of a black woman from antiracist heroine to black feminist can be only a transitory, rhetorical intervention; and the reverse slippage, the one from black feminist to antiracist that Hurston constructs for her narrative voice in *Their Eyes*, would not be possible.

Indeed, a few years later, Hurston's contribution to William Bradford Huie's book on the McCollum trial (1956) makes it very clear that the *Courier* articles' representation of black outrage over Ruby's silencing competes with other and black masculinist attitudes. Here, as in the novel, Hurston shows that these attitudes mirror racist constraints on black female speech that are harmful also to black men. Huie, a white journalist who had been Hurston's editor at the *American Mercury* and who wrote his book because Hurston "had asked [him] to help establish the truth" (7), inserts at the very center of his text a twelve-page account of the trial by Hurston (89–101). In this section, Hurston stresses "the trial was one of a smothering blanket of silence," that it "amounted to mass delusion by unanimous agreement" (89).

Although some blacks, Hurston claims, protest this silencing for its effects both on Ruby's case and on perpetuating dangerous myths about black male miscegenation, many more contribute to this silencing. Now Hurston describes how local community members, rather than offering antiracist support, "loudly denounced Ruby" in an effort not to antagonize white people (90). In this account too the spectators in the gallery are more afraid for their own lives than they are for what might happen to Ruby (91). Along with denunciations of Ruby that derive from fear and/or from jealousy of the well-off defendant, however, are those that support black male anger over her consensual affair with the prominent white man: "[T]here was human satisfaction on the part of the Negro men in that Ruby had gotten into 'bad trouble' by giving herself to a white man" (93). Although Hurston concludes her narration with an extended passage on the racist court's strategies for silencing Ruby's real motives in the killing, she has devoted as many pages to the black community's complicity with this silencing. When by way of comment on the verdict and the death sentence Hurston observes that "the Community will had been done" (101), this phrase that ends her contribution to Huie's book refers to black as well as white communities.

Thus, despite the utopian representation in her newspaper coverage of the trial, Hurston acknowledges in Huie's book that her feminist interventions in the relation between antiracism and black feminism must continually compete with the entrenched versions she wants to displace. Most promising as a strategy that can compete successfully in this contest is the demonstration of how the black masculinist silencing of black women can reify a racist silencing that is as harmful to black men as it is to black women. Accordingly, in the context of a white antiracist's efforts to make the McCollum trial, like the Scottsboro trials, reveal the truth about white racism to white America, Hurston abandons her *Courier* efforts to claim that the antiracist defense of Ruby is inextricable from the support of black feminism. Instead Hurston returns to the project meant to construct a more lasting alliance between antiracism and black feminism: the novel's efforts to make black resistance rhetorics prioritize a recognition of how racism can regulate black male subjectivity so that pursuits of male empowerment reify racist oppression. Of course, it is both ironic and troubling that Hurston now embeds this crucial reformulation of intraracial antiracist rhetoric in a text that targeted white antiracists; doing so would seem to register a complex anxiety about the reception of such feminist antiracism in black contexts.[23]

Nonetheless, together Hurston's *Courier* articles and her contribution to Huie's book attempt to appropriate for black feminism the corrective force that a publicly denounced racist trial could bring to bear. In the articles she inflects the rhetorical ease with which she accomplishes this appropriation with the intertext of the novel that predicates alliances between black feminism and antiracism on a more difficult achievement: shared analyses of how domination works with a subject's self-divisions. And in her contribution to a white antiracist's book she unambiguously indicts the slippage between misogyny and antiracism that can play into racist agendas for black men and women alike. Both the articles and the book register the importance for Hurston of bolstering the possible connections between feminism and antiracism with what she feels all black resisting subjects cannot afford to forget: the antiracist and black cultural rhetorics, forged in both urban and rural contexts, whose analyses of domination and strategies for agency have intraracial as well as interracial applications. Only these have the potential to make Hurston's description of the black female subject, by which she articulates both the structure of intraracial gendered subordination and strategies for resistance to it, at once the model for and the reflection of the black antiracist subject.

Chapter 3

WOMEN'S DEVELOPMENT

AND "COMPOSITE" SUBJECTIVITY

Feminism and Social Evolution in Ellen Glasgow

As we have seen, Hurston appropriates a range of rhetorics in her effort both to indict how intraracial codes prohibit black feminism in the name of antiracism and to formulate alternative antiracist discourses that can ground alliances between black feminists and black men. In doing so, she attempts to redress in black contexts the kinds of processes that also inform the essays discussed in chapter 1: the censoring of feminist analysis by its coarticulation with other oppositional discourses. An important consequence of these operations for poststructuralist feminism, as I have argued, is that difficulties arise in developing and pursuing a model of self-different, unstable subjectivity that could explain how patriarchal power can regulate not only multiple oppositional stances but also the dynamics between a subject's subordinate and privileged positions.

Attention to the latter dynamics would enable poststructuralist feminism to retain gender as a category of analysis when describing female and feminist subjects who are simultaneously disadvantaged in gender and advantaged in other categories (e.g., race, class, and nation). Instead of describing privileged female subjects only in terms of their privileges, such a feminist analysis could reveal how the practices that exclude and/or reify the oppression of other women also can reify patriarchal power in privileged class and race contexts. In this chapter and the next, I focus on white women writers who demonstrate the importance to feminist change of apprehending and resisting both kinds of effects. I turn now to the works of Ellen Glasgow, whose texts are persistently concerned with illuminating how gender subordination is secured and feminist agency is undermined by their respective coarticulations with privileges in race and class.

While Glasgow's representation of southern women has generated feminist critical attention in recent years,[1] within American literary criticism she remains a marginal, regional author. For historians of the New South, however, she has occupied for some time a privileged place among southern writers; in his influential *Origins of the New South* (1951), C. Vann Woodward claimed that, of the novelists who chronicled the Civil War and Reconstruction years, Glasgow deserves special recognition as the only "forerunner of the new age," the lone voice to raise "the standard of revolt" against the racist, classist, and sexist values of the Old South (434). To this I would add that Glasgow insists that such democratic progress is only possible when subordinate subjects recognize how power regulates their self-difference.

Indeed, to the extent that Glasgow's (few) historicist literary critics have not discerned her specific formulation of social development, they miss the influence of her feminism on her representation of both liberal democracy and the effects of racist discourses. Glasgow's most exhaustive critic, J. R. Raper, echoes Woodward's praise for her courageous dramatization of the clash between entrenched caste systems and democratic ideals in her early novel, *The Voice of the People* (1900),[2] but fails to discern that Glasgow's feminism brings racist democratic politics as well as class hierarchy under scrutiny (*Without Shelter* 121–48). More recently, Walter Benn Michaels notes Glasgow's feminist interests but implicates them in the Progressive racism practiced by the democratic hero in *The Voice* (142n38; 43). What he misses is Glasgow's emphasis on the difference that gendered subordination can make to a feminist subject's exercise of her race and class privileges. Although both Glasgow's narration and her characters do exhibit impulses to authorize feminist agency with racist discourses, the novels persistently expose and condemn these tendencies with analyses of the relation between racist strategies and the oppression of white women. In this vein, as we shall see, Glasgow's feminist aims in *The Voice* motivate not an appropriation but a forceful critique of her hero's faith in a democracy that perpetuates racist ideology as it promises mobility to all white people.

As Glasgow's work, which is in revisionary dialogue with a striking range of both oppositional and conservative contemporary discourses, justifiably begins to attract new historical as well as feminist attention, it is important to stress the contributions that her writing can make to the characterization of the self-different feminist subject within both critical methodologies. Accordingly, my reading of her work in the context of the rhetorics she appropriates and revises maps strategies for feminist agency (and their pitfalls) that respond to the ways dominant gender ideology regulates the simultaneously advantaged and disadvantaged female subject.

In a 1913 essay that argues for women's suffrage, Glasgow expresses high hopes for intersections between social evolutionary goals, democratic government, and better conditions for women: "I am still convinced that a democratic form of government is the . . . most beneficial to the whole people. No government is going to be perfect. . . . But I am an evolutionist, once and for all, and I believe that we are constantly and inevitably growing into better conditions, better states of mind, better possibilities" ("No Valid Reason" 128).

Nonetheless, in the same essay she weighs these hopes against her perception of the failure of social evolutionary thinking to produce change for women: while "everything else in the world has traveled forward . . . [women are] supposed to remain static and undeveloped" (24). In "Feminism," an essay published the same year, she complains that in the terms of prominent discourses on social evolution, woman exists, not as an active agent of life, but merely as the "passive guardian of the life force" (34).[3] But if evolutionists often assumed that woman was "the solitary exception to [the] natural law . . . of development" (27), women themselves too frequently concurred with this view. Constructing the surest obstacle to her own improvement, woman has "cheerfully defied nature and reshaped both her soul and body after the model [man] put before her" (27). Nonetheless, this "evolutionist, once and for all," combats sexist evolutionary models by appropriating the terms of social betterment for feminist aims. Representing the woman who cheerfully relinquishes agency to her reproductive role as coerced into following a bad model by her "habit" of "false thinking about her[self]" ("Feminism" 27), Glasgow undermines on their own terms the discourses that predicated social evolution on developing good habits and eschewing bad ones. Whereas within these discourses "bad habits" are those that threaten the supremacy of the "social fittest," Glasgow presents women's conformity to elite reproductive models as the bad habit that impedes their social development.[4]

Crucial to that development, then, would be interventions in women's "cheerful" embrace of gendered subordination. And although Glasgow's timely remarks in 1913 valorize the full participation in "a democratic form of government" as the key to bettering women's conditions, her earlier novel, *The Voice of the People* (1900), identifies democratic politics —

specifically those that exploit racism — not as the solution to women's subordination but as a model for it. Political participation in *The Voice* is a process that, in the terms of her later, better known novel *Barren Ground,* "ma[kes] democracy safe for [dominant race and class] politics" (5). Indeed, with the earlier novel's allusions to the demise of the biracial Readjuster movement in Virginia (1879–83), which vividly demonstrated how nonelite white men could be kept subordinate through appeals to their privileges in race, Glasgow hopes to illuminate as well why elite women's gendered oppression was among "the hardest conditions to shake" ("Feminism" 27). Her populist democratic hero can neither adequately redress his own subjugation nor illuminate that of other subordinate subjects because he does not apprehend how the dynamics between a subject's advantaged and disadvantaged positions produce their consent to oppression.

Thus democracy can give expression to "the voice of the people" and underwrite the inevitable social evolution of "the whole people" only when the people discern how power, including that of democratic governments, can turn a subject's voice against his or her own best interests. Indeed, in *The Voice* Glasgow undertakes to make this analysis of how power works with multiply positioned subjects indispensable for social evolution; and, like the rhetorical appropriations in her later feminist writing, she does so by resignifying key terms in prevailing discourses on human betterment. Most centrally she attempts to emancipate Darwin's "struggle for survival" from its Spencerian articulation as "the survival of the [social] fittest." In this novel the struggles that are necessary to human survival and improvement involve a resistance to the way dominant powers succeed in masking subjugation as privilege. To further illuminate these modes of subordination as well as modes of resistance to them, Glasgow also rewrites concepts from criminal anthropology: Sir Francis Galton's categorization of social types in his "composite photographs" and his theory of mental selection, which he based on the photographs' tendency to reenforce common features and eliminate diverse ones.

But even as contemporary events in American democratic politics, along with emerging concepts of subjectivity, provide lexicons with which Glasgow hopes to make visible the structure of elite women's subordination in gender, she also indicates that the mere recognition of this structure will not suffice to displace it. What it takes for her characters to resist the masking of subordination as privilege is the replacement of distinctions in race and class with cross-race and cross-class identifications. At the same time, these strategies are vexed (both for her characters and for her own narrative

voice) in ways that invoke current feminist debates about cross-cultural
identification. Even as it foils the ability of dominant ideology to use a
subject's privilege to secure her subordination, identification with disadvantaged others also leaves room to maintain significant distinctions. As
Karen Sanchez-Eppler has argued in regard to white feminist-abolitionists,
elite women's recognition of themselves in exploited others "supports both
reciprocal and appropriative strategies" (*Touching Liberty* 20). And while
the greater focus in feminist theoretical and historicist criticism has been on
white women's appropriative strategies, recent debates have emphasized
the importance of also "com[ing] to terms with the complicated . . . ways
that identity is continually compromised [and] imperiled . . . by identification" (Fuss, *Papers* 10).[5]

Glasgow hopes that cross-race and/or cross-class identification will im-
peril elite female identities, but she also recognizes and critiques the appropriative dimension of such identification (a dimension at times that her own
narration exploits). While poststructuralist feminism has illuminated the
racism and classism in the latter practices, what Glasgow's novels can contribute to feminist inquiry is the analysis of the diverse effects of identification in the context of the enabling and the disabling of feminist agency.
Giving us multiply positioned subjects for whom identification as a crucial
mode of resistance is always also potentially a mode of appropriation,
Glasgow shows how the latter mode, even as it shores up elite privilege,
also fortifies the gender ideologies these subjects seek to displace. In both
novels I discuss, cross-race and cross-class identification is both valorized
as the key to disrupting elite regulations of unstable subjects and prob-
lematized as a modality through which dominant gender ideology defends
against such interventions.

In the second part of the chapter, I discuss Glasgow's elaboration of the
"composite" feminist subject in her later novel *Barren Ground* (1925). The
heroine of *Barren Ground* succeeds, where *The Voice's* heroine fails, in
refusing the gender subordination disguised as privilege. What makes this
refusal possible, I argue, are egregious developments within the American
eugenics movement, made prominently visible by the effort in Virginia to
sterilize Carrie Buck. However, though the cross-class and cross-race identifications generated by allusions to Carrie Buck set in motion feminist
resistance, these identifications are also the first of several occasions on
which the protagonist and the narration try to authorize prohibited feminist interventions with racist rhetoric. In *Barren Ground* Glasgow's previous exploration of how self-different subjects consent to gendered subor-

dination widens to include a focus on how feminism is undermined when women seek to make it recognizable and/or acceptable by invoking the rhetorics of privilege. Ultimately, however, *Barren Ground* offers a vision of social evolution meant to foil the operations that both secure female subordination and recuperate feminist agency: a nonbiological reproduction of feminist culture accomplished by transmitting it to those whose "fitness" is measured not by their adherence to privileged ideologies but by their capacity to resist dominant regulations of self-difference.

Eugenics, Composite Subjects, and Eugenia('s) Battle

The Voice of the People charts the rise and fall of Nick Burr, a poor white farmer's son who becomes governor of turn-of-the-century Virginia. With the patronage of Judge Bassett, who is impressed with the boy's intelligence and efforts to educate himself, Nick joins the local elite children in their private lessons, where he and Eugenia Battle, daughter of the prominent General Battle, meet. When they are older they fall in love, but their plans to marry after Nick has improved his fortunes are curtailed by false allegations against Nick of sexual misconduct. Leveled by Eugenia's brother, Bernard, who is also the real perpetrator, these allegations create a "clash of class" (*Voice* 206) that permanently estranges the pair.

While Nick never marries but goes on to become governor, Eugenia marries Dudley Webb, a man of her own class and Nick's conservative political rival. On the eve of the election for a United States Senate seat, Nick tries to stop the lynching of a black man accused of "the usual thing" (321), a phrase with which Glasgow suggests allegations of sexual transgressions against white women. In the process Nick is shot by the angry mob who are also his nonelite white constituents, an outcome that Glasgow links to the way racism turns Nick as well as his constituents against their own class interests. The novel closes with Dudley, now assured of success, and Eugenia, devoted passionately to her new son, sharing a tender moment after Nick's funeral.

Thus this final tableau vividly links the survival of elite political power to what Herbert Spencer famously termed the biological "survival of the fittest." But, as Raper has importantly argued, the novel itself strongly critiques this view, recruiting both Spencer's critics and Darwin to reconcile doctrines of social evolution with ethical progress (*Without Shelter* 52–56).[6] Following Darwin's distinction in *The Descent of Man* (1871) be-

tween the instinct for self-preservation and a social instinct that keys survival to community interests and a moral sense, Glasgow finds promise in
the latter formulation but stresses how it can be manipulated in the interests of the "social fittest." The novel, Raper argues, critiques "the survival
of the clannish" by indicating the inadequacy of Eugenia's social instinct:
because it is so bound up with loyalty to her clan, her principled love for the
lower-class Nick dissolves in the family pressure to abandon her attachment (*Without Shelter* 133).[7]

However, while the novel does critique the dominant structuring of
Eugenia's moral sense, it equally critiques Nick's inability to act consistently in a way that best serves his own and the community's interests. For
both characters, the confusion of principle and/or personal survival with
the aims of the "fittest" race and class leads them to consent to their respective oppressions. A reading that poses Eugenia as the representative of an
elite caste against Nick as the democratic hero misses the novel's effort to
draw an analogy between the characters' shared modes of subordination.

This analogy goes unnoticed as well in Walter Benn Michaels's claim for
a different kind of similarity between Nick and Eugenia. *The Voice,* he
argues, traces a movement in American racist notions of "race," "through
which people cease thinking of themselves as belonging first of all to a
family and begin thinking of themselves as having first of all a color" (43). If
Nick's class rise, enabled by "race" conceived as skin color, is meant to
represent progress over Eugenia's repudiation of Nick on the basis of
"race" understood as family (and therefore as class), both notions of "race"
are racist. Moreover, Michaels implies that the racism of Nick's "lily-white
Democratic Party" (43) also informs Eugenia's (failed) feminist resistance,
as well as her ultimate submission, to her elite patriarchal family; the Progressive racism that is compatible with Progressive feminism's effort to
"replac[e] family with race" is, Michaels claims, central to Glasgow's novels (148n38).

However, such a reading misses the fact that the novel critiques the
political strategies spawned by Progressive racism and does so precisely
because of Glasgow's feminist aims. Drawing attention to the uses of coex-
isting, rather than successive, referents for "race," Glasgow shows that
when the "Democratic Party confers on Nick the race that blood could not"
(Michaels 43), it does so to recruit his own participation in sustaining the
racialization of class difference. Nick's belief in "race" as whiteness, rather
than as family/class, is precisely what enables the elite Democratic Party as

well as Eugenia's ruling class family to exploit his ignorance of their respective racializations of class. Glasgow stresses that the white male's racist faith in "race" as color underwrites the ability of elite whites to perpetuate "race" as class.

Importantly, Glasgow's interest in Nick's personal and political dilemmas has a crucial, indeed motivating, feminist dimension; it aims to illuminate by analogy how white women's classism and racism is integral to their subordination in gender. Rather than appropriate Progressive racism for feminist aims, as we shall see, Glasgow tries to appropriate a prominent critique of racist democratic politics to make visible how women willingly consent to gendered conditions. If Eugenia's desire to marry Nick, which thwarts her family's designs on her reproductive future, involves a racist replacement of "race" as family with "race" as color, the feminist dimensions of this desire are brought into question precisely by the feminist project the novel privileges: to implicate racism in elite women's subordination by exposing how Progressive racism can reify subjection for other white but subordinate subjects.

Furthermore, marriage to Nick, arguably made thinkable by Eugenia's apprehension of "race" not as family but as color, does not promise to be a feminist coup. To assume that it does is to assume that patriarchal husbands come only in the shape of elite ones. Despite the improvements that are available for white citizens in a racist democracy, patriarchal marriage maintains female subordination. Although Eugenia loves Nick for his progressive beliefs, his investment in patriarchal gender hierarchies complicates any effort to link her feminist goals to marrying this democratic hero; while her family insists on her loyalty to "the blood she bore" (206), Nick equates a troubling desire to possess Eugenia with the day that she will "[bear] his name" (183).

Nonetheless, it is the structure of ruling-class gender ideology on which the novel focuses. Even as Glasgow stresses that Eugenia's repudiation of Nick is motivated by loyalty to her clan, the novel also connects this repudiation to her own oppression. Indeed Eugenia seems meant literally to articulate the role of the elite white woman in the social evolutionary discourses that were, as Sir Francis Galton described them in his *Inquiries into Human Faculty* (1883), "connected with that of the cultivation of race, or, as we might call it, with 'eugenic' questions" (24–25), namely, "questions bearing on [what is] . . . good in stock, hereditarily endowed with noble qualities" (24n1). Very likely named to reflect Galton's terminology, Eugenia is pressured to observe a classed mode of femininity that prefigures the tenacity of "woman as the guardian of the life force" in subsequent eugenics theory ("Feminism" 34).[8]

It is against this characterization of women's role in social development, here and throughout her work, that Glasgow poses a feminist concept of women's development. Doing so, however, requires a vocabulary capable of illuminating a subordination made invisible by class status for elite women, liberal democratic thinkers, and conservative social theorists alike. Glasgow's strategy is to construct Nick as also subordinated by the stereotypes that supported the "cultivation of [the fittest] race." Every bit as much as Eugenia, the ugly, redheaded Nick embodies a cliché circulated by the discourses that linked social betterment to the reproduction of the "fittest." Both he and his father are described in terms that echo Havelock Ellis's account in *The Criminal* (1890) of a criminal type usually associated with the lower "unfit" classes: redheaded (Ellis 77), hirsute (73), and atavistic in features (207).

Indeed the novel's emphasis on the clear falseness of the criminal allegations against the redheaded Nick seems meant to invoke the striking visibility of racialized class bias in Ellis's own account of his research on English criminals. From the outset Ellis expects that a high percentage of these criminals will be redheads; but when he finds that there are far fewer in prison than he had anticipated, he is not deterred. As redheads comprise a significant percentage of the English lower class, he concludes that redheaded criminals are indeed quite numerous but do not survive long enough to be counted among prison inmates. Redheads' absence from the prison population, instead of educating Ellis about his class bias, signifies the physical frailty of the type: "Among the manifold risks of a criminal life the brightly pigmented person, with his sensitive vascular system, seems to be soon eliminated" (77–78).

However, if both Nick and Eugenia can be identified as types whose roles within social evolutionary discourses supported the reproduction of the "fittest," only Nick's oppressive construction is visible to the novel's characters. Nick's professional friends and political supporters, who range across social class, easily recognize that the criminal allegations against him are false; until the final moments of the novel, Nick transcends in the public sphere the injurious typing that curtails his attempt to marry across class boundaries. Glasgow expects, then, that readers of the novel, as well as contemporaneous liberal readers of Ellis, would discern the biases in the criminalization of class differences among white men. She does not expect, however, that readers will similarly recognize the subordination of elite women that attends their stereotypical role in conservative evolutionary rhetorics. Thus while Glasgow indicates that Eugenia suffers as she submits to her family's controls on her romantic choices, she also indicates that this submission is likely to be understood and therefore effaced only in terms of Eugenia's empowering embrace of class privilege. Certainly this is true within the world of the novel itself. Praised by the men (and women) of her class, she is vilified by Nick who both sees her only as an agent of class and measures his own rise partly by his ability to possess her in conventional patriarchal terms.

To generate a recognition of Eugenia's subjugated role within reproductive ideologies, Glasgow presents Nick as similar to Eugenia not only in his arbitrary construction by these ideologies but also in the way his privileged beliefs secure his consent to conservative reproductive agendas. For Nick's political mobility coexists with an implacable enforcement of class differences between men in the private sphere that relies on his own racism for support. At the same time, his eventual political demise is also linked to the racism of poor whites, including his own. Nick's belief that he has access to the full privileges of white male citizenship, which he repeatedly poses against an inferior black masculinity, blinds him to the perpetuation of class differences in both private and public spheres. Although in *The Voice* the first instance of the subject who willingly shapes "soul and body" (Glasgow, "Feminism" 27) to bad conditions is Eugenia, her mode of subordination becomes clearly visible only when recent political events help illuminate it in the nonelite white male, only when the "voice of the people" is revealed as a voice also orchestrated to speak against itself.

The events that initiate the emergence of Eugenia and Nick as similar subordinate subjects proceed from the "clash of class" that destroys their romance (206). When Eugenia's brother Bernard accuses Nick of seducing and abandoning the now pregnant Bessie Pollard (a white shopgirl), Eugenia initially believes his lies about Nick and is incredulous when Nick reveals the true culprit to be Bernard. Responding angrily against Eugenia's distrust of his honor, Nick vows never to forgive her. And after struggling with her competing impulses, Eugenia does not pursue a reconciliation. However, Glasgow goes on to elaborate this "clash of class," so that it can be read not only within the discourse of class struggle (in which Nick is the victim of Eugenia's class prejudices) but also as a symptom of both characters' oppression by ruling-class interests.

What Nick understands as a character flaw Glasgow elaborates as a product of Eugenia's consent to bad conditions in gender. It is true that Eugenia initially and ultimately responds to the crisis by "draw[ing] nearer in the shelter of the race . . . [and by] cling[ing] more closely to that unswerving instinct which had united individual to individual and generation to generation" (208). However, she goes on to experience her submission to elite prescriptions for whom she may marry as a defeat in terms of Glasgow's innovative referent for "the struggle for survival": the struggle against a gendered subordination disguised as race and class privilege.

To represent Eugenia's battle with the Battle family's priorities, Glasgow invokes Sir Francis Galton's theory of "composite" mental imaging, itself derived from his more famous invention of composite photographs. Through the construction of representative individual and group faces, Galton's goal was "to encourage as far as practicable the breed of those who conform most nearly to the central [ideal] type and to restrain . . . the breed" of inferior types (*Inquiries* 14–15).[9] Although his primary interest was in men of ability, Galton initially developed his photographic technique in an effort to determine if different types of criminals had particular features; as a result the composite photograph was associated with criminal anthropology. Regarding all of his composites, however, from those of families to those of criminals and ideal social types, Galton stressed that the final image articulated what all the participant faces had in common, eliminating individual peculiarities in the process. Not surprisingly Galton had preconceived notions of the commonality he would find: criminal composites reveal a common "low type" (*Inquiries* 15), while a representation of Royal Engineers demonstrates "an ideal typical form" (14).

Galton's photographs, in which the extraordinary disappears in common elements, prove very fruitful for Glasgow's project of rewriting social evolutionary discourses in the interests of feminist development. As we shall see, the trope of the composite image grounds her exposé of Galton's own biased mode of interpretation (which tolerated no exceptions to preconceived notions of social types), as well as her representation of the way both progressive and corrupt political "bodies" assimilate the individual to entrenched social types. Regarding Eugenia, Glasgow invokes the rhetoric associated with composite images to show how dominant typing leaves no room to observe differences among members of a group (for example, Eugenia's subordination by elite reproductive aims) and how such individual members can be coerced into a self-destructive identification with the type.

Most importantly, however, Glasgow appropriates Galton's related concept of "cumulative" ideation, a process in which the subject's investment in established ideas eliminates new ways of thinking. Indeed for Glasgow the subjective processes that eliminate resisting impulses in dominant ones make the self-different subject vulnerable to the strategies whereby elites maintain the composition of both privileged and disadvantaged social bodies. This concept of what might be called "composite subjectivity" follows Galton's own connection of such mental imaging both to the effects achieved by the photographs and to social regulation. He claimed that "blended memories are strictly analogous to blended pictures" in their tendency to eliminate exceptional images in general ideas. Unlike the composite photographs, however, the mind does not "blend images in their right proportion" ("Generic Images" 158, qtd. in Forrest 140). As a result, general ideas "are never to be trusted" for accuracy; indeed "when they are of long standing they become fixed rules of life, and assume a prescriptive right not to be questioned" ("Generic Images" 169, qtd. in Forrest 140).[10]

Eugenia's clinging to an "instinct" that is the commonality linking "individual to individual and generation to generation" turns out not to be a symptom of her uncomplicated allegiance to elite class categories (208). Rather, Glasgow portrays Eugenia as eventually observing a "fixed rule of life," one that maintains itself through the subjective dynamics that secure, despite her resistance, her pivotal role in reproducing the fittest class. Developing Galton's psychic analog to the way composite images exclude the exceptional and retain the common and the fixed, Glasgow traces these dynamics as Eugenia struggles with competing images of Nick. At stake in this extended passage is Eugenia's capacity to formulate a nontypical image of Nick and thus to assert her autonomous desire over her family's prescriptions.

Significantly, the starting place for Eugenia's struggle with her competing impulses is an image of Nick that echoes the clichéd images in criminal anthropology; she recalls his "convulsed features, the furrow that cleft the forehead like a seam, the heavy brows bent above the half-closed eyes, the spasmodic working of the drawn mouth" (209). Registering the "fixed," classed lexicon of criminality that holds sway with the elite Eugenia, her imaging of Nick coincides precisely with the features that, Ellis claimed, Continental anthropologists found in criminals: "the eyes are small"; "the eyebrows [are] thick and close"; there are "spasmodic contractions . . . of the face" (*Criminal* 83) and "lines of the forehead" (85).

As she retreats to the "shelter of [her] race" (208), then, Eugenia reveals the tenacity of the characterizations, ones that Nick will easily transcend in the public sphere, within the intimate family discourses meant to secure the biological reproduction of class. Yet the shelter offered by this lexicon is one that comes at the high cost of restrictions on Eugenia's sexual, reproductive, and social choices. Anticipating the analysis of the Association of Southern Women for the Prevention of Lynching in the 1930s, Glasgow implicates the protection offered by Eugenia's family in the criminalization of black men (which here extends to the racialized poor white male), meant also to severely restrict the sexual and social activities of white women.[11] Although the father who is "a bulwark against the world and its incoming tribulations" assures her that she will always be protected from the "rascals" (like Nick) who might plague her (208), the only rascal in this case is her brother, and the protection to which she succumbs will emerge as indistinguishable from a femininity felt as both imprisonment and bodily injury.

In fact, rather than empowering her, Eugenia's imaging of Nick within elite lexicons causes her to feel as if "she had emerged, defeated, from a physical contest," as if, that is, she has been vanquished in a Darwinian struggle for survival (209). The contradiction between Eugenia's inscription in empowering class and race discourses and her sense of personal, gendered defeat, then, is the occasion for Glasgow to resignify the referent for the "struggle for survival" so that it will serve (elite) women's development. In the course of this passage, such a struggle is motivated by a social survival instinct that resists the masking of subordination as privilege, the turning of self against self; it is an instinct Glasgow poses against the reigning one whose terms for class and race survival spell gendered defeat.

When Eugenia's class and race identifications produce a sense of defeat felt as "something throbb[ing] in her temple like an imprisoned bird" (209), Glasgow portrays the elite female "soul and body" turned against its gendered self ("Feminism" 27). Since the same discourses that criminalize Nick and biologize his class difference construct Eugenia's body as a "temple" to class breeding, mobilizing these lexicons against Nick instigates her body itself to police her heretical desires. Her throbbing temple becomes the paradoxical site both of a prison house and of the rebellious thoughts and desires to which it refuses expression.[12]

With this contradiction, however, comes a change in her imaging of Nick that challenges dominant lexicons. In the place of biased and racialized clichés, Eugenia remembers her lifelong compassionate friend and her recent beloved. Beginning when her bedroom hearth reminds her of the firelight in a black servant's cabin, her counterimages of Nick emerge, importantly, in the context of black faces: "She saw the negro faces in the glow of the hearth, and she saw Nicholas and herself sitting side by side in the shadow" (210).[13] Thus the poor white boy, the elite girl, and the black servants are associated in a shared difference from and opposition to elite white ideologies; and the type of such resisting subjects is represented most vividly by "the negro faces."

As Eugenia goes on to recall her love for him, an identification with Nick and the black servants seems to be the key to displacing the distinctions between herself and racial(ized) others that characterize her initial "fixed" conception of Nick's class difference. However, this identification also instigates the return of Nick's image as a stereotypical composite face:

She had loved him for his strength, his vigor, his gentleness—and she still loved him. . . .

An impulse stirred her to cross the fields to his door and fling herself into the breach that divided them; but again the phantom in the flames grew dim and then sent out the face that she had seen that afternoon—convulsed and quivering, with its flitting sinister likeness to [his father] Amos Burr. A voice . . . of her whole dead race that had decayed and been forgotten, and come to life again in her—spoke suddenly from the silence:

"When all's said and done, a Battle's a Battle." (211)

In the end Eugenia apprehends the "impulse" to violate her family's controls on her choice of a mate as a suicidal gesture; to go to Nick is to "fling herself into the breach" that divides the two classes. As her "struggle for survival" reverts to one whose terms endorse "the survival of the fittest," the images that have challenged clichés of classed masculinity give way to a return of those stereotypes: Nick, assimilated to his family type, is now indistinguishable from the "sinister" Amos Burr.

What disempowers the alternative images of Nick, then, is Eugenia's apprehension that they now represent the most forceful threat to *her* survival, and this threat proceeds from the association of the lovable images with the "negro faces" (210). At the same time that Nick's appeal is connected to his sympathy for her black servants, Eugenia's loving reverie also positions him *as* the black man. Indeed her recollection of Nick's numerous fine qualities culminates in a significant image of the grown man's kindness: "the strong man . . . bearing the old negro's bag upon his shoulder" (210).

Nick's taking up of the black man's burden plays out a slippage for Eugenia between his progressive nature and the racialization of lower-class whites in discourses like Galton's and Ellis's.

Nevertheless, Eugenia's return to such "fixed" ideas about Nick registers more than an automatic preference for what racial difference means in white, ruling-class terms. Her retreat from positive images of Nick is motivated by the fact that her heretical desire threatens Eugenia with the same kind of racialization that Nick suffers in elite discourses. We will recall that counterimages of Nick, themselves symptoms of Eugenia's rebellion, coincide with her resisting images of herself, and both are linked to identifications with her family's black servants. It is the "negro faces" that constitute the representative faces of resisting subjectivity (210). Indeed, Eugenia's location in childhood of her identification with Nick and the servants harkens back to the child Eugenia's tendency to speak in the dialect of her black playmates. Significantly, this tendency is linked to resisting the propriety required by her guardian, Aunt Chris: " 'She don't manage me,' [Eugenia] had once confided to Delphy, the washerwoman, 'but I jes' plays that she does' " (77).

As she approaches adulthood, however, identifications between the rebellious Eugenia and blacks undergo a crucial transformation. Instead of expressing her resistance to classed modes of behavior, such identifications become strategies by which her unconventional tendencies might effectively be managed. In response to Eugenia's unladylike interest in philosophy and her initial indifference to his advances, for example, Dudley will observe that she is "good-looking enough to warrant the unconventionality of a Hottentot" (187). Eugenia's firelight reverie registers this shift in the valence for "blackness" as it traces her relationship to Nick from childhood to adulthood, at which point the rebellious imaging of Nick implicates her in a dreaded racialization that revitalizes the priority of racist white identity for her "survival." As a result, the adult Eugenia retreats from the feminist resistance that means membership in a black composite type, a rejection predicated on reasserting Nick's racialized difference from herself. In the slippage of "blackness" from being the signifier of Eugenia's resistance to being the signifier of the threatening racialization of herself, potentially subversive cross-race and cross-class identifications are recuperated in reactionary ones, in the racist fear of being racialized.[14]

Thus if imperatives for women to reproduce their race and class can be challenged by women's ability to identify and love across social boundaries, those imperatives, initially tied to granting women "the shelter of [their] race" (208), reassert themselves through coercive exploitations of elite women's racism. At the end of this complex process Eugenia loses her battle against a subordination maintained by her privileged identifications, a battle that Glasgow hopes will redefine the "struggle for survival" most pertinent to elite women's social evolution. But even as the Battles succeed in shifting Eugenia's efforts from a new kind of struggle to the old one for the "survival of the fittest," readers are meant to regret this outcome. More ventriloquized by than author of "When all's said and done, a Battle's a Battle" (i.e., the referent for "battle" remains designated by the Battles), Eugenia feels a "grief [that] rose to her throat and clutched her with the grip of claws" (211). And although she again experiences one part of her self turned against another, this time the grip of the policing self, whose racism turns the resisting self's identification with oppressed others into a threatening racialization of heretical desires, wins the battle. Cross-race and cross-class identifications, the crucial components in the struggle of this self-different subject against elite ideology, are revealed as also the occasions for that ideology to defend itself against such challenges.

The point of this extended scene of mental imaging is to represent this struggle and its recuperation, to foreground the complex mechanisms that produce elite women's consent to their subordination in gender. Once completed, this process leaves no room for further resistance. Indeed at this point the novel abandons its interest in Eugenia's development; she dutifully makes a passionless marriage within her own class, accedes to being a "race mother," and takes up political sides with the elite interests that will eventually displace Nick's liberal regime.

As Glasgow shifts her focus to Nick's rise and fall, however, she retains her interest in making visible the subject turned against itself, a visibility that could complicate Eugenia's classed femininity in retrospect. Like Eugenia, Nick's racist identifications, in his case with white masculinity, make him unwittingly complicit with strategies that constrain his sexual and reproductive options to the reproduction of the fittest class. While Eugenia makes a class-appropriate marriage and eventually becomes a mother, Nick never marries or reproduces. But Nick's political adventures, reminiscent of recent state politics in Virginia, will finally make the modes of domination that are hard to perceive in the private sphere visible in the public one. If liberal democratic discourses could indict the typing of non-elite white men in elite discourses but could not critique a similar typing of elite women, Glasgow recruits recent politics to illuminate the need for democratic theory to recognize that the regulation of self-difference is crucial to maintaining dominant power in private as well as public contexts, for women as well as men.

Democratic Politics and Composite Subjects

After the scene of Eugenia's capitulation to her family's dictates, the novel turns its attention to Nick, whose privileged investments Glasgow similarly implicates in a consent to his own subordination. Whereas Eugenia's consent is secured by eliminating resistance in her elite perspectives, Nick's takes the shape of a virtually uncontested blindness to how his investment in white masculinity reifies his class subordination. We see this blindness as Nick, outraged at Bernard's malicious lies, feels that "murder [would be] too mild for the man who had lied away his friend's honor for the sake of the whiteness of his own skin. It was the injustice that he resented with a holy rage — the hideous fact that a clean man should be spotted to save an unclean one the splashing he merited" (212).

While Nick's murderous rage registers a Darwinian struggle for survival against corrupt social forces, he also misapprehends both the nature of these forces and the struggle that would best serve his interests. Rather than raging against the classed clichés that motivate Eugenia's repudiation of him, Nick directs his anger against the violation of his white male honor. "Whiteness of skin" and its opposite, being "spotted," refer metaphorically to the racialization not of class but of the honorable and dishonorable behavior of unquestionably white men. Regarding the problem as one of dishonorable acts perpetrated by one white male against another — Bernard acts hideously against his "friend" — Nick assumes an equality in masculinity among white men that veils the class distinctions that have been brought to bear so effectively on his private life.

Although it serves elite classist and racist interests, Nick's blindness is itself bound up with racist bias. At the same time that he insists on the discursivity of distinctions among white men, he naturalizes such distinctions between white and black men. "Whiteness of skin" and "spottedness," when they are metaphorical signifiers for white male behavior, circulate arbitrarily: the "spotted" man is misperceived as "white," and vice versa. Yet this insistence that meanings for white men can be falsely assigned relies on a naturalization of racial attributes per se: "whiteness of skin" is synonymous with principled behavior and "spotted[ness]" with criminality. However, it is precisely Nick's racist confidence in the literal "whiteness of his own skin," and its difference from the blackness equated with criminality, that both blinds him to the racialization of his class status and, as we shall see, enables the elimination of the nonelite white male from political power.

The structural similarity between Nick's blindness to a persistent mode of class stratification and Eugenia's acceptance of gendered subordination in return for race and class privilege is underscored when Nick, despite his forceful articulation of violations against his male honor, soon feels that "his brain was deadened by the sense of *unutterable* defeat" (214; emphasis added). The defeat (the false impugning of male honor) that can be spoken, resisted, and rather easily reversed also obscures one that is unutterable (because invisible): the masking of classed subordination in apprehensions of white male privilege.

Significantly, a symptom of this defeat occurs as the mental image Nick calls up in response to it: "[H]e beheld the pictured vision of that other student of his race — the kinsman who had lived toiling and had died learning. He came to him a tragic figure in mire-clotted garments — a youth with aspiring eyes and muck-stained feet. He wondered what had been his history — that unknown labourer who had sought knowledge. . . . [And] in his vision that other student walked not alone" (215). Displacing a focus on the loss of Eugenia with an image of economic and educational oppression he is well on his way to transcending, Nick shifts his attention from his private sufferings to a public mobility that he has already begun to enjoy. As with Eugenia, however, the mental image that marks Nick's acceptance of a fatal "clash of class" between the lovers also registers the effacement of his subordination in the apprehension of privilege (206). Importantly, privilege here is constituted by a singular belief in the mobility between positions itself; in Nick's identification with the image of his kinsman, the relation between advantaged and disadvantaged positions is one only of mobility. As this apprehension of mobility masks certain stabilizations of Nick's classed meaning, it also precludes his ability to perceive a different relation between his subordinate and privileged positions: the effacement of the one in the other, the elite masking of "race" as class in his apprehension of "race" as color.

Nick's "fixed" idea that negates any challenges to it, then, is the liberal democratic concept of mobility itself, which obscures the coarticulations of a subject's advantaged and disadvantaged positions in ways that can stabilize subordination. Although the latter operation produces oppressive conditions that are extremely "hard . . . to shake" ("Feminism" 27), they can be mistaken for conditions that are as changeable as one's garments. Unlike the relation between Eugenia's constricting skirts ("the best prisons men ever invented" [194]) and the subsequent literalization in her own body of these restrictions (when her heretical thoughts "throb in her temple like an imprisoned bird" [209]), the classed "muck-stained body" of Nick's kinsman promises to be as changeable as the "mire-clotted garments" the farmer's son has already exchanged for the lineaments of political life. Thus Glasgow identifies in the context of late-nineteenth-century democratic politics the kind of impasse that, I have argued, confronts poststructuralist feminist theory: a focus on the subject's instability as the site for mobility and performative transformations obscures the dominant regulation of self-difference.

Because this regulation relies primarily on Nick's illusions of white masculinity, it also can receive support from sexism; while Nick shares a structure of subordination with Eugenia, its particular effects further estrange him from a support of women's social progress. By way of comfort, Nick's wealthy supporter, Tom Bassett—who as a child assumed that "all heads are afire where [Nick] come[s] from" (66)—observes "gaily" that if Nick's physical attributes have a negative significance, it is simply because women "don't take kindly to [Nick's] carrot locks" (216). At one time, then, Tom obscures the elite investment in stabilizing class meanings and pits nonelite white men against white women. Indeed Tom heralds Nick's imminent election to state office, and therefore his class mobility, by noting Nick's good fortune in the fact that women "can't vote, God bless them!" (216).

Fifteen years later, when we next encounter him, Nick's political career has prospered, and he is about to become the Democratic Party's candidate for governor. Glasgow's description of the party convention that will nominate this "man of the people" is also the occasion for her to reiterate the limits of representative democracy in turn-of-the-century Virginia: "the convention had assumed the air of a carnival of males—the restriction of sex limiting it to an expression of but half the population" (238). Against such gendered limitations, however, Glasgow explicitly invokes Galton's composites to represent the *inclusion* of nonelite white men in this exclusive political body: "A composite photograph of the faces. . . . would have presented a countenance that was unerringly Anglo-Saxon, though modified by the conditions of centuries of changes. One would have recognized instinctively the tiller of the soil—the single class which has refused concessions to the making of a racial cast of feature. The farmer would have stamped his impress indelibly upon the plate, . . . that integrity of type which is the sole survival of the Virginian pioneer" (239).

Whereas Galton's composites were meant to reify exclusionary types, Glasgow's composite of the "unerringly Anglo-Saxon" political body, exclusive of blacks as well as women, both includes nonelite white men and is positively altered by them. Authorized by the "modifications" important to Darwinian evolution, the nonelite "tiller of the soil" defies the assimilation of individual features to type. Reflecting Nick's beliefs, this composite maintains that privileged groups can be both joined and modified by nonelite individuals.

Yet as the following paragraph further elaborates this composite political face, it invokes rather than revises Galton's paradigm in which individual differences are subsumed in stable types: "In the general face, the softening influences of society, the relaxing morality of city life would have appeared only as a wrinkle here and there, or as an additional shadow. Beneath the fluctuating expression of political sins and heresies, there would have remained the unaltered features of the steadfast qualities of the race" (239).

For Galton, of course, the elimination of diversity in type simply brings into focus the contours of (biased) ideal or criminal types. But Glasgow's description of the same process exposes the biases and agendas that preserve referents for prevailing types; in her composite, homogeneity both covers over the "relaxing morality" and the criminality ("political sins") of the reigning political powers and subsumes internal challenges ("political . . . heresies") to those powers.

Most strikingly, Glasgow turns Galton on his head by attributing contradictory types to this composite face; it is both a criminal composite of those who are morally lax and commit "political sins" and an ideal composite that articulates the "steadfast qualities of the race" (239). Moving from a lexicon of criminality to one of racial quality, Glasgow constructs a pointed equation between the criminal type and the ideal racial type, an equation meant to invoke recent state politics. As Glasgow's composite "general face" shifts from signifying the nonelite white male's membership in the exclusive political body to signifying the erasure of his "heresies" in a prevailing but criminal image of racial quality, Glasgow alludes to the demise of the Readjuster movement in Virginia. Integral to this demise, moreover, was the exacerbation of fears of black male miscegenation by those who tolerated and concealed white male miscegenation (thus the "relaxing morality of city life" that recedes into the shadows of the ideal racial composite [239]).

The Readjusters, a short-lived biracial party coalition between nonelite whites and blacks, provided Glasgow with a lexicon for the nonelite white male turned against himself by the very political rhetoric of inclusion in empowered white masculinity. Begun in 1879 when white farmers demanded a downward readjustment of the state debt to enable tax cuts, the movement expanded under the leadership of William Mahone to a coalition organized around shared interests of blacks and nonelite whites, including improvements in the public schools and the elimination of poll taxes. Coming to full power in the election of 1881, the coalition accomplished important changes for its constituents: channeling funds to the public schools, placing black teachers instead of white ones in black schools, and eliminating the whipping post.

Yet, as James T. Moore points out, the white Readjusters were also white supremacists; while they called for civil rights for blacks, they did so in white supremacist rhetoric meant to allay fears that white rule could be endangered and that blacks would transgress social barriers between the races, especially those that proscribed miscegenation (180). If this rhetoric enabled the construction of a biracial coalition white Readjusters could embrace, in the end the Democrats took back the white vote by capitalizing on white racist fears and by shifting the main issue from the debt to race. Mounting a vigorous white supremacy campaign, they convinced white voters that Readjustment would lead to black rule, integrated schools, and interracial marriages. While certain Readjuster improvements survived, the return of the Democrats to power effectively eliminated blacks from both voting and political office and burdened nonelite whites with new strategies for disenfranchisement.[15]

In *The Voice* Nick's youth coincides with the Readjuster administration, but his studies that prepare him for class mobility and political life are also an apprenticeship to Judge Bassett, who favors the elite Funders even as he believes in extending (private) education to the exceptionally talented Nick. Indeed the judge inflects his speeches on "Jeffersonian lustre" with a "denunciation of the Readjuster party then in power" (144). Later on he responds to Nick's Democratic nomination for governor (which takes place once the Democrats are back in power) as being the best political news since the fall of the Readjusters (250). But Nick, the voice of nonelites, often stands against the Democratic platform and for former Readjuster positions, fighting efforts to disenfranchise black voters, and pursuing black Readjuster aims when he tries, in the novel's climactic scene, to stop a lynching. Nonetheless, the judge's contradictory investment in democratic principles has its trace in Nick as well. For Nick will emerge as, like Eugenia, the heretical composite subject who, through the interarticulation of his privileged and subordinate positions, can reproduce at the level of subjective ideation the elite strategies that eliminate heretics from ideal social bodies. When in the final scene the racist rage of nonelite whites against a black prisoner results in the elimination of Nick and the return to power of the white elite, Glasgow means to implicate Nick as well as his assailants in the dynamics that defeated the Readjusters.[16]

As we have seen, Nick's laudable principles coexist with white supremacist assumptions about black men and with an investment in white male privilege and mobility. To the extent that Nick is backed by the "unerringly Anglo-Saxon" Democratic party, Glasgow implicates his prejudices in the party politics that can turn white men's racism against their class interests. Significantly, the aide who works to keep the party behind Nick, one who is distinguished by both his bias and his continual sacrifice of principle to political expediency, is named "Galt." Politics that exploit racism keep in place the typing association with Galton's composites, as regards nonelite whites as well as blacks. Thus the history of the Readjuster movement enables Glasgow to reveal the socially mobile democratic subject also as a subject recruited to obstruct his own development.

While Nick is meant to be visible as the divided classed subject of recent Virginian history, he differs from the white Readjuster in suffering the kinds of false allegations that the Readjusters believed about black men. This representation both alludes to the racialization of poor white men in social evolutionary theories and underscores the fact that trumped-up, racialized criminalizations are the tools for shoring up elite power. At the same time, this similarity to black men also introduces the possibility of displacing the racist, self-destructive distinctions that brought down the Readjusters with an identification, again represented (recalling Eugenia's cross-race identifications) as the vehicle of both resistance and recuperation.[17]

Glasgow prepares for the scene of Nick's murder by emphasizing that the now Governor Burr continues to make the racist distinctions between white and black men that defeated the Readjusters. When the old allegations are newly mobilized in an effort to thwart his imminent election to Congress, Nick reiterates his innocence almost in the same breath with which he pronounces the guilt, on hearsay, of a black prisoner who is in danger of being lynched. And if Galt is true to his namesake when he automatically types the black man as guilty of "the usual thing" (321), that is, sexual transgressions against white women, Nick is only marginally better when he accepts vague reports of the black prisoner's guilt: "I don't know the details — but there is sufficient evidence against the man, they say, to hang him twenty times. He's as dead as if the noose had left his neck — but he must die by law" (321).

Describing death by law in terms of a hanging that precedes the rule of law, Nick's insistence on the black prisoner's right to due process, Glasgow implies, is compatible with legal lynching. Nonetheless, when he prioritizes even his limited goals for the black prisoner, Nick literally positions himself to finally intuit the classed construction of his own masculinity. At the jail, Nick tries to address the mob of poor white country people "in the name of the Law" (333) but he is drowned out by words that precipitate the novel's climactic moment:

> He tried to speak again. "We'll be damned, but we'll get the nigger!" called someone beside him. The words struck him like a blow. He saw red and the sudden rage upheld him. He knew that he was to fight — a blind fight for he cared not what. The old savage instinct blazed within him — the instinct to do battle to death — to throttle with a single hand the odds that opposed. With a grip of iron he braced himself against the doorway, covering the entrance.
>
> "I'll be damned if you do!" he thundered.
>
> A quick shot rang out sharply. . . .
>
> "By God, it's Nick Burr!" [a well-known voice] said. . . .
>
> "Boys, I am Nick Burr," he cried, and he went down in the arms of the mob. (333)

In shooting Nick to death a few days before the congressional election, the lynch mob, comprised of white country folk and even friends, accomplishes a political defeat that echoes the death of the biracial Readjuster party in Virginia. Murdered by his own constituency (he dies in the arms of the contrite mob) as he tries to extend legal rights to a black man, eliminated from political power that will now go to the elite Dudley, Nick falls prey to the nonelite white racism that brought down the Readjusters and revitalized elite white rule. And although these forces are here attributed to the lynch mob, Nick's own multiple impulses seem to be distributed between his commitment to extending certain rights to blacks and the racist ire of his constituents. If he is not in sympathy with their actions, he has betrayed an agreement both with their anger against the black man and with their assumption that the prisoner is guilty as charged. Such an assumption of black male predation against white women, we will recall, was a crucial component in foiling the white Readjusters' pursuit of civic rights for whites and blacks alike.

With this dispersal of Nick's psychic impulses, the demise of the white Readjuster is also invoked to illuminate defeats at the level of the subject that heretofore have been unrecognizable for Nick. If Nick's belief in the promises of white male citizenship have until now blinded him to the persistence of his classed status within elite private spheres, an identification with the black prisoner opens his eyes. When Nick's effort to protect the black prisoner in "the name of the Law" draws the response of "[W]e'll get the nigger" from close by, he experiences the derogatory racialization as an attack against himself: "The words struck him like a blow." Unlike his earlier apprehension of the false charges as a metaphorical racialization that does not undermine his access to a literal, privileged whiteness, Nick now recognizes himself as a subject for whom false allegations function to preserve subordinate racialized categories.

In addition, as is the case with Eugenia, an identification with racial others registers a possible displacement of the dynamics that recruit Nick to participate in his own oppression: the privileged distinctions in one category that covertly bring to bear subordination in others. As a direct result of his identification with the black prisoner, Nick experiences the racist vocabulary that is compatible with his own racism as a blow to his own body, as a (soon substantiated) threat to his survival. Recalling the effects of Eugenia's sense that her own racism poses a threat to her physical survival, Nick's similar apprehension may initiate, as it does for Eugenia, a new kind of Darwinian struggle: to oppose the strategies that use race privilege to maintain (gendered and classed) subordination.

The question remains, however, of whether viscerally felt identifications with oppressed others can sustain either the potential alliances or the struggles against the forces of oppression that they initiate.[18] While these identifications are meant to register interventions in the hegemony that masks a subject's defeats in his or her apprehension of privilege, the novel also stresses the renewed assertions of this hegemony that emerge precisely in response to such potentially subversive tactics. Indeed even as Glasgow suggests that the identification with the black prisoner may inspire a new mode of resistance, she also represents the occasion as fatally dangerous to Nick; he is killed by his political supporters precisely because he cannot be distinguished from the black prisoner. At the same time, in the light of the Readjusters' demise both the punishment of white alliances with blacks and the naturalizing of (certain) racist differences are more visible as disasters for the nonelite white subject.

Nonetheless, the novel's resolution points to Glasgow's concern with the implacability of the processes her novel critiques. Indeed her own representation exhibits symptoms of this tenacity of the mechanisms that use a subject's investment in racist and classist distinctions to covertly undermine resistance to classed modes of gender. Glasgow clearly tries to differ from Eugenia in that her own representation of the white man taking up the black man's burden (Nick as subject to false allegations of sexual transgressions) allows her to construct rather than to evade a context in which nonelite white men, blacks, and elite women become visible in a shared opposition to (different) effects of elite oppression. But Eugenia's fears also gloss the novel's own wariness of identifications with blacks, if not with the nonelite white men (whose oppositional discourses Glasgow wants to extend to elite women). While *The Voice* strongly indicts the practice of using false allegations against blacks to disenfranchise both blacks and nonelite whites, that indictment is also the limit of its interest in the black citizen whose only function in the novel is to make visible the disenfranchisement of the nonelite white male, who in turn illuminates elite women's subordination.[19]

Finally, Glasgow's representations of miscegenation are especially vivid sites where her advocacy of an antiracist feminism is superseded by racist representation. While the trope of the composite image itself cannot help but invoke mixed race physiognomy, Glasgow's one use of the composite image to actually represent miscegenation also condemns it, albeit on potentially antiracist terms. "The relaxing morality of city life" that appears as wrinkles and shadows in "the general face," we will recall, indicts the hypocrisy of elite white men who conceal white male miscegenation as they use the false specter of black male miscegenation to disempower black and nonelite white men (239). However, this representation, like her feminist critique of the Battle men who take no responsibility for their black mistresses and mulatto offspring, runs no risks of violating bedrock racist attitudes toward miscegenation itself. Nonetheless, it is likely that her fear of doing so in a novel that presents as desirable the inclusion of difference in a composite social body prompts Glasgow to insert an unambiguously racist polemic against miscegenation. Describing constituents that Nick encounters on a train, the narrator notes that the mulatto is "the degenerate descendant of two races that mix only to decay" (246).[20] But, as Glasgow's effort to recast Eugenia from "the guardian of the life force" to a woman coerced to a bad model is meant to show ("Feminism" 34), such discourses on racial purity also present substantial obstacles to elite women's social development.

Thus although *The Voice* is dedicated to exposing, even criminalizing, the masking of subordination as privilege for variously disadvantaged white subjects, Glasgow's narration is not immune from the threats and seductions by which privilege monitors the success of resisting representation. To the extent that Glasgow's revision of Galton's notion of composite mental imaging succeeds in illuminating ongoing competitions for what agendas will organize "composite subjectivity," especially as regards the dynamics between privileged and subordinate positions, the novel also demonstrates the tenacity for the author of the very processes she critiques.

Women's Development in *Barren Ground*

Barren Ground, published in 1925 but concerned with the same historical period as *The Voice,* locates the composite subject who can avoid mistaking subordination for privilege only in the female protagonist, Dorinda Oakley. By the 1920s Glasgow characterizes the political common man not as the subordinate subject who can illuminate women's oppression but as the agent of strategies that in *The Voice* lead to Nick's political demise: "[T]he sons of the good people [nonelite whites] drifted away to the city, where they assumed control of democracy as well as of the political machine which has made democracy safe for politics" (*Barren Ground* 5). Significantly, this passage stresses that the young men who are now complicit rather than potentially resisting subjects are "sons" before they are (corrupt) political subjects. It is an observation that reflects, I will argue, the influence of Freud's model of oedipal development on Glasgow's understanding of male subjectivity. Indeed the novel goes on to evaluate Freud's oedipal son as the composite subject whose embrace of subordination in the name of power is implacable.

Barren Ground's Jason Greylock, who abandons the pregnant, poor Dorinda for the elite Geneva Ellgood, negotiates power and subordination not within a public, political sphere but within a patriarchal, if degenerating, family. Here the submission to powerful male authority, rather than being disguised in privileged identifications, is clearly recognized by Jason as the consequence of early childhood scenarios. But while Glasgow models this awareness on Freud's description of oedipal dynamics, Jason's account of his subjectivity also departs from the Freudian one:

It seems to me . . . that I've always been balked or bullied out of having what I wanted in life. I remember once, when I was a little child, I went out with Mother to gather dewberries, and just as I found the finest brier, all heavy with fruit, and reached down to pick it, a moccasin snake struck out at my hand. I got a fit, hysterics or something. . . . [W]henever I reach out for anything I particularly want, I have a jumping of the nerves, just as if I expected a snake to strike. . . . I wonder how much influence that snake has had on my life? (65)

In a passage clearly meant to parody Freud's notion that the father's injunction against desire for the mother grounds a strong moral sense, Jason's fear of his father makes him jumpy and weak-willed as an adult. Nonetheless, Jason's submissiveness leads to rather than curtails his accession to patriarchal power over both property and women. Despite his protests that he married Geneva Ellgood under threats from her father and brother, and despite his continued preference for Dorinda, he responds to the angry heroine who flees from him by pursuing her only "as far as the end of the yard" he will soon inherit (170).

The most egregious outcome of Jason's vulnerability to stronger men, however, is its injurious effects on the pregnant Dorinda. In Glasgow's rewriting of Freud, then, oedipal dynamics produce morally impoverished, not morally responsible, adult men, whose subordination to paternal law nonetheless makes them agents of patriarchal power over women. If *The Voice* holds out hope of instigating male resistance to more empowered men by recognizing how identifications with white male privilege can mask classed subordination, here dynamics between a *recognized* subjection to more powerful men and the eventual participation in male power leave no room for resistance. As is the case with Freud's oedipal son, Jason's continual submission is not obscured by power but rather guarantees access to it. For Glasgow, then, Freudian accounts of masculinity usher in a "composite" subject utterly coopted by the patriarchal power he will eventually wield over women (like Jason) or over citizens (like the nonelite "sons" who "ma[ke] democracy safe for politics"). No longer a potential model for the subordinate female subject, the subjugated male emerges now as embracing a submissiveness that will earn him access to (albeit degenerating) patriarchal power.

Fortunately, *Barren Ground*'s female protagonist can do without a male model. In fact the novel shifts its focus from revealing the subordination secured through a subject's privileges to exploring strategies for countering such operations, and it does so by mobilizing effective versions of the subversive identifications that cannot be sustained in *The Voice*. What enables Glasgow to imagine Dorinda Oakley's triumph over the elite strategies to which Eugenia Battle succumbs is, I will argue, the high visibility of misogynist developments within eugenicist discourses and practices themselves, practices that Glasgow hopes will inspire progressive cross-class identifications. By 1924 the American eugenics movement, which at its inception in 1900 took its name—as, I have argued, Glasgow likely takes Eugenia's name—from Galton's *Inquiries,* had codified the elite family discourse that regulates Eugenia's choices into a highly influential "scientific" polemic.[21] Especially in the wake of early-twentieth-century immigration and of World War II, in which thousands of white Americans died, eugenicist rhetoric stressed the imperative for elite white American-born women to reproduce within their race and class. The focus of this rhetoric on the pivotal role of women in reproducing the fittest class aimed to recruit elite women's "cheerful" consent, in the name of class and race privilege, to the gendered subordination this role often required. Similarly, "negative eugenics," the effort to contain the reproduction of poor white, immigrant, and black women, reenforced a hierarchy between such "unfit" women and elite women.

However, the egregious direction taken by negative eugenics in Virginia at the time Glasgow wrote *Barren Ground* had the potential to reveal that elite patriarchal agendas aimed to control all women's reproductive lives. The effort to sterilize Carrie Buck, initiated in 1924 to test Virginia's sterilization law of the same year, dramatically demonstrated that white women could be falsely characterized and arbitrarily sterilized simply for reproducing outside the bounds of marriage. Based solely on the evidence of her illegitimate reproduction, Carrie Buck was deemed "feebleminded" and eventually sterilized.

What made poor white women's illegitimate pregnancies undesirable, though, was not the need to prevent the spread of congenital diseases (which they did not have) but the fear of white female miscegenation, linked by eugenicists to poor women's out-of-wedlock sexual activity. Indeed Carrie Buck's case coincided with Virginia's Act to Preserve Racial Integrity (1924), which made it unlawful for whites to marry nonwhites; thus it is not surprising that dire measures were taken to regulate the white women whose reproductive capacity could not be contained within racially controlled marriages. Famous for eventually producing the notorious Supreme Court decision (*Buck v. Bell,* 1927) that established the right of all states to sterilize populations that were deemed "unfit," the case of Carrie Buck also revealed that strategies for maintaining race purity included the sterilization of white women whose illicit reproduction transformed them into the bearers of congenital disease.

Such an arbitrary labeling of poor white women as "feebleminded" had the potential to alert elite women as well to the regulation of female bodies and female adult lives central to all eugenicist aims. Feminist advocacy of public and professional lives for women in the 1920s often came up against eugenicist arguments that white women of "good stock" must prioritize reproduction. For feminists, then, the excessive strategies deployed to eliminate Carrie Buck's reproductive capacity would foreground as well the eugenical counter-imperative for elite women — that they *must* reproduce and within the framework of patriarchal marriages. And nonfeminist women, whose consent to oppression is Glasgow's most pressing feminist concern, certainly understood the stigma of illegitimate pregnancy. With the case of Carrie Buck, Glasgow hopes that discourses of racial purity could undermine their own aims by foregrounding elite men's regulation of women's bodies across class boundaries. She hopes, that is, that the dynamics for elite women between privileges in race and class and disadvantages in gender could shift from supporting to disrupting their consent to gendered subordination.

It is this shift that *Barren Ground* produces for its protagonist (and seeks to produce for its readers) by bringing center stage the dilemma of the figure who in *The Voice* recedes in the focus on the nonelite white male: the unmarried, pregnant, poor white woman. Read in the context of the case of Carrie Buck, the depiction of such a woman unveils elite strategies for controlling women's reproductive lives more effectively than does *The Voice*'s analogy to a political movement that excluded women. Dorinda's illegitimate pregnancy functions both to emphasize that the meaning of the poor white woman's pregnancy depends on the whims of elite men and to set the stage for Dorinda's refusal to participate in elite marriage and maternity.

Indeed Dorinda discovers that her pregnancy is illegitimate at a site, Five Oaks, that refers explicitly to the scene where Carrie Buck became a pawn for eugenicist aims. Until the early twentieth century, and thus at the historical moment of Dorinda's pregnancy in the novel, the town of Amherst, in which the Buck case was first heard, was called "Five Oaks"

(Smith and Nelson 53–65).[22] Whereas in 1924 the former Five Oaks was the site where illegitimately pregnant women were diagnosed as feeble-minded, the novel's Five Oaks is the context for revealing that a white woman's illegitimate pregnancy is not only the product of men's betrayal but also the catalyst for the most "fit" of feminist rebellions. Glasgow's Five Oaks is the property of elite but degenerate men who abandon poor white lovers, drive legitimate partners mad, and engage in the miscegenation that the polemics surrounding Carrie Buck attributed to poor white women's sexual autonomy. The novel's counter to contemporary events at Amherst is clear: the discourses that stigmatize women for illegitimate pregnancy in the name of racial purity ignore both the male abuse of white women and the widely tolerated practice of white male miscegenation.

At Five Oaks Dorinda learns that her pregnancy is illegitimate for the sole reason that Jason has given in to pressures, exerted by stronger men, to marry within his class. Illegitimacy, then, emerges not as the effect of female promiscuity but as an arbitrary category that serves patriarchal power and eugenical aims. Dorinda's story, however, disrupts these aims; rather than a stigma that generates desires for legitimate, eugenical reproduction, Dorinda's illegitimate pregnancy inspires her to repudiate the subordinate marriage and maternity that Glasgow links to a racist sense of pride in reproducing the "fittest." As she walks through the Five Oaks property musing on her imminent marriage, Dorinda initially regards the elder Dr. Greylock's mulatto children as "crawling, like small, sly animals, over the logs at the woodpile" (134). At the same time she cheerfully anticipates seeing her own "little children [play]ing under the great oaks in the grove" (145). This is precisely the kind of pride in racist reproduction, linked to the indictment of illegitimacy as the source of miscegenation, that could secure elite women's consent to the constraints of patriarchal marriage and maternity. When her own pregnancy is constructed as illegitimate, however, the Dorinda unprotected by an elite male lover or father sees very clearly the control of powerful men over female sexuality and reproduction. Perhaps most significantly, her experience of being a poor, unmarried woman grounds her antipathy, once she has risen in class, to marriage with elite men who police the valorized as well as the stigmatized reproductive body.

Along with the novel's construction of an identification between Dorinda and poor white women like Carrie Buck, it also likens the protagonist to another disadvantaged unmarried mother: the elder Greylock's mulatto mistress, Idabella. The first person that Dorinda encounters once she has learned of Jason's betrayal, and thus of her recently acquired illegitimacy, is the mother of the elder Greylock's mulatto children: "At the beginning of the sandy road . . . she met the coloured woman, Idabella, who said 'good evening,' after the custom of the country, as she went by. She was a handsome mulatto, tall, deep-bosomed, superb, and unscrupulous, with the regal features that occasionally defy ethnology in the women of mixed blood" (153).

What should we make of this passage in which Dorinda, newly stigmatized by an illegitimate pregnancy, comes face to face with a racist icon of immoral sexuality and reproduction? If, as I have argued, the larger scene at Five Oaks is meant to counter the eugenicist depiction of poor white women as immoral miscegenators, the mulatto Idabella, both product and practitioner of illegitimate miscegenation, here is blatantly characterized as "unscrupulous." However, Dorinda herself has just discovered how her own illegitimacy is an injurious construction that serves the interests of elite men. Indeed the very focus on Idabella's difference from her ethnicity seems to invoke Dorinda's intuition of how she, like Carrie Buck, is now vulnerable to being characterized in ways that defy her ethnological status (i.e., as an unprincipled miscegenator). Perhaps, then, the passage's more progressive impulse, played out in the claims that Idabella is "superb," possesses "regal features," and "def[ies] ethnology," recognizes that the racist characterization of black women as "unscrupulous" is also an arbitrary construction. In this sense Idabella's "defiance of ethnology" may register a feminist resistance to racist meanings for the mulatto woman's ethnology; an identification (Dorinda's and/or the narrator's) with this unmarried mother may be capable of defying the racist perception that also informs the passage. Certainly it is worth noting that whereas Dorinda is only passing through Five Oaks, Idabella actually lives there; that is, Idabella could also be identified with Carrie Buck as the subject of arbitrary gendered and racialized meanings.

However, precisely because Dorinda is meant to invoke Carrie Buck, the likeness to Idabella could aim primarily to remind readers of a grievous racialization of the white woman, one that leaves the raced meanings of the black woman in place. As a reflection of the white woman whose class and reproductive activities can be racialized as black, the mulatto woman would function primarily to lend a note of added horror to the injustice perpetrated against the white woman (i.e., the latter can be unfairly troped as like the black woman whose "unscrupulousness" remains unquestioned). Such a reading dovetails as well with Glasgow's racist indictment of miscegenation in this scene, which shifts the onus for what remains a loathsome practice from poor white women to elite white men. Old Greylock, who announces Jason's betrayal and thus Dorinda's illegitimacy, is a miscegenator. At Glasgow's Five Oaks the "unfit" are not unwed white women but the elite men who abuse such women; however, that "unfitness" is still made legible by a racist hallmark: the practice of miscegenation.

Thus both progressive and reactionary gestures are in play in the passage that likens Dorinda, outraged at her own vulnerability to arbitrary sexist and racist categories, to Idabella even as Dorinda perceives the mulatto woman through a racist lens. On the one hand, identifications with poor white and (more ambivalently) black women can both reveal the discursivity of race for all women and disrupt the elite woman's consent to gendered subordination in the name of class and race privilege. But on the other, once these identifications enable a feminist awareness of white women's subordination to racist reproductive aims, the articulation of this awareness can become entangled with racist rhetoric. The description of Idabella betrays the temptation to authorize what Glasgow may have regarded as an unspeakable feminist analysis with racist rhetoric, to illuminate white women's injuries by stressing their difference from the mulatto woman who retains her racist meanings. As in *The Voice,* the moment of productive identification is also the occasion to preserve distinctions, harmful both to racial others and to white women; and if the narration here indicates these problematics, it is also vulnerable to them.

However, the novel goes on to implicate such a double impulse — both to indict the racist categorization of women's reproductive bodies and to authorize feminism with racist rhetoric — in the recuperation of the elite woman's feminist resistance. While this resistance emerges when the eugenicist discourse of racist privilege is unmasked as also the discourse of female subordination, the feminist insights of Glasgow's characters and (as in the scene with Idabella) of her own narration coexist with a tendency to authorize feminism with the racist discourses that undermine it. In *Barren Ground* Glasgow explores in self-reflexive ways how patriarchal ideology profits when prohibited feminist resistance is figured forth in authorizing racist terms.

Glasgow's exploration of the relation between unspeakable resisting discourses and the authorizing lexicons that neutralize resistance is a further development of Galton's notion of the ideation in which culturally potent representations prevail over all challengers. This exploration may also owe something to Freud's elaboration of the "dream work" in *On Dreams* (1900). Indeed virtually at the same moment that Glasgow in *The*

Voice adapted Galton's ideas to an account of how dominant ideology secures subordination at the level of the subject, Freud used Galton's composite photographs to help explain an aspect of unconscious mental processes in which disparate dream thoughts are condensed into a composite dream image: "The dream work then proceeds just as Francis Galton did in constructing his family photographs. It superimposes, as it were, the different components [from the dream thoughts] upon one another. The common element in them then stands out clearly in the composite picture, while contradictory details more or less wipe one another out" (*Dreams* 28). However, Freud was most interested in the "*motive* necessitating this compression of the material" (32), and this he located in the need to disguise wishes that are inadmissable to consciousness (59). When analysis unraveled composite dream images, the products of what he more frequently called "condensation" and "displacement," into their component dream thoughts, those thoughts were revealed as linked to culturally unacceptable wishes that had been repressed. Freud's use of Galton's composite images to describe a process that both combined disparate ideas and disguised unacceptable wishes may have influenced Glasgow's exploration in *Barren Ground* of a mode of conscious ideation motivated by the need for dissemblance. Indeed Freud himself goes on to explain the dream work in terms of the kinds of conscious negotiations that for Glasgow threaten Dorinda's feminist progress: "The formation of obscure dreams occurs *as though* one person who was dependent upon a second person had to make a remark which was bound to be disagreeable in the ears of this second one; and it is on the basis of this simile that we have arrived at the concepts of dream distortion and censorship" (63).

While Glasgow shows us Dorinda's success in displacing a number of gendered restrictions, she also explores her protagonist's tendency to represent not only the "disagreeable" but also the virtually unrepresentable in the terms of culturally sanctioned discourses. But in contrast to the Freudian paradigm, where the disguising discourse succeeds in expressing the repressed wish in acceptable ways, Glasgow is interested in how the conscious mediation of prohibited representation through dominant, authorizing discourses functions to reinforce the initial prohibition. If in *The Voice* and in the early chapters of *Barren Ground* Glasgow reveals how dynamics between advantaged and disadvantaged positions recruit women's consent to gendered subordination, she goes on in the latter novel to stress that these same dynamics serve patriarchal ideology by foiling strategies for feminist agency.

Freed from her desires for elite but subordinate marriage by an illegitimate pregnancy resonant with the abuse of Carrie Buck, and freed from illegitimate reproduction by a fortunate miscarriage, Dorinda embarks on an adult life structured by production (she develops the family property into a thriving dairy farm) rather than marriage and reproduction. Along the way, however, Glasgow represents a number of instances where Dorinda uses a racist vocabulary in the effort to make otherwise prohibited feminist interventions seem appropriate. In several cases, however, the narration immediately indicates how racist rhetoric dovetails with the power that propertied white men exert over female sexuality and reproduction. Consider this exchange between Dorinda and Bob Ellgood as she is buying cows from Ellgood's stock farm for her dairy farm:

> "By the way, [said Bob] those Jerseys have never been milked by a woman. I don't know how they'll take to it. Will you hire a man?"
>
> "Not at first. Until I get started well, I'm going to do my own milking. I can put on Rufus's overalls, and when I milk myself I can be sure of the way the cows are handled. With negroes you can never tell. . . . [T]hey don't take the trouble to milk them thoroughly. And they won't be clean, no matter how much you talk to them."
>
> "That's the trouble [said Bob]. Cleanliness is a joke with most of the farmers about here, but it's the first step to success in dairy farming. It keeps down disease, especially contagious abortion, better than anything else. Yes, you've got the right idea."
>
> His eyes were shining as he looked at her. (293–94)

Dorinda begins by making the unreliability of black labor the alibi for the shift she wants to make in gender roles. But with Ellgood's response, Glasgow reminds her readers of the connection between racist discourses and the eugenicist imperative that elite women organize their lives around reproduction. Just as the productive role of her dairy cows reflects Dorinda's own life choices, Ellgood's stock farm, emphasizing the cows' reproduction, reflects his inscription in the human reproductive economy Dorinda resists. It is useful to recall at this point that Ellgood's earlier goals for his sister, linked to the aims of same-class marriage and reproduction, have helped to construct both (the then poor) Dorinda's illegitimacy and the elite Geneva's marital misery. Thus when Ellgood approves of her racist alibi for gender shifting ("You've got the right idea"), it is because her racist discourse on the uncleanliness of blacks easily dovetails with a discourse that recognizes abortion among "prized stock" as a disease: "[I]t [cleanliness] keeps down disease, especially contagious abortion."

As it is the only allusion the novel makes to the termination of pregnancy that enables Dorinda's independence, Ellgood's equation of miscarriage with disease is telling. If poor white women's illegitimate pregnancy could be troped as a vehicle for spreading congenital diseases, Glasgow suggests, elite "women's" failure to reproduce could be similarly understood in terms of a disease that must be controlled.[23] When the now elite Dorinda tries to vindicate her feminist transgressions with racist rhetoric, Glasgow embeds a reminder that the plight of Carrie Buck, directly linked to racist ideology, is inextricably tied to eugenicist imperatives that elite women must reproduce within patriarchal marriages. Importantly, the recognition that earlier intervenes in Dorinda's desire for a subordinate marriage and maternity now functions to register the dangers of authorizing feminist resistance with racist rhetoric. Just as an elite woman's racism can function to recruit her consent to gendered subordination, so can her racism function to foil her strategies for feminist agency.

Any question that Glasgow encourages an analogy between Dorinda and the cows in this scene or that she wants to portray racism as detrimental to feminism is dispelled by a passage that directly follows the exchange with Ellgood. "If you're going to keep cows," a workman tells her, "you'd better see that Doctor Greylock [now Jason] mends his fences. . . . That old black steer of his is a public nuisance" (295). Dorinda's surprising response is to wish Jason dead, "as impersonally as if she were thinking of the black steer that trampled the ploughed fields" (295). For the workman's remarks have reminded Dorinda of Jason's alluring presence in her dreams, over which she has no control. Likening him to the "black steer" that sexually menaces cows betrays Dorinda's translation of the emotional threat Jason poses into a racist one from which white women could expect protection: the black man from whose rapacity white women are allegedly in danger. But such rhetoric, of course, was famous for securing white women's subordination to white male prerogatives; we need only recall that Glasgow stresses its use in *The Voice* to recruit Eugenia for elite reproduction. If such a slippage between feminist and racist discourses constitutes an effort to recruit a powerfully criminalizing discourse to indict Jason for his sexist crimes, the remainder of this passage underscores how this strategy simply reifies the privileges such rhetorics are meant to secure for white propertied men.

First the menace Jason poses takes the form, not of his physical violation of her or her property, but of her own longings over which she has no control: "the unforgettable ecstasy [that] came back to her in her dreams" (296). That is, Jason's threat is constituted precisely as the control of her sexual desires that racist allegations against black men are meant to secure for white ones. Accordingly, when Jason literally begins to pursue Dorinda as she makes her way home, he does not, like the menacing black steer, violate the boundaries of her property by transgressing those he should observe (the fences that must be mended). Rather he retreats to his own property where the gate is very much in place: as he nears the entrance to Dorinda's farm, "he wheeled about and alighted to open the red gate of Five Oaks" (298).

Recalling that Five Oaks is the site, both historically and in the novel, where elite patriarchal meanings are constructed for the female reproductive body, the real danger Jason presents stems not from his invasion of Dorinda's property. Rather the danger consists in her continued, helpless desire for a man who adheres to rather than overrides the boundaries, cultural as well as physical, of Five Oaks. In an effort to articulate the desire that threatens her feminist agency as a recognizable transgression, Dorinda invokes a racist analogy between Jason's presence in her dreams and the transgressive black male. That is, she avails herself of the privileged rhetorics to which she has access in order to articulate an oppression that otherwise would not be recognizable as such. But this impulse that promises to make resistance effective, Glasgow suggests, turns out to reify dominant gender ideology; the rhetoric of black male violation of white women legitimizes rather than criminalizes white men's control over white women's sexual desire.

Dominant ideology, then, profits when the subject, who occupies both advantaged and subordinate positions, figures forth unrepresentable resistance to subordination in privileged lexicons. Indeed this passage eventually shifts its strategy for resisting the threat posed by Jason from the activation of racist myths that also oppress white women to the repudiation of paternal and patriarchal discourses, of which such myths are notoriously an example. After refusing to listen to Jason's entreaties as he follows her, Dorinda arrives home to discover that her father has died before he could articulate any final words to her. The chapter, whose final several pages are devoted to refusing to listen to Jason, ends with her exclaiming about her father: "I'll never know now what he tried to tell me. . . . No matter how long I live, I shall never know" (299). In the end, freedom from paternal legacy at the moment of inheritance, one that cannot help but resonate with the refusal to hear Jason's entreaties, takes the place of the resort to racist rhetoric. Resistance to the danger represented by Jason now consists in the inheritance of property without the transmission of patriarchal culture.

That racism turns a feminist subject against herself is further dramatized when racist discourses support one of the biggest obstacles to Dorinda's feminist rebellion: achieving feminist "birth control" by repudiating all sexuality as repugnant. Such a strategy for birth control may well register a critique of Margaret Sanger's notorious alliance between feminist birth-control advocacy and the eugenics discourses that the novel forcefully indicts.[24] However, Dorinda's own strategies are equally dangerous to feminism. Her troping of her desire for Jason as a black male violation of her body builds on her earlier racialization of her sexual feelings as the site of a dark, junglelike part of her self (239). But if this strategy accomplishes the feminist goal of preventing her participation in patriarchal reproduction, it also functions to proscribe her access to nonreproductive sexuality or to a reproduction whose impact on her adult life she can control.

Nevertheless, Dorinda's ultimate strategy registers Glasgow's hopes for an effective feminism that is not entangled with the discourses that undo it: a grounding of social evolution in the transmission of feminist culture through the inheritance of property. Posed against a restitution of the failed romantic marriage plot, the novel's happy ending comes when Dorinda equates her resistance to romantic marriage with her intentions to bequeath her property, which now includes Five Oaks, to a subject distinguished by his support of productive women and his immunity to oedipal masculinity.

Dorinda's eventual purchase of Five Oaks from the now bankrupt, drunken Jason is the crowning achievement in her feminist modification of the world she inhabits. As she develops a prosperous dairy business on her own inherited property, she also constitutes a nonbiological, interracial family in which adult women produce rather than reproduce and men are "emasculate in [their] unselfishness" (372). For the first ten years after her affair with Jason she lives only with her black servant, Fluvanna, whom she regards as family; in a rhetoric that flouts the law against interracial families whose racist aims involved the policing of white female reproduction, Glasgow notes that "[t]he affection between the two women had outgrown the slender tie of mistress and maid, and had become as strong and elastic as the bond that holds relatives together" (349). And a sexless marriage to the unattractive but respectful, pragmatic Nathan Pedlar brings a maternal relationship with Nathan's crippled son, John Abner, which fulfills very different desires from those Freud attributed to mother-son relations.

What interests Dorinda is not an eroticized relation to the representative of patriarchal power but the opportunity the crippled stepson presents for the nonbiological transmission of feminist culture. John Abner is her chosen heir, it seems, not only because he esteems Dorinda highly but also because he has a clubfoot. Like Dorinda who gives the lie to eugenical categories when her illegitimate pregnancy initiates a life of exemplary fitness, John Abner's infirmity seems to be the condition that prepares him to carry on Dorinda's project for cultural change. If in Freud's account of male development the son's acceptance of metaphorical castration is the key to his eventual accession to patriarchal power, John Abner's literal impaired extremity makes him a good candidate for evading the pitfalls of oedipal masculinity. His affliction impairs his ability to accede to patri-archal power, enabling him both to resist subordination to this power and to be an agent for displacing it.

John Abner differs dramatically from Jason, whose acceptance of meta-phorical castration produces a fearful retreat from moral action and an implacable subordination to the patriarchal dicta that injure women. In-stead of embracing a racist and classist masculinity that depends on the con-trol of women's reproduction, John Abner, at the moment that inspires Dorinda to tell him that he will be her heir, is represented as emphatically lame and in pursuit of a self-image mediated through identifications both with "blackness" and with Dorinda: "[T]urning at the gate, she went back to meet John Abner, who was limping toward her over the dead leaves in the walk. His long black shadow ran ahead of him, and while he approached her, he looked as if he were pursuing some transparent image of himself" (525–26). John Abner's limping pursuit of a "black" image of himself may promise a productive identification of the impaired white man with other disenfranchised males (reminiscent of Nick's identification with the black prisoner), an identification here made possible when there is little hope of acceding to empowered white masculinity.[25] The latter hope, as we have seen, covers over classed modes of subordination for Nick and makes sub-mission a permanent feature of the privileged Jason. Moreover, at the same time that John Abner "pursu[es] some transparent image of himself" in his black shadow, he is also pursuing Dorinda; reproducing Dorinda's subjec-tivity in John Abner appears to involve the identification with disadvan-taged others so crucial for Glasgow to breaking the hold of dominant ideol-ogies on subjects who are simultaneously advantaged and disadvantaged.

Indeed John Abner presents a more vivid challenge to racist notions of family than does Dorinda's nonbiological relation to Fluvanna when he suggests that "Idabella's mulatto children," who are "still hanging about Five Oaks," (492) could, because they are Jason's kin, be called upon to take familial responsibility for the dying alcoholic. His willingness to acknowledge that Greylock's interracial offspring are related to the white son challenges the racist aims of the Racial Integrity Act. Indeed this challenge made by the heir to Five Oaks to the discourse that most authorized the eugenical regulation of women's adult lives is good news for Dorinda's (and Glasgow's) project of displacing patriarchal culture with feminist culture.

The bad news is that it is not clear whether Glasgow is fully up to this challenge. John Abner's recognition of a family relation between races is undermined by what seems to be disdain for Idabella's children who "hang around" Five Oaks. And his willingness to connect them to Jason may betray a desire to racialize as black the degenerate and injurious Jason — the same impulse that Glasgow criticizes in Dorinda. And Dorinda's response to John Abner's suggestion is similarly marked by ambivalence: "[S]he shiver[s] with disgust" and remarks, "What the law doesn't acknowledge, I suppose it doesn't bother about" (492). While these remarks are ambiguous — Dorinda's disgust may be directed toward miscegenation or toward the law that doesn't acknowledge it — that very ambiguity registers the contest, in force for both Dorinda and Glasgow, between a feminism that requires antiracism and a racism that recuperates the feminism it is meant to support.

Thirty years later, in her autobiography *The Woman Within* (1954), Glasgow represents *herself* as the kind of subject she articulates in her protagonists.[26] Invoking the dilemma of her characters, Glasgow presents an identification with "whiteness," especially as regards meanings for the female body, as the occasion to make privileged distinctions that both afford protection and inscribe her in gendered subordination (*Woman Within* 1–10). It is not surprising, then, to find here the temptation, like the ones Dorinda faces, to authorize an intervention in gendered roles with the discourses that can support white supremacy.

While Glasgow does make the straightforward claim that "maternal instinct, sacred or profane, was left out of me by nature" (108), she also invokes eugenics to cement her right not to reproduce: "I felt that my increasing deafness might be inherited, and that it would be a sin against life to pass on an affliction" (153). Supporting her decision not to marry or reproduce with such proscriptions, despite prominent opinion that hereditary deafness could be overcome by marriage with the hearing, risks underscoring the elite regulations that eugenics made for female reproduction generally.[27]

Certainly the appeal to eugenics constitutes another instance of the effort we have seen in both novels to appropriate the terms of social evolution for feminist aims. But it also demonstrates how that appropriation can play into the very processes Glasgow understands as being most responsible for retarding women's social development. The opposition to controls on biological heredity that *Barren Ground* makes central to its concept of feminist social evolution is here undermined by the very strategy the novel identifies as so threatening to feminist interventions: the impulse to authorize an "unacceptable" resistance to conventional gender roles with the dominant discourses that can recuperate it.

Glasgow's autobiographical representation of the "woman within," then, implicates her own subjectivity in the ongoing contests that pressure both her characters and her narrative voice. If Dorinda is as attached to Fluvanna as to a relative, Glasgow goes on to make this heretical idea palatable by noting that the attachment remains informed by "an inherited feeling of condescension" (349). If, in the exchange with Ellgood about bovine production and reproduction, Dorinda's stereotyping of black labor instigates the narrative's allusion to the fact that racism motivates reproductive imperatives for elite women, elsewhere Dorinda's autonomy finds support in stereotypes of black labor without registering the risks that racism poses to feminist aims.

Despite and perhaps because of Glasgow's own narrative lapses, displacing the strategies whereby the subject's privileges either reify gendered subordination or foil feminist agency is a crucial component in the novel's construction of a happy ending. The final passage of *Barren Ground* presents the transmission of feminist culture from and to subjects who can resist mistaking subordination for privilege as the explicit replacement for the resolution of a marriage plot:

"Bear with my fancies now, John Abner. When I am gone both farms will be yours."

"Mine?" John Abner laughed as he looked at her. "Why, you may marry again. They are saying at Pedlar's Mill that you may have Bob Ellgood for the lifting of a finger."

Dorinda smiled, and her smile was pensive, ironic, and infinitely wise. "Oh, I've finished with all that," she rejoined. "I am thankful to have finished with all that." (526)

Marriage to Bob Ellgood, as John Abner makes clear, means relinquishing control over inheritance to the man whose imbrication with elite controls on white women's reproduction the novel has emphasized. Importantly, being "finished with all that," repudiating the romance that leads to subordinate marriage and maternity either as the poor shopgirl or as the elite landholder, has also meant avoiding the investments in race and class privilege that shore up white women's subordination. Being through with desire for men like Ellgood, whose condemnation of "contagious abortion" in prized "stock" dovetails with Dorinda's use of racist epithets to support feminist change, may herald a commitment to "being through" as well with seeking to authorize feminist interventions with racist rhetorics. In the pensiveness, infinite wisdom, and irony that distinguish Dorinda's final resolution, there may be the awareness that can foil the way that dominant ideology manages a self-different subject. But, of course, repression of sexual and romantic desire (being "finished with all that" [526]) has also been characterized by the impulse to authorize resistance with racism, including the racialization of Dorinda's own desire. There remains, then, the possibility that her feminism will continue to resort to a racism that Glasgow knows supports dominant gender ideology.

Finally, and perhaps most importantly, the progressive vision of this feminist transmission of culture, the one that empowers female and male subjects who can resist dominant regulations of their advantaged and disadvantaged positions, may be threatened by the particular structure of property inheritance on which it relies. Glasgow's antidote to elite patriarchal hegemony over cultural meanings, made possible by the ownership and transmission of property, consists of simply wresting control over both property and its transmission. As a result, the pitfalls of controlling the subordinate (even if productively impaired) subject through inheritance that Glasgow implicates in the oedipal relations that make Jason a pawn of oppressive power might well affect the novel's feminist scene of inheritance. That is, the very aspects of John Abner's subjectivity that Dorinda/Glasgow wants to reproduce may be eliminated, and on the terms of her own analysis, in the mode of their reproduction. Nevertheless, if in its final passage *Barren Ground* registers the competition between these possibilities, it also emphasizes what both novels and the autobiography do make clear: that dominant regulations of how advantage and disadvantage intersect for the "composite subject" are among the "hardest conditions to shake" ("Feminism" 27), even when the object is both to expose and to eliminate them.

Chapter 4

"CAUGHT IN A SKEIN OF VOICES"

Feminism and Colonialism in Elizabeth Bishop

At the end of *Barren Ground* Glasgow envisions transmitting feminist cul-ture, which stresses an awareness that gendered oppression can be secured through privileged beliefs, to a nonoedipal man, whose physical impair-ment immunizes him against embracing subordination in the guise of male privilege. Nevertheless, Dorinda's own resisting subjectivity, also posed against male oedipality, is represented in the novel both as prototypical for her intended heir and as precarious. Despite (and also because of) the cross-cultural identifications that save her from mistaking privilege as subordina-tion, Dorinda remains vulnerable to authorizing her feminist rebellion with the racist rhetoric that sustains patriarchal interests. Just as dominant gen-der ideology is capable of recruiting women's consent to oppression in the name of privilege, so is it able to recuperate the feminist resistance that aligns itself with privileged positions.

Elizabeth Bishop also explores the similarity between structures of fe-male subordination and the operations that can undermine feminist agency. And like Glasgow, Bishop identifies the interarticulation of subordinate and privileged positions as being integral to both processes. However, whereas Glasgow's feminist subject becomes vulnerable to oedipal-type effects because she authorizes her resistance with discourses of domination, Bishop's makes such vexed alliances because she is the product of oedipal dynamics. Influenced by the psychoanalysis of both Freud and Melanie Klein, Bishop links adult feminist subjectivity to a childhood development that makes the price of resistance the loss of crucial familial and social relations. As a result, the child learns to disguise feminist protest in the discourses that preserve these relations. When the adult feminist subject makes alignments with the discourses that promise to legitimate but actually undermine feminism, dominant gender ideology builds on the psychic structures established in childhood.

In this chapter, I trace Bishop's numerous feminist revisions in her poetry and prose of the autobiographical scene of development she records in the short story "In the Village" (1965). As it strives to authorize critiques of the mother-child dynamics that serve patriarchal ideology, this repetitive re-writing also attempts to extricate Melanie Klein's mother-centered description of development from its affiliation with Freudian paradigms. Most centrally, Bishop tries to disentangle the "good mother," on whose internalized image Klein predicates successful female development, from her definition by masculinist interests. My primary focus, however, is on Bishop's simultaneous preoccupation with scrutinizing her own strategies for this project of feminist resignification, which in the Brazil writing relies on colonialist representations of Brazilian culture.[1] Indeed this project is always as much about tracing the lures, pitfalls, and potential successes of strategies for feminist signification as it is about reformulating key concepts in gender ideology.

As a result, Bishop charts a complex contest between the feminist subject's desire to avail herself of the rhetorics that promise to legitimate prohibited feminist representations and her desire to articulate the dangers to feminism of its alliance with colonialist discourse. Her deliberate, persistent representation of this contest illuminates both how her feminist project of resignification is pressured toward fatal alignments with colonialist rhetorics and how her intersecting feminist and anticolonialist aims eventually produce a renunciation of them. Although the latter impulse prevails, it does so only after a lengthy process that Bishop's final retelling of the "Village"'s scene of development (in the late poem "In the Waiting Room" [1971]) will attempt to render unnecessary. Like both Hurston and Glasgow, Bishop comes to prioritize for feminism an awareness of how domination governs the interarticulation of multiple discourses for self-different subjects. In Bishop's case, her final feminist revision of Kleinian psychoanalysis provides the terms for imagining that this awareness might be installed early in life as a permanent feature of the daughter's subjectivity.

Female Development and Feminist Subjectivity in "In the Village"

Published in *Questions of Travel* (1965), "In the Village" is situated at the very center of that book, as if to mark the importance to the volume's poems of this story that traces the child Bishop's development in relation to domestic maternal and public "paternal" voices.[2] Significantly, the story divides the collection into poems that represent North America and those that represent Brazil; while the former section includes poems that elaborate the story's focus on the construction of female subjectivity, the latter includes ones that project both this construction and an effort to resist it onto a Brazilian scene. In the Brazil poems Bishop stakes her feminist desire for a different world on a colonialist empowerment to realize emancipatory dreams in a new world, but at the same time she problematizes this impulse. As these poems enact the American feminist's projection of her agendas onto Brazilians, they are also the occasion to document how dominant gender ideology profits from such a strategy. Illuminating the unrepresentable with authorizing discourses emerges as a vehicle for undermining the feminist speaker, a symptom of how resistance can be monitored by the dynamics between a female subject's disadvantage in gender and her privilege in race, class, and national identity.

The story's main event is a mother's scream that the adult narrator characterizes as all-pervasive for her, yet unheard by the "public": "A scream, the echo of a scream, hangs over that Nova Scotian village. No one hears it; it hangs there forever, . . . unheard, in memory" (47).[3] The scene that generates the scream, narrated now by the child the speaker once was, is the fitting of the mother for a new purple dress. As she evaluates the dress that will mark her emergence from mourning for her husband, the mother, who is also prone to nervous breakdowns, expresses anxiety about the fitting as a helplessness to control or evaluate her relation to the "colors" she is about to assume. Echoing Bishop's interrogation in "The Map" (1935) of the correspondence between arbitrary assignation of signifiers ("colors") and the nature of the signified ("Are they assigned, or can the countries pick their colors?" [*Complete Poems* 3]), the anxious mother asks, "Is it a good shade for me?" Is it too bright? I don't know" (*Questions* 48). Aesthetic questions about the arbitrary attribution of meaning in the early poem translate here into questions of the female subject's choice in assuming the signifiers of normative femininity.

As the mother worries about her fitting, sounds of another "fitting" ring out from Nate's blacksmith shop and appear to precipitate the mother's scream of rage against her own situation:

> Clang.
> *Clang.*
> Oh, beautiful sounds, from the black-
> smith's shop at the end of the garden! Its
> gray roof, with patches of moss, could be
> seen above the lilac bushes. Nate was
> there — Nate, wearing a long black leather
> apron over his trousers and bare chest,
> sweating hard, a black leather cap on top
> of dry, thick, black-and-gray curls, a black
> sooty face; iron filings, whiskers, and gold
> teeth, all together, and a smell of red-hot
> metal and horses' hoofs.
> *Clang.*
> The pure note; pure and angelic.
> The dress was all wrong. She screamed.
> The child vanishes. (48–49)

Whereas for the child the sounds of a "domestication" explicitly gendered as male are "pure and angelic" messages from the world of freedom outside the troubled home, for the mother they precipitate a scream against the "fitting" she endures within the home. What the child understands as a juxtaposition to and an escape from the scene of domestic "fitting," the mother understands as an analogue for it.

If the "vanishing" of the child registers the loss of childhood in the experience of adult pain (Kalstone 15), Bishop pointedly connects this loss to an entrance into cultural constructions of female subjectivity. The child who vanishes from the domestic scene becomes a speaker who has entered a public, masculine world that, importantly, she apprehends as a comforting alternative to her troubled "female" home. However, her experience of Nate's world soon also introduces her to the dangers of embracing such comforts. Although the blacksmith's shop is appealing and even homelike, once there the child notices that the freshly shoed horse "expresses his satisfaction . . . as he backs into the shafts of his wagon" (56). It is this kind of satisfaction that the raging mother refuses; and as the child takes note of the horse's complacency about its domestication, she registers an incipient sympathy with the mother's resistance to hers.

Nonetheless, such an intuition must compete with the fear of the resisting maternal voice and of its consequences: the loss of maternal care that the child craves. On returning home, the comfort supplied by the grandmother is threatened by the possibility of again inciting the mother's scream. Fearing another outburst, the grandmother cries as she cooks, and the child tries to cheer her up (57–58). The mother-daughter bond, initially severed by the mother's rage against her "domestication," is restored for the child as a reward for helping the grandmother adhere to the requirements of domestic propriety: to both repress her own sorrow and to repress the rage of the daughter. Both the price and the sine qua non of the restoration of this mother-daughter bond is the repression of anguish over the domestication that produces good mothers.

Accordingly, the child's desire to eradicate both the mother's scream and the grandmother's sorrow turns out to have implications for her own self-expression; she feels herself to be "caught in a skein of voices, my aunts' and my grandmother's" (72). In response to the child's own "shriek" of fright (69), we are told, her aunt "almost shouts": "Don't cry!" . . . "Don't *cry!*" (70). In exchange for the comfort of a mother-daughter bond that assuages the terrors of maternal rage, the child learns, she must censor her own expressions of anguish. As a result, the ability of her own voice to resist the discourses that enforce prohibitions by conferring familial and social relations becomes the central issue in the final passage of the story, where the child demonstrates a much more ambivalent response to the blacksmith's sounds that "turn everything else to silence":

> Clang.
> *Clang.*
> Nate is shaping a horseshoe.
> Oh, beautiful pure sound!
> It turns everything else to silence. . . .
> *Clang.* . . .
> Now there is no scream. . . . surely it has gone away, forever.
> Clang.
> It sounds like a bell buoy out at sea.
> It is the elements speaking: earth, air, fire, water.
> All those other things — . . . things damaged and lost,
> sickened or destroyed; even the frail almost-lost scream —
> are they too frail for us to hear their voices long, too
> mortal?
> Nate!
> Oh, beautiful sound, strike again! (76–77)

Now the "Clang!" that drowns out the scream in a solacing way is understood as also repressing it. The initial gratitude for the disappearance of the scream coexists with a mourning for the "sickened and destroyed" voice of the resisting mother. This contradictory yearning — both to silence the maternal voice that shatters mothering and to resuscitate its resistance to gendered restrictions that also affect the child — constructs the child's feminist subjectivity as the site of contradictory meaning. Following her mournful meditation on the mother's frail, lost voice, the child exclaims, "Nate!," an utterance that may be read as an outraged accusation similar to the mother's cry in response to Nate's "clang" (she has just finished mourning the loss of the mother's voice drowned out by Nate's sounds). But the cry also can be read as an appeal for Nate to repress the mother's scream again.

Indeed these contradictory agendas appear to coincide in the child's utterance that seeks at one time to retain a coveted mothering and to preserve the mad mother's discourse of resistance to the restrictions that structure conventional mothering (and the gendering of the child that Bishop implicates in those restrictions). Doing so means the cry "Nate!" simultaneously expresses both dismay at Nate's silencing of the maternal scream and, paradoxically, an appeal to Nate and his "language" as the comforting vehicle for expressing this dismay. The paradox, however, is a necessary one; without aligning resistance with the discourse that underwrites crucial familial and social relations, resistance will always mean the loss of those relations.[4]

The rhetoric that can accommodate such contradictory referents is a "poetic" one, whose multivalence in Bishop's work ranges from an inscrutable coding of privatized meaning to the more recognizable disguises of irony and allegory.[5] Inscrutable representation is the mode of the child, desperate for maternal care, who models her expression on that of the repressed maternal figure. In "Sestina," which is published two pages after "Village" in *Questions of Travel* and revisits the story's thematics, the tears that the grandmother hides in "laughing and talking" preoccupy the child. As a result, the child sees the repressed tears everywhere in the domestic scene; the teakettle has "small hard tears" (80), and the "teacup [is] full of dark brown tears" (81). But like the mother's scream that permeates the village but is heard only by the child, the tears are part of private perception. Thus like the grandmother, whose approbation encourages the process, the child also hides the tears in her incipient art:

> With crayons the child draws a rigid house
> and a winding pathway. Then the child
> puts in a man with buttons like tears
> and shows it proudly to the grandmother. (81)

Indeed, the poem goes on to conclude by emphasizing that the child's artistic expression will continue to reproduce the grandmother's self-policing of expression: "The grandmother sings to the marvelous stove / and the child draws another inscrutable house" (81).

In the story and the poem, the development of the child's speaking and artistic voice invokes both Freudian and Kleinian paradigms. With the flight from a frightening, disappointing mother to a comforting paternal figure, "Village" stages the turn that in Freud's view is motivated by the child's repudiation of a mother who has produced her daughter as female and/or failed to give the child adequate love or food ("Female Sexuality" 203). But the opposition between "bad" and "good" mothers and the subsequent ambivalent characterization of reliable, loving maternal figures allude to Melanie Klein's theories, which Bishop found compelling.[6] Indeed, Klein's ideas figure so centrally in Bishop's subsequent rewriting of the story's thematics that it is useful at this point to review the concepts that Bishop tries to appropriate and revise.

Klein differs from Freud in locating fundamental developmental processes not in interactions with the father but in ones with the nursing mother in the first year of life: "From the beginning the ego interjects objects 'good' and 'bad,' for both of which the mother's breast is the prototype" ("Psychogenesis" 282).[7] The good breast is the one that provides plenitude and the bad one is fantasized as withholding what the child craves. These dynamics are complicated by the infant's sadistic feelings toward the withholding breast/mother, manifest in fantasies of fragmenting and destroying the mother's body. When it projects its own aggressive feelings onto the bad object, breasts and mothers are fantasized as interjected persecutors from whom the infant's body is also at risk. Importantly, such fantasized persecution is the first manifestation of a superego ("Psychogenesis" 287).

When at four or five months the child comes to recognize the mother as whole and, therefore, that the loved object is also the hated object, the mother emerges as an ambivalent figure ("Psychogenesis" 306–8). This ambivalence extends superego functions from the persecutory bad mother to the demands of the good one (288) and creates as well an uncertainty about the goodness of the good mother who can readily transform into the bad one (287–88). At this point aggressive fantasies against the bad mother, which involve fragmenting and destroying the mother's body, also threaten the well-being of both the good mother and of the child who has internalized her ("Oedipus" 370). Finally, as a result of the guilt and sense of loss generated by these aggressive fantasies, the infant desires to make reparation to the mother by reconstituting her fragmented body. With such reconstruction, the child restores a good internal object that is necessary to the child's successful future development ("Weaning" 295–96). In artistic creation, Klein links such reparation to constructions of maternal figures ("Creative Impulse" 232–35).

But while Klein departed from Freud by attributing the earliest formation of the superego to maternal rather than paternal relations, her sense of successful female development did not differ from the classic psychoanalytic account. For Klein, resolving ambivalence about the mother by reconstructing the good internal mother is the foundation for the female child's "surrender[ing] herself completely to her paternal super-ego" (*Children* 321). If Klein reformulates Freud's Oedipus complex as a development that builds on early maternal relations, the purpose of the female Oedipus complex remains the same: to lead the girl toward marriage and maternity, "to achieve increasingly a feminine and maternal attitude" ("Oedipus" 376). In "Village" and "Sestina" Bishop represents this fit between the two paradigms; in both texts the Freudian flight from the bad mother to the appealing "father" has the same effects as does the Kleinian restoration of good mothering: the production of a female voice that represses anguish and resistance as it adheres to paternal dicta for that voice. There is no difference, finally, between Nate's silencing "clang" and the "good" maternal figure's "Don't cry!" Indeed, maternal nourishment in "Village" is vividly indistinguishable from repression, from swallowing the tears that the grandmother stirs into the potato mash (57). Likewise, the price of maternal approbation and nourishment in "Sestina" is the reproduction of the grandmother's disguising of her pain.

At the same time these two texts also imply a critique of the Kleinian fit between the child's restoration of a good mother and patriarchal requirements for female development. The lament for the resisting mother's scream in "Village" and the (failed) effort to retrieve and express the grandmother's hidden tears in "Sestina" prefigure Bishop's careerlong project of representing the resistance these maternal figures, as well as the child they influence, must repress. In a number of works this project takes the shape of reconstructing a resisting mother—the mother who shatters conventional bonds and/or challenges patriarchal controls on mothering—as Klein's good, nurturing mother.

Klein's prioritizing of maternal rather than paternal relations for the construction of subjectivity enables Bishop to imagine feminist interventions in patriarchal development. But such interventions require the disentangling of "good mothering" and the female development it produces from the patriarchal paradigm to which Klein subscribed. As a result, Bishop takes poetic license with Klein's lexicon: the ambivalent figure, whose meaning shifts on the basis of the nurturing she provides or withholds, becomes the grounds for turning the bad mothers who resist patriarchal regulations into good ones and loving but conventional mothers into bad ones. In Bishop's final version of this project, the late poem "In the Waiting Room," the interrelated dissolution of maternal and daughterly bodies/selves that is the price of aggression against the "bad" mother becomes necessary to a process of emancipating maternal-child relations from the hold of patriarchal ideology. Such dissolution paves the way for reconstructing a feminist version of the maternal figure who shapes her daughter's subjectivity.

Whereas for Klein women's artistic construction of mother figures represents the reparation to the mother that grounds normative female subjectivity, Bishop's artistic reconstructions of "good mothers" aim at one time to retain the maternal relations that Klein valorized and to make feminist interventions in mothering itself. This project, however, must buck precisely the psychic structure of female subjectivity that Bishop represents in "Village" and "Sestina"; it is the child's craving of security and mothering that makes her both renounce the resisting mother who cannot supply it and disguise her own rebellious voice in the appropriate representation required by the patriarchal maternal figure. Such a child is the precursor of Bishop's adult speakers who make vexed alliances with colonialist discourses in order to release the resisting feminist voice from inscrutability. In the course of the Brazil writing, Bishop connects the need for these authorizing affiliations to the fear of psychic and social reprisals that attend the violation of the conventionally "good" mother's demands.

Nevertheless, the signal feature of the Brazil writing is precisely the way the texts register an awareness of such dynamics even as they participate in them. This awareness, in turn, relies on the tension between Bishop's progressive beliefs and the appeal of colonialist rhetorics as an authorizing framework for what she regards as prohibited feminist and homoerotic representation. A crucial consequence of this tension is that Bishop strives to distinguish her feminist strategies from imperialist and patriarchal colonialism. But at the same time, the texts persistently record the failure of this distinction by embedding realizations that colonialist discourses are inevitably the vehicles of patriarchal ideology. Each one of the texts I discuss records how the rhetorics that promise to authorize feminist representation dupe the speaker into reproducing the discourses she wants to critique. The strategies meant to intervene in the silencing of resistance that is the price of coveted maternal and (paternal) social relations turn out to be a renewed version of Nate's "clang," the discourse, we will recall, that reifies subordination as it promises liberation. That is, the psychic dynamics that make the child long for both the maternal and paternal comforts that demand repression are reproduced as the dynamics that make vexed but authorizing discourses appealing to resisting speakers.

However, in the course of the first chapter of the travel book *Brazil* (1962), these strategies prove to be their own undoing when the distinction between feminist and imperialist colonialism collapses. Precisely as the consequence of forging such distinctions, the feminist representation authorized by a "better" colonialism ultimately comes also to signify the imperialist discourse Bishop wants to repudiate. Yet *Brazil*, like the other texts I discuss, also registers the ongoing contest between such recognition/resistance and the continual lure of crossing prohibited with authorized representation. Only late in her career does Bishop abandon her repeated representation of this contest for a clear renunciation of colonialist discourse. Doing so also instigates a rewriting of "Village" 's scene of female development in North American rather than Brazilian contexts and a final shift in the referent for "good mothering."

Feminism and Colonialism in Bishop's Representation of Brazil

"Brazil, January 1, 1502" (1960),[8] also published in *Questions of Travel* (1965), initiates the effort to distinguish between imperialist and feminist colonialist rhetorics that Bishop will continue to pursue in the subsequent Brazil writing. It also initiates her concern with the lures and the liabilities that colonialist representations hold for authorizing the articulation of feminist difference. Initially the poem declares an equivalence in perspectives between the speaker and the early Portuguese soldiers as regards their expectations "for a different world, / and a better life" ("Arrival at Santos," *Questions* 3):

> Januaries, Nature greets our eyes
> exactly as she must have greeted theirs:
> every square inch filling in with foliage —
> big leaves, little leaves, and giant leaves.
> ("Brazil," *Questions* 5)

Such an "exact" equivalence derives from a "Nature" that, rather than being a projection of the viewers, has the autonomous power to "greet [the] eyes" of the explorers and the speaker alike. In the subsequent stanzas, however, interpreting nature from the vantage point of the earlier colonialists both brings to mind the soldiers' imperialist violence and raises the question of the speaker's relation to that colonialist tradition:

> Just so the Christians, hard as nails,
> tiny as nails, and glinting,
> in creaking armor, came and found it all,
> not unfamiliar:
> no lovers' walks, no bowers,
> no cherries to be picked, no lute music,
> but corresponding, nevertheless,
> to an old dream of wealth and luxury
> already out of style when they left home —
> wealth, plus a brand-new pleasure.
> Directly after Mass, humming perhaps
> *L'Homme armé* or some such tune,
> they ripped away into the hanging fabric,
> each out to catch an Indian for himself. (6–7)

As this passage acknowledges that the speaker is like the soldiers in having "not unfamiliar" expectations of newness and freedom in the "different world," it also registers the disturbing shape these expectations take for the soldiers: violence against women and nature.[9] Now "Nature," initially regarded as autonomous from its spectators, is revealed as the soldiers' violently imposed "fabrication" of Brazil. And when the speaker's equation of "Nature's" femininity ("she" greets the eyes) with its freedom from cultural construction is echoed in the soldiers' violent feminization of nature, the former's feminist expectations of difference in Brazil are at once likened to and strongly alienated from those of the early colonialists.[10]

The double valence of the "just so" that begins the passage plays out the feminist speaker's contradictory relation to patriarchal imperialism. On its most overt level "just so" functions to reiterate her implication in a projection of "not unfamiliar" (if different) desires of her own onto the landscape and the inhabitants of Brazil. But in the context of the passage's indictment of the soldiers, "just so" announces the speaker's recognition that the soldiers' perspective is injurious in ways "just like" the ones she goes on to describe. The passage attempts to resolve the speaker's contradictory positioning when her own projections of meaning onto the Brazilian landscape characterize the native women as resisting the soldiers' "dream" of Brazil:

> [the soldiers] ripped away into the hanging fabric,
> each out to catch an Indian for himself, —
> those maddening little women who kept calling,
> calling to each other (or had the birds waked up?)
> and retreating, always retreating, behind it. (7)

While Bishop's native women valiantly resist the soldiers, they do so in ways that enact Bishop's concept of feminist subjectivity. As with the child's voice that emerges at the end of "Village," the Brazilian women's voices encode feminist resistance in overt meanings as they "retreat" behind the "fabric" of nature constructed by the soldiers.[11] Especially with this retreat, the native women reproduce Bishop's own double relation to authorizing discourses.

Locating the North American child's subjectivity in Brazilian women seems to have two interrelated but also competing aims. First Brazil is presented as the pristine "different world" where Bishop both imagines an effective version of encoded feminist resistance and is able to reveal such coding as a necessary, cumbersome feminist strategy. But this fantasy itself plays out a version of Bishop's own coded representation: the disguising of her own subjectivity in that of the native women, a disguise meant to authorize her revelation of such feminist strategies by representing them as instances of Brazilian cultural difference. As a result, Bishop's account of the native women's voices also has the contradictory aim of illuminating the consequences, only implied in "Village," of legitimating feminism with the discourses that oppose it: a "retreat" that leaves patriarchal culture dangerously in charge, that undermines the "calling" that speaks in the very language that is out to annihilate such speech.

The poem's interest in these dynamics, of course, also glosses Bishop's project of bringing feminism to light in a representation of the Brazilian women that, despite its feminist aims, also resembles the soldiers' arbitrary projections onto this different world. Thus the native women's "calling and retreating" acknowledges the dangers, underscored by the poem's concern with the speaker's inscription in patriarchal colonialism, in her own strategies for "calling and retreating": her authorization of feminist representation with colonialist projections. In the end, the poem charts a contest between two feminist impulses: to authorize feminist resistance with colonialist appropriations of cultural difference and to analyze the way in which such authorizations are complicit with the discourses that support dominant gender ideology.

A number of Bishop's subsequent feminist representations of Brazilian culture remain torn between these impulses. "Squatter's Children," also published in *Questions of Travel,* documents these competing desires as it explicitly replays and revises "Village"'s scene of childhood development in a Brazilian context. At the outset the poem emphasizes the speaker's physical distance from the scene, one that reflects the cultural distance that informs her account of the Brazilian children: "On the unbreathing sides of hills / they play, a specklike girl and boy, / alone, but near a specklike house" (11). Moreover, this perspective is initially presented, as is the perspective in "Brazil," as simply recording what is illuminated by nature itself: "The sun's suspended eye / blinks casually, and then they wade / gigantic waves of light and shade" (11).

When the speaker zooms in for a close-up, however, what she sees is Brazilian children negotiating a version of "Village"'s scene of development:

> The children play at digging holes.
> The ground is hard; they try to use
> one of their father's tools,
> a mattock with a broken haft
> the two of them can scarcely lift.
> It drops and clangs. Their laughter spreads
> effulgence in the thunderheads, . . .
> apparently the rain's reply
> consists of echolalia,
> and Mother's voice, ugly as sin,
> keeps calling them to come in. (11–12)

Here, a culturally dominant speaking position underwrites a change in the story's account of the child's relation to maternal and paternal discourses; the child flees the acculturating not the resisting mother, and paternal "language" articulates only resistance to domestic imperatives. The same "clang" that in the story signifies a repressive discourse disguised as a liberating one here constitutes a discourse that, as a consequence of the impairment of the poor Brazilian father's tools, is identical with the children's laughter and the sounds of nature. In Brazil, if not in Nova Scotia, the paternal "language" that represents an emancipating "outside" to a vexed scene of maternal domesticity lives up to the promise that is broken in "Village": in tune with the natural world, it liberates the children from an "ugly" maternal voice and the domestic scene it defines.

This utopian "paternal" discourse, moreover, is a trope for the rhetoric that authorizes Bishop's own emancipatory gesture, her resignification of "Village"'s construction of the female child's voice. That is, a fantasy of Brazilian children's access to paternal but emancipatory modes of representation tropes Bishop's hope that colonialist discourse can authorize the resistance to repressive gendering that, for the child in the North American story, is drowned out by "paternal" discourse. That Bishop vividly describes the "good" rather than the withholding mother's voice as "ugly as sin" is a symptom of this hope; she feels authorized to critique as Brazilian the sanctioned figures that regulate the child's representation in North American contexts.

The final stanza further dramatizes Bishop's hope that colonialist perspectives and rhetorics can underwrite resistance to the good, acculturating maternal voice:

> Children, the threshold of the storm
> has slid beneath your muddy shoes;
> wet and beguiled, you stand among
> the mansions you may choose
> out of a bigger house than yours,
> whose lawfulness endures.
> Its soggy documents retain
> your rights in rooms of falling rain. (12)

The speaker's maternal invocation of "Children," which usurps to contradict the "ugly" maternal voice that directly precedes it, resonates with overlapping parental, colonialist, and class authority as it comes out in support of the children's resistance to the more conventional mother. However, even as this voice gives substance to the poem's earlier fantasy of appropriating an emancipatory paternal "law" to support resistance to domesticating mothers, it also inspires the speaker to shift from an unambiguous celebration of Brazilian "nature" to an ironic representation of it.

If the stanza initially seems to trope the natural world as a site of expansive freedom for these children, it also presents them as "beguiled" by a confusion that the line breaks emphasize.[12] To choose mansions "out of a bigger house than yours / whose lawfulness endures" overtly means to have access to the vast home of the natural world. But the line "out of a bigger house than yours" calls attention to a contradictory meaning: to be forcefully excluded from a bigger actual house, the site of an enduring "lawfulness" that determines stratified social positions. What looks like access to a free natural world is really exclusion from a privileged, governing one. In the final line the irony comes to the fore: "rights in rooms of falling rain" are, of course, rights to poor housing, exposure to the elements, and so on.

As the speaker's lofty speech on the children's access to an unsocialized natural world embeds the recognition that this natural freedom is really a symptom of the children's oppression, it again articulates the plight of the North American child, "beguiled" by apparently emancipatory rhetorics that are really subordinating ones. At the same time, the passage glosses the predicament of another beguiled subject: the speaker herself, who continues to hope that colonialist rhetoric can provide the emancipatory "lawfulness" that authorizes the representation of feminist difference in the "different world." Registering the predicament, however, does not here inspire a refusal of it. In the end, the poem's representational stakes continue to include both producing Brazil as the site where perceived emancipatory discourses actually underwrite resistance to conventionally "good" mothers and representing in Brazil the child's dilemma in "Village": seduction by a liberating discourse that in fact is a regulatory one. Thus the doubled discourse of the final stanza plays out once again a contest between the appeal of representing feminist difference with discourses on Brazilian difference and the feminist resistance to this appeal.

Resignifying Feminism in *Brazil*

Such a contest also drives the narrative trajectory in the first chapter of Bishop's Time/Life travel book, *Brazil* (1962),[13] where she attempts to authorize feminist critiques of patriarchal culture with successive representations of Brazilian difference. These critiques have explicit Kleinian dimensions; they aim to resignify from a feminist perspective the referents for good and bad mothering, respectively. Mothers who expose and/or resist the patriarchal regulation of biological mothering are presented as good nurturers, while conventional, biological mothers are portrayed as literally poisoning their children.

Each of these representations also replays the discovery of the poem "Brazil": that colonialist discourses are imbricated in patriarchal imperialism. But also like "Brazil," each effort inspires the vexed hope that a renewed feminist use of colonialist rhetoric can combat the patriarchal and imperialist aspects of colonialist discourse itself. Eventually, however, the repetition of these dynamics makes a difference. When the final representation of a Brazilian difference in mother-daughter relations comes to signify also the liabilities of the processes that have produced it, the feminist project of authorizing alternative configurations of good mothering can no longer be kept distinct from the feminist project of recognizing the dangers of doing so with colonialist rhetorics.

The chapter's trajectory, then, enacts a project of feminist resignification that it simultaneously analyzes, critiques, and ultimately reformulates, demonstrating that agency can emerge as a product of the operations that initially recruit the subject's participation in the ideologies she wants to displace. As a consequence of this process, a vexed project of feminist resignification transforms into one of resignifying feminist analysis itself to prioritize the resistance to the coarticulation of feminism with the dominant discourses that undermine it.

Bishop begins the opening chapter of *Brazil* by representing "Brazilian difference" not as difference but as an instance of a universalized scene of criminal maternal desire. Most characteristic of Brazil is a "human" scene that traverses cultural boundaries—"one of those 'human interest' dramas . . . that take place every so often in New York or London or Rome": "A newborn baby was kidnaped from a maternity hospital. Her name was Maria da Conceicao, or Mary of the Conception, but the newspapers immediately abbreviated this, Brazilian-fashion, to Conceicao-zinha, or 'Little Conception.' . . . One of the hospital nurses, who had lost a child of her own by miscarriage shortly before, had stolen her" (9–10).

Kidnapping babies to fulfill maternal desire is, clearly, a symptom of dominant ideology gone awry; the nurse's maternal desires, linked to her financial dependence on her mate, are entirely consistent with what the patriarchal organization of reproduction requires. When the nurse's normative desires exceed the social constrictions on them, however, her story has the potential to illuminate how patriarchal power governs the relation between economics, maternal desire, and biological female reproduction. But such stories "in New York or London or Rome," because they sanctify the biological mother and criminalize the impostor mother, tend to fortify rather than call into question the connection between "good mothers" and patriarchal ideology.[14] Bishop's initiation of her text on Brazil with a scene that in first world countries should but fails to expose the dominant structuring of maternal desire registers her agenda for the meaning of Brazilian difference: the enabling of resisting representations that she regards as being unspeakable in North America.

Accordingly, while the story of "Conception" is similar to others all over the Western world, its Brazilian difference takes shape as Bishop's critical exposition of the structures of maternal desire that the story would reify in "New York." "So far," the narrator says, "it all could have happened in New York or London or Rome." "But," she adds by way of introducing an analysis of the nurse's (rather than the offended family's) predicament, "now the story *becomes Brazilian*" (emphasis added):

The white nurse's mulatto lover, owner of a small grocery store, had promised her a house to live in if she had a child. . . . So the nurse—determined, she told reporters, "to have a decent place to live in" with "home atmosphere," and also because she really wanted a baby—concealed her miscarriage and told her lover that the baby would be born on such and such a day. Until then she boarded Conceicaozinha with her laundress, an old woman living in a *favela* shack. The nurse was arrested as she took them food. The baby was fat and well. (10)

Throughout *Brazil* miscegenation has a positive valence for Bishop, often standing in for other transgressions of social norms that she advocates (especially homosexuality and nonbiological families). In this passage miscegenation sets the stage for Bishop to represent the nurse's criminal desire as the simple extension of a normative but troubling structure of maternal desire. What the news story presents as a crime against the father now becomes Bishop's critical illumination of patriarchal hegemony over female desire and reproduction. The nurse's longing for a child ("she really wanted a baby") is bound to an economy wherein women trade their reproductive capacity for a "decent place to live in" with "home atmosphere." Most importantly, "the nurse [that] was arrested as she took . . . food" to a thriving baby emerges as the Kleinian "good mother" at the moment she is criminalized for an illegitimate exercise of mothering. Thus Bishop's retelling of the nurse's story critiques patriarchal parameters for mothering as it relocates the "good mother" outside of the biological family, outside of imperatives to reproduce race, and outside the law.

But the chapter goes on to emphasize that such resignification fails to be achieved by mere cultural displacement. First, Bishop pointedly observes that the return of "Little Conception" is both a restoration to the father (not the mother) and a triumph of the bond between the father and the law: When the father was told the good news he sobbed and said, " 'This is the strongest emotion I have ever felt in my life.' He was photographed embracing the police" (10). Yet the very observation meant to illuminate the complicity between the father and the police also points to the impotence of Bishop's interventions in the story of "conception" against this hegemonic configuration. The return of "Little Conception" to the father, whose control over female conception Bishop has tried to expose, is greeted by the "applause and cheers" of the community whose strong emotions support the patriarchal law (10).

Moreover, this applause also marks the futility and the end of Bishop's initial strategy for representing the nurse as a "good mother." Finding a receptive audience for her version of the nurse's story in her North American readers, as the subsequent passage implies, also encounters the obstacle of *their* "strong emotions." For the "happy ending" to the story, Bishop tells us, also reflects North American expectations of "predictable" Brazilian difference: "Brazilians love children. They are highly emotional and not ashamed of it. Family feeling is very strong. They are Roman Catholics, at least in outward behavior. . . . So far it is all fairly predictable" (10). Whatever distance is gained on American patriarchal ideology by interrogating its operations in terms of Brazilian scenarios disappears because Americans' notions of "predictable" Brazilian difference support the father's hegemony over "family feeling." As a result, Bishop's strategies for resignifying the "good mother" shift from mere cultural displacement to invoking discourses that can turn "strong family feeling" against Brazilian conventional families. That is, because the strategy of cultural displacement generates not a critique of patriarchal ideology but its reification through "predictable" American stereotypes of Brazilians, Bishop herself now looks to established discourses on Brazilian difference to underwrite changes in the representation of the "good mother."

Accordingly, Bishop goes on to note that the nurse's story also "brings to mind" a lethal Brazilian *perversion* of "family feeling," an alarming indifference to the "shocking" rate of infant mortality in Brazil (10). And this recognition is inextricable from a questioning of the outcry over illicit maternal desire: "Why all this sentimental, almost hysterical, concern over one small baby, when the infant mortality rate in Brazil is still one of the highest in the world?" (10). Indeed when, instead of supporting the father's position, strong feelings appropriately decry the infant mortality rate, the nurse is transformed into a heroine: "During the three days when Concei-caozinha ['Little Conception'] was hidden in the washerwoman's shack, and survived, it is a safe guess that more than 60 babies died in Rio" (11). More harmful by far than the nurse's illicit mothering, the failures of the sanctioned family challenge prevailing notions of good mothering. More clearly than in her initial story of the nurse, Bishop is able to suggest the importance of rescuing female "conception" from its normative structures, harmful to mothers and infants alike. While the nurse who steals "concep-tion" and hides her/it from the father is arrested as she brings food to a fat, healthy baby, normative Brazilian family love poisons its children into pa-triarchal gender: "The masses of poor people . . . love their children and kill them with kindness by the thousands. The wrong foods, spoiled foods, worm medicines, sleeping syrups — all exact a terrible toll: the 'little angels' in . . . gilt-trimmed coffins, blue for boys and pink for girls" (11). Thus for the resignification of "good mothers" to be effective, it must recruit dis-courses that have hegemonic force, ones that can appropriate for feminist critique the strong family feelings that are sutured to dominant ideology. The effective resignification of charged concepts is not simply a matter of, for example, shifting contexts and/or exploiting the double meanings in a term like "conception" — but of recruiting "strong feelings" to underwrite new meanings. Related to the compunction to authorize unpalatable femi-nist representation with the discourses that preserve familial and social relations (Bishop's sense of the psychic motivation) is the need to fortify feminist interventions with the "strong feelings" of her readers.

Nevertheless, the chapter immediately registers Bishop's apprehension that recruiting strong colonialist feelings must backfire against the project of disentangling good and bad mothering from their patriarchal meanings. Within this version of a "predictable" colonialist discourse on the need for change in underdeveloped Brazil lurks the development fantasy that, as Bishop emphasizes in the poem "Brazil," includes an egregious patriarchal construction of the female body. This realization seems to surface, directly following her remarks on murderous family love, in a passage that both invokes the development fantasy and alludes specifically to the poem:

Nevertheless, the population of Brazil is increasing rapidly. . . . It is like the banana tree that grows everywhere in the country. Cut it back to a stump above ground, and in a matter of days it sends up a new shoot and starts unfolding new green leaves.

Indeed, the banana tree is a fairly good symbol for the country itself. . . . *Brazil struck all the early explorers as a "natural paradise," "a garden," and at its best moments it still gives that impression* — a garden neglected, abused and still mostly uncultivated, but growing vigorously nevertheless. Great resources have been squandered, but even greater ones are still there, waiting. But it is the mismanagement and waste of both human and material wealth along the way that shocks the foreigner as well as the educated, sensitive Brazilian. (11; emphasis added)

As the startling metaphor of the banana tree for the female reproductive body makes clear ("Cut it back to a stump" and it will still produce "new green leaves"), the feminist colonialist rhetoric that invokes development fantasies paradoxically entails the translation of the female body into material resources available for the development of a colonialist "paradise." For this image follows directly from and extends the logic of her condemnation of patriarchal families in the guise of primitive, exotic practices in Brazil. As such, this troubling image may play out for Bishop herself the dangerous, logical consequences of her own discourse. In any case, when she follows it with a direct allusion to the poem "Brazil" 's comparison of early and modern-day foreigners — "Brazil struck all the early explorers" — the passage goes on to repeat the poem's trajectory. The rest of the passage is devoted to advocating present-day foreign interventions that can redress the effects of previous exploitative ones.

Bishop's initial appeal to colonialist dreams is immediately followed by an effort to realign them with desires for a different paradise, achieved by an intervention that reflects the vision rather than involves the exploitation of "educated, sensitive Brazilian[s]." Although "[g]reat resources . . . are still there, waiting," much of the "garden" is "neglected, abused"; as a result, the foreign intervention Bishop advocates is one that redresses the effects of earlier ones. As in the poem, a colonialist vision initially shared by early and latter-day foreigners becomes a desire, shared by sensitive latter-day foreigners and Brazilians, to combat the effects of earlier colonialism.

Moreover, just as the poem shifts from the speaker's identification with rapacious colonialist perspectives to a fantasy of Brazil as a feminist and homosocial utopia, so does this passage instigate a similar shift in the chapter. If the failure of Bishop's first effort to effectively resignify "good mothers" by shifting cultural context and exploiting puns pressures her toward colonialist discourses that activate "strong feelings," the implacable sexist dimension of the latter compels her to represent Brazil as an a priori utopia. And, as in the poem, this latter gesture is symptomatic of Bishop's efforts to displace an injurious colonialist rhetoric with a feminist colonialist one.

Having registered the liabilities of the development fantasy for both women and nature, Bishop now presents Brazil as the site where strong feelings automatically, without the aid of authorizing, dominant rhetorics, extend beyond the nuclear biological family to authorize homoerotic, inter-racial, and alternative mother-daughter relations. All this is made possible, moreover, by Brazil's a priori "feminine" language: "The tendency in Brazil is . . . to lighten the language with constant diminutives (as Maria da Conceicao became Conceicaozinha). In fact the Portuguese regard Bra-zilian Portuguese as 'effeminate' — charming when women speak it, but no language for men" (12). In the utopian version of the different world, the flexibility of its language translates into a progressive feminist culture where "Conception" is easily relieved of her/its Catholic, patriarchal fram-ing. While the passage also registers a continued debt to colonialist authori-zation for such transformations — a Portuguese effeminization of Brazilians supports the author's case for a utopian women's language — this acknowl-edgment disappears in the elaboration of Brazil as a feminine utopia. In-deed Brazilian culture's remarkable "atmosphere of familiarity, of affection and intimacy" means that "strong feelings" support not the patriarchal family but rather relations "in social life," including, most prominently, same-sex relations (12): "Part of the same emotionalism in social life is the custom of the *abraco*, or embrace. Brazilians shake hands a great deal, and men simultaneously embrace each other casually with their free arms. Women often embrace, too, and kiss rapidly on both cheeks: *left! right!* Under strong feeling the *abraco* becomes a real embrace" (12).

Recasting the embrace that earlier sutured public feeling and the law to the father's interests, in this passage the *abraco* — articulated in the terms of Brazil's "women's" language — ties the emotions of the public to homoso-cial affection. Here the strong feelings that earlier supported the heterosex-ual family urge homosocial interactions toward bigger and better embraces.

But the real test for such a flexible, counterhegemonic language is its ability to forge an interpretive framework for the chapter's initial feminist retelling of the story of "Conception." Now Bishop attributes to indigenous Brazilian "familiarity" the production of an alternative "good mother." Indeed Brazilian Portuguese turns out to be the perfect vehicle for such a manifestation of familiarity; the language that is singularly receptive to resignifying the contexts that define "Conception" is so precisely because it is itself modeled on a nontraditional mother-child relationship. In an extended footnote, Bishop tropes the relation between Portuguese and Brazilian Portuguese as that between a mother and a racially different child: "[T]he Brazilian version [of Portuguese] has 10,000 more words than the mother tongue, most of them introduced by Indians and Negroes" (13n).

It is not surprising, then, that this utopian Brazilian language and the familiarity it sponsors provide the cultural context for a mother-daughter relationship in which interracial bonds structure a good mothering freed from the reproductive, economic, and emotional imperatives of patriarchal marriage:

[O]ne occasionally sees an elegant lady out walking, leaning on the arm of a little dressed-up Negro girl, or taking tea or orangeade with her in a tearoom; the little girl is her "daughter of creation" whom she is bringing up.

In such relationships there is complete ease of manner on both sides. *Sometimes Brazilians seem to confuse familiarity with democracy,* although the attitude seems rather to be a hold-over from slavery days, or feudalism, or even the Roman Empire, when every rich man had his set of poor relations and parasites. Nevertheless, a sense of natural responsibility underlies the relationship and certainly contributes something toward the more difficult and somewhat broader *conception of what democracy generally means today.* (12–13; emphases added)

By the end of this passage, Bishop finally achieves a new symbolic register for "conception": a "conception of what democracy generally means today." As the term for female reproduction is replaced by its homonym, shifting the determining referent for mothering from the female body to ideas of social "responsibility," the mother-child relations governed earlier in the chapter by patriarchal hegemony transform into the "daughter of creation" model governed by democratic principles.

However, the passage also registers the liability of invoking colonialist discourses to get from the one interpretive framework to the other. "Familiarity," until now a Brazilian concept that extends "family feeling" beyond patriarchal and heterosexual strictures, emerges as also "a hold-over" from slavery, feudalism, and ancient imperialism. Although Bishop attributes such troubling notions of "familiarity" to Brazilians, her own feminist resignification of "good mothers" relies on the class and race hierarchies that trigger her comments on imperialist "familiarity." The Brazilian (and specifically the "mother of creation" 's) confusion of an "[imperialist] familiarity with democracy," then, also projects Bishop's own anxieties about authorizing the alternative mother-daughter relationship with a colonialist notion of "familiarity."

Having registered the implication of her own representational strategies in vexed discourses of national, race, and class domination, Bishop characteristically attempts to disengage her narration from them. As characteristically, she does so by criticizing the racism and imperialism of the early colonialists, against whom she poses her better and modern-day foreign intervention. While elite Brazilians can "confuse [imperialist] familiarity with democracy," her own invocation of Brazilian familiarity is synonymous with "a conception of what democracy generally means today." In distinguishing this "conception of democracy" from Brazilian ones, moreover, Bishop deliberately presents an ideal of ethical democracy as a modern American one.

However, there is a problem in valorizing as utopian "what [American] democracy means" as Bishop writes her travel book. Locating American-type democracy in Brazil would invoke contemporary American policy that rhetorically promoted democracy in Brazil while prioritizing American business and political interests over the policies of Brazil's democratically elected government. In 1962, United States relations with Brazil were structured by Cold War security policies and articulated in the Alliance for Progress, created in 1961. But although Alliance agendas overtly advocated democracy in Brazil, they, in fact, often resisted the populist movements and the constitutional government of Joao Goulart, whose attempt to increase national control over the economy threatened United States hegemony in the hemisphere. Although Bishop was no supporter of Goulart, whom she regarded as "a real old crook from the dictator gang" ("Aunt Grace" 401), she was critical in 1961 of United States policies; in a letter to Pearl Kazin, Bishop declared that "we [the United States] couldn't be doing much worse here as things are now" (400).[15]

Indeed Time/Life's desire to publish *Brazil* was a timely effort to represent Brazil as part of the American democratic family. As John Moors Cabot (a former United States ambassador to Brazil) states in the introduction, Brazil is "our South American sister republic" where a hallmark "warmth of hospitality" is manifest as "contributions to inter-American [democratic] ideals" (7). But Bishop was aware of the self-serving aspects of United States policy, as she was aware of and resistant to Time/Life's investment in supporting United States interests in controlling the trajectory of Brazilian democracy.[16] Thus her explicit effort to distinguish her use of "democracy" from ones that confuse it with an imperialist "familiarity" may constitute an attempt to mobilize a more equitable concept against the very American usage of the term she invokes in contrast to Brazilian confusions. That is, even as Bishop appropriates the prevailing discourse on bringing American-style democracy to Brazil, she tries to distance herself from it. Her description of the "daughter of creation" model as an instance of a "more difficult and somewhat broader conception of what democracy generally means today" (13), then, seems to register the "difficulty" of renouncing United States uses of "democracy" while appealing to them for authorization. Rather than displacing those meanings, such strategies can only "broaden" them.

Thus this complex passage, which finally succeeds in extricating good mothering from patriarchal hegemony over "strong feelings," is also devoted to a metacritique of the strategies that produce this success. Indeed this passage revisits the discoveries of the Brazil poems and of the previous segments of this chapter twice in the space of a paragraph. The trajectory of all the texts on Brazil—the discovery that feminism is recuperated by colonialist discourses and the consequent effort to distinguish a feminist colonialist discourse from an imperialist one—is here played out twice in the course of a single passage. First she attempts to counter the imperialist implications of the "familiarity" that underwrites her feminism by an invocation of American versions of "democracy"; but because this term is itself imbricated in neocolonialist aims, Bishop registers the difficulty of distinguishing her referent for "democracy" from contemporary United States agendas for Brazilian democracy. Such a condensed repetition of this process presents the recognition of how patriarchal ideology (always for Bishop a benefactor of colonialist agendas) benefits from feminist alignments with colonialist discourses as itself a crucial feminist representation. Accordingly, this recognition is no longer veiled; as much as it articulates feminist "good mothering," the "daughter of creation" model signifies overtly a collapsing of colonialist "familiarity" with the feminist version of "democracy" embodied in the alternative model of maternal relations.

Prioritizing for feminism a vigilance about such dynamics is the end product of a process that Bishop documents in the course of the chapter as the need to complicate the relation between discursive instability and resignification. Disentangling female "conception" from its imbrication in patriarchal ideology is not simply a matter of invoking the multiple referents for the term, nor, as the chapter initially attempts to do, of denaturalizing tenacious meanings by displacing their cultural context. The desire to displace a patriarchal representation of the mothering traditionally bound to female biological reproduction with a feminist critique of such mothering provokes alignments with discourses that both authorize the resisting representation and lend it the support of the interpretive community's "strong feelings." Yet this kind of authorization does not yield the emancipatory effects it promises; rather, it reifies dominant categories.

Even as Bishop emphasizes the dangers in the pressure to recruit "strong feelings" to combat the dominant hegemony over such feelings, she also demonstrates that the resulting affiliations with colonialist rhetoric inspire both a repudiation of these strategies and a renewal of them. In *Brazil* as well as in the poem "Brazil," repudiation of the discourses that are harmful to both women and Brazilians fuels rather than halts the feminist speaker's efforts to construct a "different world" in Brazil. The desire to disentangle feminist perspectives from rapacious colonialist ones generates the search for kinder, gentler ones. In contrast, it is in the context of utopian representation that distinctions between bad and good deployments of colonialist rhetoric finally become impossible to sustain. Any apprehension that imperialist colonialism underwrites utopian representation leaves no room for such distinctions: the good representation *is* the bad one. In Bishop's Brazil, utopian feminist "familiarity" ultimately emerges as indistinguishable from imperialist and patriarchal valences for the term; and this fact is registered by the confusion (between imperialist familiarity and democracy) that marks the "good mother" sponsored by Bishop's notion of "familiarity." When destructive colonialist rhetoric becomes visible in utopian feminist representation, there is no better colonialist space that Bishop can imagine.

What takes the place of Bishop's repeated failures to make progressive distinctions within dominant, authorizing rhetorics is the desire to extricate feminist representation from colonialist authorization altogether. And this desire arises from the realization that the colonialist rhetorics that promise to enable what for Bishop are prohibited representations will always be a version of Nate's domesticating discourse: the language that promises emancipation even as it brings dominant regulations to bear. If this realization nullifies the feminist "good mother" underwritten by colonialism, it nevertheless constitutes in itself a new mode of feminist articulation that analyzes the effects of alliances with dominant rhetorics even as it seeks a counterhegemonic framework for, say, "good mothers." Both projects are central themes in the most well known of the poems in Bishop's late collection *Geography III* (1976), to which I now turn. Here Bishop explicitly implicates feminist colonialism in activating in the feminist subject the fears and guilt that serve patriarchal culture. But she also formulates a counter-model of Kleinian maternal relations, meant to produce a daughter for whom the mediation of resistance with the discourses of domination always triggers the critique of such "unlikely" configurations.

Restoring an "Unlikely" Maternal Body

"Crusoe in England" (1971) introduces the topic of maternal relations not in order to construct new referents for good and/or bad mothers but to illuminate the social and psychic reprisals triggered when the speaker uses a colonizer's power to make a difference in maternal relations. Bishop's rewriting of Defoe's *Robinson Crusoe* (1719) emphasizes how colonialist power works against rather than for the kinds of differences the speaker wants it to underwrite:

> One day I dyed a baby goat bright red
> with my red berries, just to see
> something a little different.
> And then his mother wouldn't recognize him.
>
> Dreams were the worst. Of course I dreamed of food
> and love, but they were pleasant rather
> than otherwise. But then I'd dream of things
> like slitting a baby's throat, mistaking it
> for a baby goat. (15–16)

Making a representational "difference" in babies in this different world now produces precisely the kind of effects that, for Bishop, colonialist authorization is meant to evade: the loss of a mother's approving care ("his mother wouldn't recognize him"). As my reading of *Brazil* has shown, constructing a feminist colonialist difference in the mothering of children always reifies the dominant notions of the "good mother" that Bishop wants to displace. Here, this process is registered both by equating the difference the speaker wants to make with the "child's" loss of a "mother" and by triggering unpleasant psychic events.

To the extent that the speaker's search for "something . . . different" is bound up with her own dreams "of food and love," with the desires for maternal nurture that, for Bishop, always threaten feminist resistance, her colonialist transformations instigate self-incriminations for having violated existing maternal relations. What this passage shows, then, is Bishop's sense that colonialist authorizations of feminist resignifications, because they are imbricated with patriarchal ideology, activate rather than foil the psychic mechanisms that bind the need for maternal nurture to dominant gender ideology.

Finally, and in contrast to *Brazil* where the unstable, contradictory referents for a homonym play out Bishop's effort to resignify "conception" by invoking colonialist discourses, the homonymic referent for the overt meaning of "dy[ing] the baby goat" registers how colonialist authorization undermines the speaker's efforts to construct "something different." The "dying" (changing of color) that uses colonialist authorization to make a difference in "babies" refers in the nightmares to a murder for which the speaker feels self-incriminating remorse. Thus the shift from a feminism that counts on colonialist authorization to resignify key concepts to one that analyzes how alliances with dominant discourses recuperate such efforts also entails a shift in characterizing the effects of unstable reference. In the first instance, such instability underwrites a hoped-for emancipatory resignification, achieved by constructing multiple meanings for "conception"; in the second, the multiple referents for "dying" register that such strategies for resignification can revitalize dominant meanings in the guise of emancipatory ones.

Like "Crusoe in England," "In the Waiting Room" (1971) critiques Bishop's previous feminist-colonialist interventions in "Village"'s scene of female development. Returning both bad and good mothers to North American contexts, Bishop's efforts to resignify these figures are part of a new feminist project: to indict and to foil the pressure of feminist resistance toward the legitimating discourses that undermine it. For this purpose Bishop returns in this poem to the formative events of "Village" in order to rewrite the emergence of the child's voice in relation to maternal and "paternal" voices. We will recall that, in the story, a Freudian flight from a troubling mother to a comforting "father" builds on and is itself in turn fortified by a Kleinian desire to please the "good mother" who trades nurturing for the child's repression. The product of these complementary processes is a divided subjectivity, manifest for the North American child as the need to disguise resistance to the point of annihilating it. The poem's retelling of the story, however, locates the developing child on the side of the resisting mother and ultimately imagines a maternal discourse that can underwrite feminist resistance, thus freeing it from the mandatory disguises that lead in adulthood to vexed feminist alliances.

What first frightens the poem's child is not, as in the story, a terrifying mother who refuses maternity but rather intersecting patriarchal and colonialist constructions of maternal and child bodies. This child learns early in life what Bishop's adult speakers learn the hard way: that colonialist representation cannot be distinguished from patriarchal ideology. Thus, as we will see, the frightening patriarchal images in the *National Geographic* refer as well to the images produced when feminist critiques of mothering are mediated through colonialist representation. And these mediations are recognized, as they finally are apprehended in the Brazil writing, as versions of the repressed maternal voice that "Village" 's child reproduces in order to preserve the good mother. When the fear of being identified with the magazine's images turns the child from them, she also turns from rather than to the repressed maternal voice, whose effects are implicated in the magazine's patriarchal and colonialist representation.

The repudiation of the "good" repressed mother also means an identification with the "bad" resisting one, a reversal at the heart of the poem's feminist revision of Klein's account of female development. Although incorporating the resisting aspect of the "bad" maternal voice results in a recognizably Kleinian loss of identity and fragmentation of bodies, this process underwrites the child's resistance to rather than inscription in patriarchal female identity. For the cry of resistance that in the story shatters the child's sense of well-being here productively disrupts the child's obedient education in patriarchal and colonialist culture. And while this shattering also instigates a Kleinian restoration of the maternal body, Bishop predicates this restoration on a questioning of this body's "unlikely" construction both by patriarchal-colonialist ideology and by the female speakers who are regulated by that ideology.

"Waiting Room" begins as a record of a young girl's response to images in the *National Geographic,* including constructions of the female body in which colonialist and patriarchal representation are inextricable. Significantly, the intersection between privileged national and subordinate female identifications that inspires *Brazil's* narrator to authorize feminist representation with colonialist discourses here disrupts the child's sense of mastery over the meanings for her world. Because pride in her reading skills conflates with her learning of the text's meanings for female bodies and for mothering, that mastery, along with the culturally superior perspective it entails, becomes indistinguishable from identifying with subordinate femininity.[17]

As she waits for her aunt in a dentist's waiting room, the child expresses a pride in her reading ability that transforms into horror at the images in the text:

> while I waited I read
> the *National Geographic*
> (I could read) and carefully
> studied the photographs: . . .
> Osa and Martin Johnson
> dressed in riding breeches,
> laced boots, and pith helmets.
> A dead man slung on a pole
> — "Long Pig," the caption said.
> Babies with pointed heads
> wound round and round with string;
> black, naked women with necks
> wound round and round with wire
> like the necks of light bulbs.
> Their breasts were horrifying.
> I read it straight through.
> I was too shy to stop. (*Geography* 3–4)

In "First Lessons in Geography," which is the epigraph to *Geography III*, Bishop links a child's learning of geography to the rote memorization of the parts that are included in the whole of a particular geographical category. "Waiting Room" presents the *National Geographic*'s representation of the relation between body parts and the wholes to which they belong, then, as lessons in the cultural geography of the body. At first this "geography" consists of expected relations between parts and wholes: "Osa and Martin Johnson / dressed in riding breeches, / laced boots, and pith helmets." With the dead man described as an animal to be prepared for a feast, however, bodies themselves emerge as part of interpretive frameworks that assign arbitrary meanings. And this discovery ushers in the child's apprehension of arbitrarily constructed meanings for female and maternal bodies, recognizable when familiar conceptual wholes (mothers and babies) include unfamiliar parts.

Of the strange parts attached to a recognizable female and maternal body, the African womens' "horrifying" breasts are most prominent and invoke the terrifying ones Klein associates with the infant's fantasy of the "bad" mother. But if this image recalls Bishop's feminist projection of bad (as well as good) mothers onto culturally different women, here she pre-

sents such projections as one and the same with the patriarchal constructions of the eroticized female body. Now it is impossible to distinguish what
may be a feminist cultural displacement of "horrifying breasts" from those
that are meant to titillate North American heterosexist readers.

But even more dramatically, these breasts turn out also to be part of the
white, North American female body. In its compatibility with patriarchal
ideology, feminist colonialist representation reifies grievous masculinist
constructions not only of the exoticized other woman but also of the eroticized North American female body. For a single female body, one that
includes nationally and racially different parts, encompasses the description of different women's bodies in this passage. The body of Osa Johnson,
whose status as American explorer of third world countries seemingly immunizes her from female gendering (there is no difference between the
description of her body and that of her husband's), has neither torso nor
breasts: we see only her unigendered breeches, boots, and helmet. The torso
with its "horrifying" breasts belongs to the culturally and racially different
female body. However, in terms of the "whole body" assembled in this
passage from its various parts, these breasts also are part of the Western
explorer's female body.

Bishop's selection of the parts that here add up to the whole female body
is deliberate and arbitrary. As critics have noticed, the poet constructs
rather than faithfully records the contents in the "February, 1918" issue of
the *National Geographic,* where neither "Osa and Martin Johnson" nor the
African women and children appear.[18] While Bishop has attributed the in-
accuracy to her combination of two issues of the periodical,[19] Lee Edelman
has persuasively argued that another text—Osa Johnson's autobiographical *I Married Adventure* (1940)—is the primary source for the passage that
juxtaposes the identically dressed "Osa and Martin Johnson" to the naked,
"distorted" African women (Edelman 188). It is *I Married Adventure,* Edelman notes, that contains the photographs of African women and children
on which Bishop likely modeled the poem's images. Moreover, Johnson's
text also contains complaints about the constrictions of female dress, an
equation of "identical" (male) dress with "adventure," and an indictment of
the bodily distortions suffered by African female bodies. Bishop's image of
the identically dressed Johnsons, Edelman suggests, echoes Osa's juxtaposition of liberating unisex outfits to a constrictive femininity whose distortions show up so clearly in the African women and children (189–92).

In contrast, I submit that the poem critiques rather than endorses Osa's
feminist representation. Not only, as I have suggested, does Bishop impli-

cate Osa's unisexed body, because it is authorized by its culturally superior position, in the magazine's patriarchal and colonialist construction of female bodies. Johnson's description of the African scene of mothering also points to her deployment of the very feminist strategies that the poem repudiates: "The narrower and longer the head when the basket contrivance was removed, the greater the pride of the mother. That her baby had cried almost without ceasing during this period of distortion was of no concern whatsoever" (*I Married* 151). Such an account of a harmful mothering trapped in proud consent to oppressive convention recalls Bishop's own projection of "bad" acculturating mothers, as a strategy for legitimating critiques of patriarchal families, onto Brazilians. In *Brazil,* I have argued, Bishop comes to recognize that such projections of both bad and good mothers serve to reify the patriarchal conventions supported by colonialist discourse.[20] Thus the poem relocates Osa Johnson's description of "bad" African mothering as an image in the *National Geographic,* a magazine notorious for its intersecting heterosexist and colonialist representations of naked female bodies.

Accordingly, Bishop goes on to link the child's resistance to the magazine's patriarchal images to her repudiation of a harmful "good" maternal figure not in Africa or Brazil but "in Worcester, Massachusetts":

> Suddenly, from inside
> came an *oh!* of pain
> — Aunt Consuelo's voice —
> not very loud or long.
> I wasn't at all surprised;
> even then I knew she was
> a foolish, timid woman. . . .
> What took me
> completely by surprise
> was that it was *me:*
> my voice, in my mouth. . . .
> I was my foolish aunt,
> I — we — were falling, falling,
> our eyes glued to the cover
> of the *National Geographic,*
> February, 1918. (*Geography* 4–5)

Clearly this maternal cry, whose reproduction as the child's voice is so alarming, echoes the mother's scream in "Village," instigated by a cultural "shaping" of the female body. Indeed in the poem the child's education through reading in the meanings of the female body replaces the mother's fitting for the garments that signify her return to a normative femininity. However, there is also a very significant difference in this distressing cry; it issues not from the mad, resisting mother but from the maternal figure who modulates her rebellious utterance. When the child recoils from this disciplined voice, it is part of her horrified retreat from patriarchal constructions of femininity, like those in the *National Geographic.*

At the same time, this renunciation is also predicated on an identification with the mad mother's cry of rebellion. The aunt's "*oh!* of pain," which Bishop separates by a line from the description of its modulation, also recalls that of the mad resisting mother. It is this recollected voice, finally retrievable from the repressed maternal voice, that underwrites the child's refusal of the repressed aspects of this voice on the occasion of crying out against patriarchal, colonialist images of the female body. On the occasion of being "fitted" through obedient reading for femininity, the child, like the mad mother, resists a gendering that now vividly is an effect not only of a shaping paternal discourse but also of the repressed maternal voice.

At first the child pays the same price that the mad mother pays for such resistance: a disconnection from a stable sense of self and from her social world, the falling off the world "into cold, blue-black space" (6). But this alienation also has an important critical dimension; she is able to apprehend that a vexed gendering is a condition for integration into the social group: "But I felt: you are an I, / you are an *Elizabeth,* / you are one of *them*" (6). Significantly, this critical perspective on her relation to cultural definition leads to a refusal to connect body parts to their socially defined wholes:

> I scarcely dared to look
> to see what it was I was.
> I gave a sidelong glance
> — I couldn't look any higher —
> at shadowy gray knees,
> trousers and skirts and boots
> and different pairs of hands
> lying under the lamps. (6)

This breakdown of the whole body into its parts resonates with Klein's description of the infant's fear that anger against the bad, internalized mother results in a fragmentation of the child's own body. But Bishop's "bad" mother is Klein's "good" one; thus the "good," repressed maternal voice is the entity that, in retaliation for the child's aggressive feelings against it, invades the child's "inside[s]" and destroys bodily integrity.

Furthermore, this rendering of whole bodies into their parts is also good news; it inhibits the child's ability to recognize oppressive constructions of whole female bodies, especially when they are reified by apparently emancipatory but actually subordinating bodily formations. Indeed the body parts she cannot shape into a whole recall precisely the "familiar," lower part of the body that belongs to Osa Johnson, whose unisex immunity from patriarchal femininity is linked to her status as a Western explorer. Rather than masking the patriarchal distortion and objectification of the female body, now familiar "trousers and skirt and hands" entail a recognition of that distortion, played out in the child's inability to "look any higher" at torsos and breasts.

What remains, in Kleinian terms, is to restore the fragmented mother but without destroying the possibility for the resistance proscribed by the patriarchal "good mother." If subjective integrity depends on such restoration, than resisting subjectivity entails the ability to "look . . . higher" on the female body without accepting masculinist constructions of that body and/or effacing them in familiar versions. Accordingly, the child goes on to reconstruct the maternal body precisely as it has appeared in Bishop's version of the *National Geographic:* familiar body parts intertwined with "those awful hanging breasts" of culturally and racially different women. But in contrast to the magazine, the reconstruction of this body is inextricable from an interrogation of the discourses that produce it:

> Why should I be my aunt,
> or me, or anyone?
> What similarities —
> boots, hands, the family voice
> I felt in my throat, or even
> the *National Geographic*
> and those awful hanging breasts —
> held us all together
> or made us all just one?
> How — I didn't know any
> word for it — how "unlikely." (6–7)

What literally holds these arbitrary body parts together into a whole female body is the child's critical questioning of them. The parts that add up to one female body in the magazine are here cohered most vividly in the frame of that questioning; as a result that body is not embraced but rather discerned as an "unlikely" configuration that can be analyzed, broken down, and potentially reconfigured. Such analysis, the legacy of the fortunate fragmentation inspired by resistance to the repressed aspect of the aunt's voice, foregrounds the notion that what is familiar (comforting and/or linked to social authorization) about this body is inextricable from what is "awful" about it.

From the maternal body in question in the passage, glossed by the Brazil writing, we can infer the specific directions Bishop would like this analysis to take. There is the question of the relation between the repressed "family voice" and maternal support of patriarchal constructions of femininity. There is the question of how the repressed mother's voice is reproduced "in [the child's] throat" through the exchange of nurture for regulation. There is the question, as the reconstructed body refers back to Bishop's representation of the *National Geographic*'s assembly of the body, of the role of this regulation in the impulse to authorize unspeakable feminist configurations with dominant discourses. Specifically, there is a feminist recognition of the intersection between patriarchal colonialist representation (the exoticized, objectified breasts) and the feminist representation authorized by colonialism (the displaced, horrifying breasts of the "bad" mother).

While this body that calls itself into question is underwritten by the child's identification with a resisting maternal voice, willing to chance the disintegration of self and world, the very need to restore a maternal body registers Bishop's subscription to Klein's emphasis on the importance of such reconstructions to the child's further development. Thus it is the socially viable, repressed maternal figure that the child both makes reparation to and restores, but with a critical difference. When the child directs her questioning of the restored maternal body to an interrogation of its mediated "family voice," she imagines new referents and consequences for the modulated maternal "cry of pain":

> How had I come to be here,
> like them, and overhear
> a cry of pain that could have
> got loud and worse but hadn't? (7)

Now the maternal figure's censured "cry of pain" always also signifies both the unmitigated cry and a regret over the failure to fully articulate it. Thus the aunt's voice, already distinguished by the split between its repressed aspects (repudiated by the child) and its "cry of pain" (on which the child models that repudiation), becomes a model for the automatic questioning of utterances whose mediation of feminist resistance inspires gratitude for participation in the community at large ("be[ing] here, like them"). If "a cry of pain that could have / got loud and worse but hadn't" appears to express gratitude for the mediation of the cry, it also expresses regret that the "cry of pain that could have" was prevented from fulfilling its resisting promise. As this observation at one time expresses gratitude for the repression that confers crucial relations and regret for what is lost as a result, the mechanisms that recruit consent to oppression come under scrutiny by virtue of their very effects. That is, Bishop imagines that the kind of scrutiny to which her adult speakers come with great difficulty could be installed at the formative moments when the daughter's subjectivity is shaped by the maternal voice.

"Waiting Room" 's reformulation of the child's relation to the discourses that shape her voice, then, aims to redress at (what Bishop regards as) its origin the production of a divided subject that is vulnerable to patriarchal regulation. For her adult speakers that regulation works through the coarticulation of subordinate femininity with privileged positions in nation and class. Whereas Bishop's writing about Brazil makes these alliances as a consequence of the feminist subjectivity produced in "Village," in "Waiting Room" she imagines an alternative development for the feminist subject that both eliminates and guards against such alliances. And whereas in the Brazil writing Bishop's feminist project is to resignify good and bad mothering with colonialist discourses, in "Waiting Room" she wants to resignify bad mothering as that which encourages such alliances and good mothering as that which creates in the daughter a vigilance against forming them. As the latter mode of resignification eschews such alliances, it looks instead for authorization to a reformulation of Kleinian psychoanalysis; the result is a valorization of the very disintegration of the "whole" subject and her bodily integrity that feminist disguises and dominant alliances guard against.

At the same time, "Waiting Room" points to the continuing impulse to avoid the kind of terrifying separation from familiar, empowering contexts that underwrites Bishop's vision of the new feminist subject. While the poem unambiguously registers a resistance both to the magazine's sexist presentation of the African woman and to the related repression of her own timid aunt, the critique of the recuperated *feminist* voice — at the level both of repressed maternal speech and the colonialist feminism of the resisting daughter — remains a subtext to be interpreted. One troubling result is that Bishop's description of the African women's breasts as "awful" leaves the racializing of this awfulness in place. The subtext that makes such racializing "awful" for the North American women who practice it lets stand the overt racist signification.

Bishop herself, then, has difficulty complying with the strategies that the poem now prioritizes for feminist practice. For this very reason, however, her imagining of a female subject for whom vexed feminist alliances always signify their liabilities becomes even more compelling. Yet, in the terms of Bishop's own analysis, such subjects can act effectively on these insights only when supported by counterhegemonic discourses that underwrite the dissolution of regulated selves and, therefore, render unnecessary the resisting subject's affiliations with authorizing rhetorics. Bishop's psychoanalytic version of such a discourse — the voice of a maternal figure whose provision of care is bound up with transmitting a wariness of such affiliations — shares similarities with the remedies both Hurston and Glasgow, as a consequence of their own respective dilemmas of feminist representation, also prioritize. All three authors link feminist (as well as other modes of) liberation to a resignification and transmission of culture made possible when discourses that cohere personal and community identity expose rather than enforce the affiliations, both dominant and oppositional, that recruit subordinate subjects' consent to oppression.

EPILOGUE

Toward a Poststructuralist Feminist Counterhegemony

Throughout *Unsettled Subjects,* I have argued that poststructuralism's emphasis on the subject's self-difference and on the instability of social and analytic categories should enhance rather than limit the capacity of feminist theory to analyze dominant gender ideology. Feminist theory encounters a stubborn impasse, I have further argued, when it marshals the insights of poststructuralist analysis only for the critique of feminist identity and for its complement, an unnuanced valorization of emancipatory resignification. Because these modes of analysis have shifted attention away from the workings of patriarchal power, they have functioned to impede the pursuit of what Nancy Fraser has recently described as the most urgent task for poststructuralist feminist inquiry: to "maximize our ability to contest the current gender hegemony and to build a feminist counterhegemony" ("Pragmatism" 158).

When, as a result of historicizing diverse representations of female subjectivity, we recognize that gender hegemony relies in large part on managing the interarticulations of a subject's multiple positions, building "a feminist counterhegemony" becomes a matter of making effective interventions in this specific mode of regulation. What might such interventions look like, and what should be the role of poststructuralist theory in helping to formulate them? By way of conclusion, I would like to revisit the strategies that have emerged in the course of this study. The specific shape these interventions take in particular cultural contexts, along with the difficulties the respective authors encounter in producing effective change, gesture toward future directions for poststructuralist feminism.

As all the texts I have considered show, dominant gender ideology is capable of securing female subordination and neutralizing feminist agency

via the articulation of gender with a subject's other beliefs, both conservative and oppositional. Feminist agency, therefore, depends on discerning
these operations that function precisely through the slippages and sleights
of hand that, as we have seen, make such processes difficult to detect. From
here crucial tasks for a counterhegemony become, on one hand, to forge
beneficial alliances with the other emancipatory rhetorics with which feminism is coarticulated and, on the other, to change a feminist subject's investment in the dominant race, class, and/or national identifications that both
oppress others and often undermine feminist aims.

As regards the mechanisms that censure feminism in the name of other
emancipatory politics to which female subjects subscribe, Hurston offers us
a powerful remedy: emphasizing the importance to all oppositional politics
of recognizing how power regulates self-difference. Hurston pursues a
black feminist counterhegemony meant at one time to indict codes of silence and to persuade black men to renounce the censoring of feminism in
antiracist terms. Crucial to this counterhegemony is the empowering of the
antiracist discourses that illuminate how racist ideology secures a subject's
consent to oppression by making antiracist rhetorics indistinguishable
from harmful agendas. Black feminism can then use the terms of such
antiracist analyses to indict intraracial codes of silence. This kind of remedy
for the interception of one oppositional discourse by another has implications for poststructuralist feminist theory as well. Clearly, reigning emancipatory models of the unstable subject would be unable to hinder the feminist formulation of models that strongly link subjection to self-difference if
the other progressive politics with which a critic's feminism is articulated
helped illuminate such an analysis. Indeed the centrality of inquiries into
domination and self-difference for current radical democratic politics can
be motivated by attending to analyses that have emerged historically in
both feminist and other American emancipatory rhetorics (for example, as
we have seen, in the populist rhetorics of the 1880s and 1890s, the antiracism of the 1930s, and both black and white feminist writing throughout
the century).

Will the analysis of power's regulation of unstable, plural subjectivity be
able to ground a cross-cultural feminist counterhegemony, one that underwrites alliances between different women around shared structures (if not
content) of oppression and strategies for resistance? Any utopian hope of
this kind, of course, must be mediated by the recognition that white feminist alliances with third world women have historically involved the effacement of the racist and classist dimensions of white feminism (Carby 6). Yet

we might cautiously explore the possibility that attention to a structure of power in one cultural context can illuminate heretofore obscured and/or unrepresentable modes of local domination elsewhere, thus providing both mutual benefit and "a parallel for allying with others" (Chow 114). We will recall, in this vein, how Johnson's attention to the structure of multiple address in Hurston is the (ultimately unmet) condition both for illuminating the prohibitions on her own authorship and for underscoring Hurston's effort to make visible similar prohibitions in black contexts. Moreover, alliances other than specifically feminist ones can emerge from the cross-cultural feminist analysis of how power regulates self-difference. In her final novel, *Seraph on the Suwanee* (1948), for example, Hurston foregrounds how the white protagonist's racism dovetails with her husband's racist, tyrannical dictates for what kind of offspring she must reproduce. In this case, a black woman's cross-race feminist analysis, meant to illuminate for white women the relation between their gendered domination and their racism, aims to inspire primarily an *antiracist* alliance between white and black women.

When feminists do pursue the examination of the relation between female subjection and self-difference, they stress that a feminist counterhegemony requires the complication of poststructuralism's notions of emancipatory resignification. On the one hand, the texts I have discussed offer some support for a faith in the possibilities generated, without specific agendas for change, by a decentered subject's negotiation of unstable terms. Some progressive reformulations do emerge without deliberate calculation and even as a consequence of the dynamics on which dominant hegemony relies. Thus antilynching analyses of unfair allegations "automatically" awaken in Janie Woods the feminist anger submerged by her commitment to race solidarity, and the excesses of eugenicist sexism instigate, without deliberate reflection, the cross-cultural identifications that make a feminist of Dorinda in Glasgow's *Barren Ground*. However, all the literary authors I have discussed emphasize that the most effective modes of resignification are products of an energetic, deliberate reformulation of intersections between the multiple rhetorics that a particular feminist subject negotiates. Concepts of emancipatory resignification that do not stress the conditions for successful transformation run the risk of invoking aleatory processes that simply emerge from such multiplicity. Durable resignification, in contrast, requires deliberate strategies both for breaking the hold of dominant gender ideology on self-different female subjects and for reconfiguring intersecting discourses and subject positions.

However, not only is feminist resignification continually in competition with entrenched meanings; it also encounters obstacles at the level of the feminist subject herself. While both Hurston and the theorists I have considered show us interceptions of feminist resignification by its coarticulation with other oppositional discourses, Glasgow and Bishop stress that these obstacles can emerge when feminist speakers attempt to authorize unspeakable interventions with the dominant rhetorics at their disposal. In the latter case dominant gender ideology asserts itself precisely through the discourses that are meant to authorize feminist change. And as Glasgow's novels dramatize, feminist investments in culturally enfranchised positions also threaten the very strategies that can break the hold of dominant gender hegemony over self-difference. Her representation of these dynamics in the contradictory effects produced by elite women's cross-cultural feminist identifications indicates an important future direction for poststructuralist feminism. Instead of asserting that such identifications are either emancipatory or reactionary, feminists could pursue analyses of and interventions in the slippage between these progressive and appropriative effects.

An important project for a feminist counterhegemony, then, is to expose and indict the consequences of feminist alliances with dominant discourses in a way that is "sufficiently compelling to persuade . . . [feminists] to reinterpret their interests" (Fraser, "False Antithesis" 71). Poststructuralist feminism has already demonstrated its capacity for making forceful critiques of feminist affiliations that exclude and/or appropriate other women, and these critiques have been extremely effective in persuading feminists to scrutinize their assumptions. Constructing a feminist counterhegemony, however, also requires an emphasis on the costs to otherwise privileged women's *feminist aims* when feminist discourses reify dominant agendas. With this emphasis, such feminists have another compelling reason for both analyzing and guarding against the desires of subordinate female subjects to redress disadvantage by mobilizing their advantages.

The capacity to fully apprehend the dynamics that produce and sustain female subordination by coarticulating a subject's gender with dominant and/or oppositional commitments, then, relies on coordinating poststructuralist insights with the historicization of female and feminist subjectivity. Together these modes of inquiry have the potential to make a compelling case for displacing the tenacious debate that effectively pits a polemic about the need to critique feminism's terms (and its attendant celebration of future but unarticulated possibilities) against the pursuit of specific feminist change. Certainly, as Robyn Wiegman points out, feminists must not assume that their introduction of race and class into feminist analysis eliminates the need to continually interrogate feminist categories and methodologies (185–86). At the same time, in view of the prevailing feminist practice of scrutinizing terms and methodologies and in view of increasing inquiries (ones that often are indebted to black and third world feminist analyses) into the relation between unstable subjects and subordinate gendering, the poststructuralist feminism that continues to displace rather than to enhance feminist critique with the critique of feminism may become more visible for its conservative effects. In the final analysis, in order for poststructuralist feminism to fully benefit from the counterhegemonic strategies that its own insights can produce, its attention to the operations of dominant gender ideology at diverse cultural sites must include the continual scrutiny of its own historical tendency to retreat from gender as a category of analysis.

NOTES

Introduction

1 Others have expressed similar hopes for an intersection of poststructuralist
theories and the enhancing of feminism's analysis of women's subordination:
Hartsock cautions that a deconstruction of political identity must not stop
there but should also contribute to a systematic understanding of the political
subject ("Foucault on Power" 163); Sawicki argues that an effective "politics of
difference" (28) needs to recognize the way "power utilizes difference to frag-
ment opposition" (18); de Lauretis poses against the arguments for a difference
that renders impossible a feminist subject the fact that diverse women claim
feminism as a ground for difference within their respective cultural contexts
("Upping" 257).

2 Describing the effects of such negative critiques, Modleski notes that poststructuralist feminism's "unimpeachable observations" about differences between
and within women function to "dissuad[e] feminists from claiming commonal-
ities across class and racial lines" without elaborating how gender is coarticulated with race, class, ethnicity, and so on (18).

3 For example, Sandoval calls attention to an "oppositional consciousness,"
manifest by a range of third world women writers, but neglected by mainstream feminism (9–17). See Grewal ("Autobiographic Subjects") for the discussion of instances where plural subjectivities enable both progressive coali-
tions and contingent identity politics. For other specific elaborations of the
relation between resistance and self-different subjectivity see Alarcon, "Theoretical Subjects," and Anzaldua, *Borderlands*.

4 Classic articulations of this argument include Hartsock's "Rethinking Modernism" and, in the specific context of literary theory, Miller's "Changing the
Subject."

5 When the critique of feminist identity does lead to the consideration of interarticulated positions, critics tend to investigate how dominant race and class
ideologies articulate gender with a subject's other positions. These investigations are extremely important ones. I am arguing for the need to address similar
inquiries to the workings of dominant gender ideology.

6 In contrast to poststructuralist feminists who have keyed their analyses to
developments in theories of the unstable subject, women of color have long

foregrounded, in the context of specific cultural femininities, the relation between gendered domination and the multiply positioned female subject. As Carby points out, since its earliest moments, black feminist literary criticism has stressed "the interrelation of sexual and racial politics" (8). For specific elaborations of this interrelation see B. Smith, and Collins (163–98). Moraga examines such interarticulation for Chicana women. See Cheung for a discussion of how these dynamics affect Asian American women.

7   Newton also notes that new historicist readings reveal how gender supports class hierarchy but not how it supports gendered oppression itself (158). And Romero shows that the new historicism reproduces more than it analyzes nineteenth-century discourses on women as agents of normalization.

8   For a compelling analysis of how the new historical faith in "the power of rhetorics" effaces the power of dominant ideology see Porter, "What We Know."

Chapter 1   *Poststructuralist Feminist Subjects*

1   The former mode of contestation resonates with Paul Smith's description of agency as "a veritable *product* of ideological interpellation" (xxxi). That is, these essays show how patriarchal regulation can be undermined by the very oppositional discourses it also mobilizes in its own interests.

2   Butler does acknowledge that dominant as well as resisting meanings can be produced by self-different subjects who constitute "the permanent possibility of a certain resignifying process" ("Contingent Foundations" 13). But dominant regulations of discursive and subjective instability function in her argument only as unelaborated "risks" that are inextricable from the emancipatory possibilities created by repudiating stable terms: "That the category [of 'woman'] is unconstrained, even that it comes to serve antifeminist purposes, will be part of the risk of [a democratization that relies on contesting foundations]" (16). Butler's valorization throughout the article of resignification as the means of a destabilizing feminist agency mutes her acknowledgment of its role in shoring up power. As importantly, the article does not even raise feminist questions of how patriarchal power profits from complex resignifying processes.

In a recent essay, Butler clarifies her definition of resignification as a "domain of possibility [that] is *immanent* to power," even when resignification opens up emancipatory possibilities ("Careful Reading" 138). Yet "Contingent Foundations" considers the implication of resignification in the field of power only as regards the feminist assertion of stable terms and not, significantly, as regards the feminist critique of those terms nor as regards the way dominant gender ideology can monitor reformulations of meaning.

3   See Fraser and Nicholson, "Social Criticism." Like Chow, and Modleski (see my introduction, note 1), de Lauretis is concerned with making differences between women inflect feminist politics rather than function to define conflicts between feminism and other categories of analysis ("Upping" 265). For a theory of constructing alliances based on shared structures of oppression both between different women and between women and other subordinated groups, see Mouffe, "Feminism."

4   Because my focus is on the way white feminist critiques of white identity can hinder postmodern feminist politics, I here discuss instances of this critique's most prevalent form: interrogations of the feminist interpretation of black women's texts. While this discourse at its best constitutes a dialogue with black feminists, such a dialogue is itself part of a larger exchange between white feminists and feminists of color generally. For discussions that expose the limits of and chart the possibilities for postmodern and/or cross-cultural feminism from third world women's diverse perspectives, see Alarcon, "The Theoretical Subject(s)"; Anzuldua, *Borderlands;* Enloe; Grewal; Allen, *The Sacred Hoop;* Mohanty; Moraga; Sandoval; and Spivak's "Three Women's Texts" and "French Feminism Revisited."

5   On white academic feminism's marginalization of black feminist production, see Collins chs. 1 and 2; and du Cille, "The Occult of True Black Womanhood"; for critiques of white feminist categories and critical agendas, see Carby ch. 1; hooks, "Critical Interrogation," "Postmodern Blackness," and "Representations"; and V. Smith, "Black Feminist Theory."

6   By stressing that Stansell does not implicate dominant gender ideology in white feminism's preoccupation with white identity or in the reluctance of white feminists to challenge Thomas's nomination before Hill did, I do not mean to diminish the importance of the motivations she does examine. Stansell usefully situates white feminists' wariness of critiquing black men in the context of a "painful division between antiracism and feminism [that] goes back to the days of turmoil and hope after the Civil War" (251). But she does not consider how late twentieth-century gender ideology, white and black, may deliberately exploit such divisions. And her critique of Catherine MacKinnon for supporting Thomas on the basis of his "authentic" experience of racial oppression is entirely persuasive (254–60); the problem here, however, is the essay's implication that MacKinnon's rather idiosyncratic response to Thomas was prototypical for the white feminists who did not make a feminist critique of Thomas until Hill came forward.

7   Stansell also notes that the left generally felt discomfort about questioning Thomas's nomination because of his race: "[T]he right had succeeded in paralyzing a liberal opposition which, because Thomas was black, shied away from discussing" Thomas's intraracial misogyny (254–55). But the culprit here is only "the right," not (also) the aims of patriarchal ideology supported in the context of Hill/Thomas by both dominant and oppositional political rhetorics. Although she thus observes how the politics of race eliminates feminist ones, Stansell blames a hierarchy of oppositional positions (antiracism takes precedence over feminist analysis) without stressing the patriarchal appropriations, white and black, of this hierarchy.

8   I refer to Johnson's "Metaphor, Metonymy, and Voice in *Their Eyes Were Watching God,*" whose argument I elaborate below.

9   See Abel, "Black Writing"; and Todorov.

10   See Abel, "Black Writing" 480–84; and Todorov 379–80. Abel argues that "Thresholds" is an instance of a white feminist's projection of her deconstructive critical dream onto a black woman, one that departs from Johnson's previous feminist attributions of reference for political categories. "Thresholds"

displays a "difference within [Johnson's] practice of deconstruction, the undoing of a counterpart for race to the feminist resistance to deconstruction,"
and this difference "facilitates the project of writing across race" (483). Abel
persuasively shows how the slippage between "race" and "a discourse on posi-
tionality" authorizes Johnson's reading across racial boundaries (482). Yet, I
will argue, this crossing does not dissolve other impasses that structure Johnson's reading of Hurston, including prohibitions against feminist reading itself.

11   For another reading of "Sis Cat" that prioritizes intraracial gender struggle, see
Boxwell.

12   While I stress Hurston's efforts to reconcile black feminism to discourses of
antiracism, a project always prioritized in her subsequent works, the possibility
the tale sets up for the slippage between interracial and intraracial "manners"
might also register how her feminist aims can be pressured, especially when
silenced by intraracial alliances, toward alignments with the aims of white
patrons. That is, Sis Cat's reverse trick arguably could be read also as a besting
of the black male trickster by adhering to the "manners required by her patrons." Even if Hurston also invokes the submission to such protocols in order
to counter intraracial sexist prohibitions, however, there is no evidence that she
here is critical of such strategies.

13   See Roberts for a discussion of how the valuation of "lawlessness as heroic"
becomes in postslavery contexts bound up with defeating a version of lawlessness itself — the "badman trickster" who turns his skills against the black community. In this context, the heroic trickster matches wits with both white law
and the black badman trickster (250). This is precisely the structure of the
trickster competition in Hurston's "The Bone of Contention," which, I argue in
chapter 2, she references in the "Sis Cat" tale.

14   Washington suggests that this is a "spurious comment," motivated by Hughes's
anger over the *Mule Bone* feud, and one that translates Hurston's insistence
that she had been betrayed into allegations that she had a tendency to violate
protocols of race representation (10). It seems possible, that is, that Johnson is
guided by the very kind of tricky discourse I have argued "Sis Cat" critiques
when the former projects the self-critique, ventriloquized by Hughes, onto
Hurston.

15   To the extent that this move shifts attention from the dominant to the resisting
uses of self-difference and self-critique, it is also easily compatible with the
influences Johnson does note at the outset: the linking of "difference as suspension of reference" to the self's critical agency reaffirms not only her own previous deconstructive work (328) but also that of the "black critics" who "adapt
the textual strategies of literary theory" to black literature (317), some of
whose voices are prominent in the anthology where the essay appears, *"Race,"
Writing, and Difference*. And such assimilation of black subjectivity to deconstruction's universal claims for a liberatory self-difference would likely appeal to the universalizing, if not the other humanistic tendencies, of the "white
critics" she addresses as well.

16   I do not mean to suggest that the critique of white feminist identity, especially in
the context of cross-race reading, is anything other than essential. I *am* arguing
that we need to discern productive instances of this critique from its use as an

alibi to interdict feminist reading itself, and it is this kind of interdiction, I have argued, that occurs in the course of "Thresholds."

Chapter 2   Antiracist Rhetorics and the Female Subject: The Trials of Zora Neale Hurston

1   For a discussion of the vernacular versus urban speech debates about authentic black representation, see Gates, "Dis and Dat" and *The Signifying Monkey* 176–80. Hurston was attacked for her use of the vernacular, and, as Washington points out, at times her alleged "minstrelsy" could not be distinguished from the "triviality" of her gendered subject matter (16).

2   Franchot claims that in all of his autobiographical writings Douglass suppresses race and class differentials in a "discourse of self-reliant virility" (142). Valerie Smith argues that Douglass's text resembles other slave narratives in troping "the journey from slavery to freedom" as "the journey from slavehood to manhood" ("Loopholes" 217). She also notes that Harriet Jacobs's slave narrative, *Incidents in the Life of a Slave Girl* (1861), explicitly counters Douglass's linking of freedom to achieving "enshrin[ed] cultural definitions of masculinity" with a narrative that celebrates strategies available to female slaves (217).

3   Gates notices that Hurston's rewriting of Douglass's meditation on the ships projects male desire "onto an object, beyond his grasp or control, external to himself" (*Signifying Monkey* 171). Although he reads this description as setting up a contrast with Janie's "active" control of "the process of memory" (172), he does not read Hurston's passage as itself implicating Douglass's tropes in a relinquishing of control to specifically racist "external" powers.

4   As McKay points out, *Their Eyes* both critiques black culture for its sexism and represents it as the context in which Janie's development, her effort both to belong to the group and to attain "freedom from intragroup oppression," occurs ("Crayon Enlargements" 57).

5   As Awkward has argued, critics tend to gloss over Tea Cake's failings in favor of the improvement he represents over Janie's other husbands. For an extensive review of Tea Cake's sexism and dominating tendencies, see Awkward, *Inspiriting Influences* 36–39; for a similar reading of the importance of Tea Cake's misogyny, see Cassidy. For readings that weigh this misogyny against his good sides, including his class contrast to the bourgeois bully Joe, see Wall; and Willis.

6   Cassidy similarly reads the rabid dog as a stand-in for Tea Cake's violent jealousy, one that allows Janie to disguise feminist rage as self-defense against a wild creature (264). Cassidy further reads this device as one that permits Janie to absolve herself of responsibility for her murderous anger (267). I am arguing that Hurston constructs this plot device as a symptom of the "code of silence" that makes such anger unspeakable, especially in white contexts. Once in place, Hurston makes her own coded narration the occasion to denounce both the imperative to disguise feminist anger and this imperative's effects on black women and men alike.

7   Davies argues that the novel demonstrates Hurston's complex adherence to codes of silence, an effort both to represent black feminist resistance and to

protect black men with a coded representation (148). In contrast, I argue that Hurston's narration largely violates these codes. Only in the instance of Tea Cake's death does the narration (blatantly) disguise Janie's feminist rage, and it does so for the purpose of using the trial scene to indict such masquerades. While I agree with Davies that the trial "conveys the threat of judgment against the articulation of black women's rage and the urgent need [to disguise it]" (155), I argue that Hurston uses the trial to represent these threats and the coded speech they produce as dangerous to black men.

8   For a documentation of the *Mule Bone* feud along with various interpretations of it, see Hughes and Hurston.

9   This description occurs on the back cover of the recent edition of the play. See Hughes and Hurston.

10   The appeal process begun after the first trials involved court battles and public lobbying that after several years resulted in the release of the defendants, the last of whom was not freed until 1950.

11   For those who supported the verdicts, however, the very fact of the allegations elevated the accusers to the status of white women who must be protected from black male savagery. Victoria and Ruby may have been fallen women, but they were *white* women (Hall 204); by advancing the false allegations that functioned to prohibit sexual relations between white women and black men, the women's sexual promiscuity disappeared in their white femininity.

12   As historians have emphasized, the "protection" of white women most often involved their elimination from the rape trials in which charges of their violation were key; alleged victims of black male rape rarely testified. Instead the white woman's story, also circulated to the public through the press, did its work independently of her, assuring that the accusation was synonymous with guilt and that evidence of what really happened would be concealed (A. Raper 18; Hall 150).

13   Kaplan also stresses that Janie's "various courtroom audiences [are] either inaccessible, incompetent, or somehow antagonistic" (131). Whereas I read the trial scene as an effort to reformulate the antiracist discourses that prohibit black feminism, Kaplan sees the trial scene as "an allegory of the dilemma Janie faces in seeking [a competent] audience" for her self-revelation (128). While this reading importantly underscores the failure of Janie's testimony to find competent listeners at the trial, I argue that Hurston holds out hope that the novel's readers, if not its characters, could be a competent audience for the parallels she constructs between antiracist and black feminist analysis.

14   As I have suggested earlier in this chapter, Hurston no doubt wanted to mobilize the analyses of the ASWPL, which contributed substantially to the reduction of lynching in the thirties. By the time Hurston wrote *Their Eyes,* both the ASWPL's implication of the oppression of white women in the logic of lynching and their willingness to violate codes for white women's speech about black men had produced crucial and well-publicized results. But the ASWPL's involvement in the Scottsboro trials was another story, one that could pose problems for Hurston's project of authorizing black feminism with Scottsboro's antiracist discourses. For one of these was the NAACP's indictment of the ASWPL's response to Scottsboro. As Hall has shown, early on in the campaign Scottsboro "challenged the adequacy of the ASWPL's law-and-order argument"

(197). Nonetheless, the ASWPL refused to take a position against the verdicts, arguing that the organization could only be effective when it focused on the importance of due process over mob rule (Hall 199). When, directly following Mr. Prescott's racist admonition to the unruly black "mob," Hurston's first observation is that "[t]he white women made a little applause" (*Their Eyes* 277), she may well mean to invoke the ASWPL's support of the corrupt legal process. Doing so flags the liabilities the ASWPL's racist response to Scottsboro could pose to Hurston's invocation of their otherwise effective analysis of the relation between the lynching of black men and white patriarchal aims. That is, if a white feminist analysis that coincided with Scottsboro can contribute importantly to Hurston's project of forging an alliance between black feminism and antilynching rhetorics, the racist limitations of this analysis also threatens the very possibility of this contribution.

15 Rachel Blau DuPlessis argues that Janie's testimony is one of several instances of "undepicted speech" in the novel by which Hurston withholds narrative from particular audiences and delivers it to others. Thus the testimony truncates and reports indirectly the large narrative Janie addresses to Phoebe (108). Yet such a reading does not account for the coding of male violence and feminist rage in the context of the novel's narrative, which is explicitly addressed to Phoebe.

16 For a different account of the rendering of Tea Cake as bestial, one that also implicates Janie in a strategy that "perhaps would appeal to stereotyped images of African Americans as being animalistic," see Cassidy 261.

17 Additionally, in the desire to persuade her listeners that she did not act "out of malice," the truth of Janie's feminist motivations, rather than the prescribed disguise of it, begins to emerge in a way that would likely not be readable by whites. At the same time that it triggers prohibitions against black feminist speech recognizable to whites, the mandates both to "remember she was not at home" and to adhere to the terms prescribed by the code also open a space to articulate feminist resistance (which Janie understands as righteous rather than malicious) in the black vernacular that would not be recognizable to white jurors (or white readers). In this vernacular, "dog" is a trope for a man who is unfaithful and emotionally, if not physically, abusive.

18 In her discussion of contemporary black male outrage over recent black feminist literary representation, McDowell notes that one critic, implying that such representation panders to white male racist stereotypes, invokes this well-known saying: "An old folk expression reasserts itself here — 'the freest people on earth are a black woman and a white man' — to explain the vagaries of the literary marketplace" ("Reading Family Matters" 82). As Hurston uses this saying to register the tenacious obstacles she encounters to reconciling black literary feminism with antiracism, then, she points to obstacles that have survived into the present day.

19 The quote is from the local newspaper, the *Suwanee Democrat,* qtd. in Huie 45. Although all reporters were barred from interviewing Ruby McCollum, she wrote to her lawyer that when the doctor "[would] get mad at me he'd tear into me like a lion, and then give me a big shot of medicine to almost kill me" (Huie 75). Adams used "shots of medicine" to make her do his bidding, including the bearing of his child against her will. After the birth of the "white" child, Adams

abused her and refused to give her an abortion when she got pregnant again; her mental health deteriorated and she was hospitalized several times (184). In an interview with Huie, the doctor's nurse claimed that he was planning to kill Ruby. At the time of the killing, Ruby was still pregnant with Adams's child, and he had just beaten her in front of a waiting room full of patients (Huie 77).

20   In actual fact, Hurston was extremely frustrated because the McCollum trial was not getting mainstream coverage. In 1953 she wrote to the conservative white William Bradford Huie, entreating him both to recognize that "there was truth that needed telling" in this trial and "to break down the walls and tell it" (Huie, "The Strange Case" 16, qtd. in McCarthy 180). Huie did respond with an article in *Ebony* and in a subsequent book about the trial, *Ruby McCollum: Woman in the Suwanee Jail*.

21   For an account of the restrictions on the press, see Huie 16–17. Huie also unearthed Ruby's letter to her lawyer describing the forced abortion (78).

22   See my discussion below of Hurston's contribution to Huie's book on the McCollum trial.

23   Hurston's location of her most clearly articulated, antiracist indictment of black male misogyny at the center of a white author's text, and one aimed to enlighten white audiences about the racist dimensions of the McCollum trial, has a number of other implications as well. This strategy likely registers a desire for her feminist analysis to benefit, as black men had recently benefited, from white antiracist support for the defendants in publicized racist trials; in this vein, she may have further hoped that black male enthusiasm for such support could extend in the context of the McCollum trial to white antiracist support for black antiracist feminism. At the same time, using Huie's text as a vehicle for her analysis may well also register a freedom to pursue such bold connections between feminism and antiracism outside of black contexts. Of course, the pursuit of the liberation granted by white contexts and discourses, as Hurston stresses in her analyses of black masculinist antiracism, also risks playing into racist agendas.

Chapter 3   Women's Development and "Composite" Subjectivity: Feminism and Social Evolution in Ellen Glasgow

1   See, for example, Carpenter; Chandler; Saunders; Scura; and Wagner.

2   Subsequent references will be to the annotated edition (New Haven, 1972).

3   For example, Spencer, whose theories of the "survival of the fittest" Glasgow both links to elite female subordination and tries to revise in *The Voice,* felt that a woman's "good physique" and her use of it for reproduction were her most important contributions to the evolution of the race (Spencer, "Physical Training" 395, quoted in Paxton 31). In 1913, however, Glasgow would be referring as well to the central role of elite women's reproduction in the eugenics discourses that *The Voice* anticipates.

4   James's *The Principles of Psychology* identifies "good habits" as those that secure social boundaries in the interests of elite power and "bad habits" as those that threaten them (79). I am indebted to Wardley's work on social evolutionary discourses for illuminating the context in which Glasgow deploys her feminist notions of "bad habits." See her "Reassembling Daisy Miller."

5 Sanchez-Eppler's *Touching Liberty* offers a strong example of the critique of nineteenth-century white feminist identification as appropriation. The white feminist-abolitionist equation between marriage and slavery, she argues, both highlights the exploitation of the female slave and "betrays an opposing desire to deny any share in this vulnerability" (22). Similarly, Wexler's critique of "affective sympathy" as the normative nineteenth-century disposition toward the socially stigmatized implicates sentimental cross-race identifications in the reification of racial subordination (38).

    What Sanchez-Eppler sees as "the essential dilemma of feminist-abolitionist rhetoric" — "the difficulty of preventing moments of identification from becoming acts of appropriation" (20) — is a central concern for the Glasgow novels I discuss in this chapter. This difficulty is also the focus of recent contributions to psychoanalytic theories of identification. In addition to Fuss, see Silverman's *Threshold of the Visible World,* in which she explores the conditions under which we might "identify with bodies we would otherwise repudiate" while "respect[ing] the otherness" of those bodies (2).

6 J. R. Raper provides an informative overview of Glasgow's favorable response to Huxley and others who criticized Spencer. He also importantly notes that Glasgow critiques the ethical and social justice evolutionists as well for their faith in social instincts they do not adequately analyze (*Without Shelter* 52–56).

7 In complaining that "class conflicts [in this novel] come down to problems of romance and manners rather than political issues" (*Without Shelter* 139), J. R. Raper insists on the division between the politics of class and gender that, I argue, Glasgow attempts to displace by making visible how class and gender intersect. As I discuss below, it is precisely because racialized and classed modes of gender play such a crucial role in the downfall of the Readjusters that Glasgow can construct an analogy between white male class politics and elite female feminist ones.

8 Although Galton coined the term "eugenics" in *Inquiries* (1883), it was not until 1900, following his lecture to the Royal Society in London, that Americans appropriated the term for their own movement dedicated to "racial betterment" by monitoring reproduction (Haller 17). See my discussion below of the eugenics movement in the context of *Barren Ground.*

9 Glasgow was likely directed to Galton by Ellis's *The Criminal,* which introduced Americans to composite photography (Haller 16); Galton himself detailed the practice he had developed and its uses for pursuing "questions of eugenics" in his *Inquiries.*

10 See also *Inquiries* 83–112.

11 See Hall 145–53.

12 Chandler notes that Glasgow records in her autobiography, *The Woman Within,* that she suffered from severe migraines that she understood in terms of a "self as a locus of conflict" (98).

13 With her choice of the hearth as the frame for competing images of Nick, Glasgow may well be invoking Galton's understanding of "home" as the most unreliable of the "faulty cumulative ideas" that become fixed for the subject (*Inquiries* 183). Eugenia's inability to sustain competing ideas of home enlarges on Galton by stressing how resisting images are eliminated in privileged identifications.

14   Although Glasgow clearly indicts the racialization of whites as a strategy for maintaining elite power over subordinate white women and nonelite white men, it is not as clear whether she similarly critiques the fear of racialization itself that ultimately wins Eugenia for elite aims. Indeed as I discuss below, a fear of clearly identifying with blacks can be discerned in her own narrative voice.

15   See Moore for a concise history of the Readjuster movement. For further elaboration, see Pearson; and Blake.

16   F. McDowell also argues that Nick's rise and fall reflects the Virginia reform movements of the eighties and the nineties that were defeated, as Nick is defeated, by southern white supremacy (60, qtd. in Santas 43).

17   As Dailey has argued, the rise and fall of the Readjusters dramatized in the case of black men the differentials in masculinity masked by both democratic theory and dominant gender ideology. The coalition was defeated when the Democrats exploited racist fears that boundaries for *male* privilege could not be contained. See Dailey ch. 5. By positioning Nick in class terms that invoke the rhetoric meant to deny black men access to the privileges of masculinity, Glasgow underscores how elite discourses enforce a differential masculinity for nonelite white men precisely by exploiting the racist differentials the latter embrace.

18   In the later novel, *Virginia* (1913), Glasgow makes the impulse to risk one's life defending the oppressed an even more arbitrary convergence of multiple and contradictory impulses; in this case the white male Gabriel dies defending a black man who unambiguously has been falsely accused of affronting a white woman. But Gabriel's impulse arises only from an elite sense of responsibility toward former slaves combined with the love of a good fight he has discovered as a Confederate soldier (380–81).

19   Like the Readjusters whom she supported, Glasgow wanted a biracial politics that advanced interests shared across race lines but one that in no way threatened white rule or racial barriers in social life. While campaigning for Henry Anderson in 1921, Glasgow ridiculed her audience for believing elite predictions that black political participation could pose a threat to white rule. Indeed here she likens such "threats" to equally false allegations about black male sexuality ("Fellow Virginians" 60). Because both rhetorics were deployed to turn white voters against a black political presence Glasgow favored, she refutes them equally, betraying a capacity to mobilize a critique of racist practices in the interest of what remain racist notions of democratic government. Yet I argue throughout this chapter that Glasgow's feminist aims continually compel her to condemn racism, including her own, because in all its forms it supports white patriarchal power.

20   This racist indictment of miscegenation may have another source as well. J. R. Raper reports that Glasgow condemned her father for his sexual involvement with black women; we have no information on how these activities affected the black women involved, but Glasgow's mother suffered a breakdown that had injurious effects on her daughter (*Without Shelter* 28–29). In this context, then, a racist repudiation of miscegenation would be meant to have white feminist consequences; but this is the very support of feminism with racist rhetoric that Glasgow links to the recuperation of feminism in *Barren Ground*.

21 Eugenics, a development of nineteenth-century ideas that social evolution could be monitored by controlling the breeding of mankind, was officially founded by Galton in England in 1901. In America, interest in restricting the propagation of the dependent and the delinquent, dating from 1870, first took root in the context of reform concerns for the care and treatment of the feeble-minded, the insane, and the poor. The use of the word "eugenics" in America and the actual movement were early-twentieth-century developments that followed the English movement. In the period from 1905 to 1930, racism and anti-immigration became central themes of the American movement as elite attitudes toward "inferior" races and classes infiltrated the scientific inquiry into hereditary infirmities (Haller 5–7, 17, 58).

22 The Amherst trial resulted in recognizing the legality of the Virginia law and the right of the state to sterilize Carrie Buck. The Virginia decision was appealed to the Supreme Court in 1927 as *Buck v. Bell* where it was upheld, setting a legal precedent for arbitrary sterilizations of the "unfit" in America (see J. Smith and Nelson 173–84).

23 Indeed the link eugenics made between poor white women's illegitimate pregnancy and the reproduction of congenital diseases would be exacerbated in the actual *equation* between illicit pregnancy and disease articulated by Oliver Wendell Holmes in his delivery of the Supreme Court's majority decision in the case of *Buck v. Bell* in 1927: "It is better for all the world if . . . society can prevent those who are manifestly unfit from continuing their kind. The principle that sustains compulsory vaccination is broad enough to cover cutting the Fallopian tubes" (qtd. in J. Smith and Nelson 178).

24 Dorinda's method of birth control may be meant to counter as it calls attention to Margaret Sanger's vexed alliance with eugenics in her quest to legalize birth control. Sanger supported the use of birth control for limiting poor women's reproduction for both economic and eugenicist reasons. At the same time she hoped that the eugenicist authorization of birth control could provide middle-class white women with sexual freedom (see *Woman and the New Race*). But by the mid-twenties the contradiction between her aims for freeing middle-class white women from mandatory reproduction and eugenicist demands for such reproduction were in open conflict, proving that feminist efforts to appropriate eugenics were doomed to make bedfellows of those who required elite women's reproduction (see "Race Suicide" 25). That Glasgow predicates Dorinda's feminist resistance and class rise on a range of scientific and medical technologies but eschews entirely the issue of birth control may register a critique of Sanger's alliance between feminist birth control and the eugenics Glasgow saw as so detrimental to women's development.

25 Such a connection between disenfranchised males and the resistance to empowered masculinity anticipates Silverman's claims in her study *Male Subjectivity at the Margins*.

26 In a story of development that seems to be influenced by Freud's *Leonardo da Vinci*, Glasgow reveals identifications with whiteness and blackness that correspond to successive black and white maternal figures. As with Freud's Leonardo, the loss of the first mother, for Glasgow her black "mammy," determines a resistance to dominant gender relations in later life. For Glasgow this

resistance is a rebellion against the coarticulation of gender and the losses represented for her by "whiteness."

27 Hereditary deafness was an object of investigation by the American eugenics movement, and Alexander Graham Bell was a central figure in this inquiry. Rather than proscribing the biological reproduction of the deaf, Bell felt hereditary deafness could be overcome by marriage into hearing families (Haller 31–33). Thus, there is no medical reason for deafness to proscribe Glasgow's maternity entirely; her use of the eugenical alibi needlessly reifies eugenical aims of policing female reproduction precisely at the moment she hopes to authorize a feminist resistance to maternity.

Chapter 4   *"Caught in a Skein of Voices": Feminism and Colonialism in Elizabeth Bishop*

1 Throughout this chapter I use the terms "colonialism" and "colonialist" to describe Bishop's relationship to Brazilian culture in the poems and prose that make Brazil the scene of feminist resignification. Strictly speaking, of course, a colonialist relationship to Brazil would describe Portugal's early colonization of the country. The United States's mid-twentieth-century efforts to install an accommodating "democratic" regime in Brazil would more accurately enact "neocolonialism." Both *Brazil* and the Brazil poems of the sixties were written during this latter period, and *Brazil* directly invokes American neocolonialist agendas. My use of "colonialism," however, is meant more generally to describe Bishop's stance toward Brazil, authorized by discourses of cultural and national superiority, from which she attempts to make differences in North American concepts. As Bishop herself emphasizes, this stance informs the projects of both early and latter-day foreign interventions.

2 Kalstone has also noted that the location of "In the Village" at the book's center indicates that Bishop's "questions of travel" that she explores in the poems derive from the story's themes (17–18). While for Kalstone the important theme of the story is the child's quest for "paradise," I emphasize how the child's divided yearnings at the end of the story show up in the poems.

3 Bishop's preoccupation with a disembodied maternal voice (here and in "Squatter's Children" and "In the Waiting Room") displays an affinity to a fantasy Silverman describes, in which the daughter disembodies a resisting maternal or female voice that "coexist[s] with the female body only at the price of its own impoverishment and entrapment" (*Acoustic Mirror* 141).

4 Harrison reads this ambiguous intersection of meanings for the sounds and utterances at issue in this passage as a configuration of "vitally conflicting sounds" that gives the mother and child "the history, companionship and compensation of a village of relations" (121). Yaeger similarly sees Nate as providing a symbolic register for the mother's scream (135). My reading, in contrast, links the passage's multivalence to the child's assumption of a feminist voice that, in exchange for coveted social relations, must disguise itself in a patriarchal symbolic.

5 Bishop's linking of feminist subjectivity to the embedding of subversive meanings in conventional overt ones resonates with feminist accounts of women's writing as marked by such strategies—most famously, Gilbert and Gubar's

account of how the subplots of nineteenth-century women authors dramatize the "desire both to accept the strictures of patriarchal society and to reject them" (78).

6   Millier notes in her critical biography that Klein's influence shows up in both the story and the poem (267). And Harrison quotes a 1956 letter in which Bishop claims she is rereading Klein and finding her "superb" (225). I argue that Klein's paradigms motivate Bishop's efforts, in several texts about Brazil and in two later poems, to link effective feminist signification to resignifying the referents for "good" and "bad" mothers. I am interested in the intertextuality between Bishop's feminist project and Klein's theories, not in a Kleinian reading of Bishop's works. For an instance of the latter mode of interpretation, see Diehl.

7   For an extraordinarily lucid and thorough overview of Klein's theories of development and their relation to Freud, see Abel, *Virginia Woolf* 10–13.

8   The date in the title, "January 1, 1502," is the day of the first Portuguese arrivals in Guanabara Bay. Because they mistook the bay for the mouth of a great river, they called it "Rio de Janeiro." That the date brings to mind this legendary mistake in perception foreshadows and underscores the point the poem is concerned with: that even "untouched nature" is subject to projections.

9   This double linkage accomplished by the "just so" has generated opposing critical readings. On the one hand, Bromwich reads it as restating in a critical mode the initial equivalence between the soldiers and the speaker — "we are like the conquistadors in supposing we can make Nature over in a language we know" (88). And on the other, Parker claims that the speaker rebels against this perspective, which at the outset included her voice as well, for "such language is so pervasive that even she who will criticize it cannot help being infected by it" (92). I agree with Parker, but I think the poem plays out this "infection" even as the speaker poses herself against it.

10   Parker similarly reads this "fabrication" of nature as the speaker's revelation of the initial "objective" natural world as a feminization of nature that constitutes an objectification of the feminine (92). Yet the tenacity of the very fantasies of "untouched nature" that Bishop seeks to expose is evidenced by other critical response to the poem. For both Bromwich (88) and Kalstone (21–22), the "retreat" of the "maddening little women" translates into the immunity of nature from the impositions of language. Of course, the point they are missing is that Bishop regards notions of objective, autonomous nature (not to mention the easy slippage between "women" and "nature") as a naturalization of arbitrary meanings that can have dangerous colonialist consequences.

11   Critics have noted two important sources for the "little women" whose language is birdsong: W. H. Hudson's *Green Mansions,* whose heroine, Rima, is an Indian girl who lives in the forest and sings like a bird; and Clarice Lispector's "The Smallest Woman in the World," which Bishop translated in the winter of 1962–63. In this story, an ethnologist pursues Pygmy women who make animal noises in order to alert each other of danger. See Goldensohn 204; and Lombardi 142–43.

12   While I argue that the double meaning of this passage is crucial to its representation of Bishop's self-division in relation to colonialist rhetoric, critics tend to see one meaning or the other, rather than both. Readers that stress the overt level of meaning see the speaker as offering the children an "enabling and

therefore consoling power" (Goldensohn 42) and recognizing that "each individual has a place" in the house of the world (McCabe 184). Those who focus on the embedded ironic meaning see Bishop as identifying with the children's homelessness (Millier 6) and "formally reprehend[ing] the children's place in the rain" (Harrison 152). Reading Bishop as a master poet seems incompatible with apprehending her representation of her division between assuming and critiquing a vexed mode of power, however "consoling."

13   In an interview with Starbuck, Bishop complains about editorial interference with *Brazil,* indicating that only two-thirds of the writing is her own (313). However, critics agree that the first chapter, which I discuss here, is part of Bishop's two-thirds. Millier, relying on Bishop's unpublished letters, claims in her recent critical biography that Bishop had a "sense of triumph" from "managing to preserve most of the first three chapters of her prose intact" (326). MacMahon, a Bishop bibliographer, asserts that the editorial revisions pertained primarily to the "political chapters" (54), which would not include the first one on "A Warm and Tolerant People." I have also reviewed Bishop's personal copy of the published manuscript, now at Harvard's Houghton Library. This copy has penciled-in revisions throughout, but changes in chapter 1 are limited to a word here and there, apparently aimed at using more precise language.

Moreover, chapter 1 exhibits what I argue is Bishop's persistent concern with resignifying female voices and mother-child relations in her representations of Brazil. These themes occur not only in "Brazil, January 1, 1502" and "Squatter's Children," but also in "Under the Window, Ouro Preto," and the later poems "Pink Dog," "Crusoe in England," and "In the Waiting Room" (the latter two of which I discuss later in this chapter).

14   I am suggesting that Bishop understands this scene of "baby stealing" as one that should expose the arbitrary organization of female reproduction, desire for children, and proper practice of mothering, but instead functions to bolster and renaturalize the patriarchal family. For a similar analysis of how the "Baby M" case, in which adoptive parents are pitted against a biological surrogate mother, both exposes and stimulates dominant family ideology, see Doane and Hodges 67.

15   For an in-depth treatment of United States/Brazil relations in 1961, see Leacock 79–103. For a history of relations leading up to the sixties, see Black 1–17.

16   In her critical biography of Bishop, Millier reports that one of Bishop's complaints against her meddling editors was that they were "dead set on promoting the United States and the democratic future of Brazil" (325).

17   This tension between the speaker's control over what she reads and its control over her has been read as an effort to make the strange conform to familiar terms (Vendler) and as a rather abstract struggle of the poet against received meaning (Pinsky 57). Edelman's very acute account also emphasizes the crucial significances of gender, sexuality, and culture in this tension.

18   See Mazzaro 193; and Edelman 184.

19   "My memory had confused two 1918 issues of the *Geographic.* . . . [T]he African things, it turned out, were in the *next* issue, in March" (Starbuck 318). Edelman points out, however, that the March issue "has no essay about Africa at all" (184).

20 *I Married Adventure* also includes a photograph of Osa holding a Pygmy mother in her arms with the Pygmy woman's children gathered around the pair; Osa grins for the camera while the mother scowls, and the caption points out that "[f]ive-foot Osa lifts a Pygmy, the mother of five children" (330). This photograph may well have struck Bishop as another instance of the colonialist appropriation of the "other" maternal woman that "Waiting Room" renounces.

WORKS CITED

Abel, Elizabeth. "Black Writing, White Reading: Race and the Politics of Feminist Interpretation." *Critical Inquiry* 19.3 (1993): 470–98.
——. *Virginia Woolf and the Fictions of Psychoanalysis.* Chicago: U of Chicago P, 1989.
Alarcon, Norma. "The Theoretical Subject(s) of *This Bridge Called My Back.*" Anzaldua 356–69.
——. "Traddutora, Traditora: A Paradigmatic Figure of Chicana Feminism." Grewal and Kaplan 110–33.
Allen, Paula Gunn. *The Sacred Hoop: Recovering the Feminine in American Indian Traditions.* Boston: Beacon Press, 1986.
——. *Borderlands — La Frontera: the New Mestiza.* San Francisco: Spinsters/Aunt Lute, 1987
Ammons, Elizabeth. *Conflicting Stories: American Women Writers at the Turn of the Century.* New York: Oxford UP, 1991.
Anzaldua, Gloria, ed. *Making Face, Making Soul.* San Francisco: Aunt Lute, 1990.
Awkward, Michael. *Inspiriting Influences: Tradition, Revision, and Afro-American Women's Novels.* New York: Columbia UP, 1989.
——, ed. *New Essays on* Their Eyes Were Watching God. Cambridge: Cambridge UP, 1990.
Benhabib, Butler, Cornell, and Fraser. *Feminist Contentions: A Philosophical Exchange.* New York: Routledge, 1995.
Bishop, Elizabeth. *Brazil.* New York: Time, 1962.
——. *The Collected Prose.* New York: Farrar, Straus and Giroux, 1984.
——. *The Complete Poems: 1927–1979.* New York: Farrar, Straus and Giroux, 1980.
——. *Geography III.* New York: Farrar, Straus and Giroux, 1984.
——. *One Art: Letters.* Ed. Robert Giroux. New York: Farrar, Straus and Giroux, 1994.
——. *Questions of Travel.* New York: Farrar, Straus and Giroux, 1965.
——. "To Aunt Grace." 26 Aug. 1961. *One Art*: 401.
——. "To Pearl Kazin." 13 Aug. 1961. *One Art*: 399–400.
Black, Jan Knippers. *United States Penetration of Brazil.* Philadelphia: U of Pennsylvania P, 1977.

Blake, Nelson Morehouse. *William Mahone of Virginia: Soldier and Political Insurgent.* Richmond: Garrett and Massie, 1935.

Boxwell, D. A. " 'Sis Cat' as Ethnographer: Self-Presentation and Self-Inscription in Zora Neale Hurston's *Mules and Men.*" *African American Review* 26.4 (1992): 605–17.

Bromwich, David. "Elizabeth Bishop's Dream-Houses." *Raritan* 4.1 (1984): 77–94.

Butler, Judith. *Bodies That Matter.* New York: Routledge, 1993.

———. "Contingent Foundations: Feminism and the Question of 'Postmodernism.' " Butler and Scott 3–21.

———. "For a Careful Reading." Benhabib et al. 127–43.

———. *Gender Trouble.* New York: Routledge, 1990.

Butler, Judith, and Joan Scott, eds. *Feminists Theorize the Political.* New York: Routledge, 1992.

Carby, Hazel V. *Reconstructing Womanhood: The Emergence of the Afro-American Woman Novelist.* New York: Oxford UP, 1987.

Carpenter, Lynette. "Visions of Female Community in Ellen Glasgow's Ghost Stories." *Haunting the House of Fiction: Feminist Perspectives on Ghost Stories by American Women.* Ed. Lynette Carpenter and Wendy Kolmar. Knoxville: U of Tennessee P, 1991.

Carter, Dan T. *Scottsboro: A Tragedy of the American South.* Baton Rouge: Louisiana State UP, 1969.

Cassidy, Thomas. "Janie's Rage: The Dog and the Storm in *Their Eyes Were Watching God.*" *CLA Journal* 36.3 (1993): 260–69.

Chandler, Marilyn R. "Healing the Woman Within: Therapeutic Aspects of Ellen Glasgow's Autobiography." *Located Lives: Place and Idea in Southern Autobiography.* Ed. J. Bill Berry. Athens: U of Georgia P, 1990. 93–106.

Cheung, King-Kok. "The Woman Warrior versus the Chinaman Pacific: Must a Chinese American Critic Choose between Feminism and Heroism?" Hirsch and Keller 234–51.

Chow, Rey. "Postmodern Automatons." Butler and Scott. 101–21.

Collins, Patricia Hill. *Black Feminist Thought: Knowledge, Consciousness, and the Politics of Empowerment.* Boston: Unwin Hyman, 1990.

Crenshaw, Kimberle. "Whose Story Is It, Anyway? Feminist and Antiracist Appropriations of Anita Hill." Morrison 402–40.

Dailey, Jane. "Race, Sex, and Citizenship: Biracial Democracy in Readjuster Virginia, 1879–1883." Diss. Princeton U, 1995.

Darwin, Charles. *The Origin of Species by Means of Natural Selection; or, The Preservation of Favoured Races in the Struggle for Life.* 1859. Ed. J. W. Burrow. Harmondsworth, Eng.: Penguin, 1985.

———. *The Origin of Species by Means of Natural Selection; or, The Preservation of Favoured Races in the Struggle for Life and The Descent of Man and Selection in Relation to Sex.* 1859 and 1871. New York: Modern Library-Random, 1936.

Davies, Kathleen. "Zora Neale Hurston's Poetics of Embalment: Articulating the Rage of Black Women and Narrative Self-Defense." *African American Review* 26 (1992): 147–59.

De Lauretis, Teresa, ed. *Feminist Studies/Critical Studies.* Bloomington: Indiana UP, 1986.

———. *Technologies of Gender.* Bloomington: Indiana UP, 1987.

———. "Upping the Anti (sic) in Feminist Theory." Hirsch and Keller 225–70.

Diehl, Joanne Feit. *Elizabeth Bishop and Marianne Moore: The Psychodynamics of Creativity.* Princeton: Princeton UP, 1993.

Doane, Janice, and Devon Hodges. "Risky Business: Familial Ideology and the Case of Baby M." *Differences* (Winter 1989): 67–82.

Douglass, Frederick. *Narrative of the Life of Frederick Douglass, an American Slave.* 1845. Ed. Houston A. Baker Jr. Harmondsworth: Penguin, 1982.

Du Cille, Ann. "The Intricate Fabric of Feeling, Romance, and Resistance in *Their Eyes Were Watching God.*" Grant 93–108.

———. "The Occult of True Black Womanhood: Critical Demeanor and Black Feminist Studies." *Signs* 19.3 (1994): 591–629.

DuPlessis, Rachel Blau. "Power, Judgment, and Narrative in a Work of Zora Neale Hurston: Feminist Cultural Studies." Awkward 95–123.

Edelman, Lee. "The Geography of Gender: Elizabeth Bishop's 'In the Waiting Room.'" *Contemporary Literature* 26 (1985): 179–96.

Ellis, Havelock. *The Criminal.* London: Scribner's, 1890.

Enloe, Cynthia. *Bananas, Beaches, and Bases: Making Feminist Sense of International Politics.* London: Pandora, 1989.

Fetterly, Judith. "Commentary: Nineteenth-Century American Women Writers and the Politics of Recovery." *American Literary History* 6 (1994): 600–611.

Fisher, Philip, ed. *The New American Studies: Essays from Representations.* Berkeley: U of California P, 1991.

———. Introduction. Fisher vii–xxii.

Forrest, D. W. *Francis Galton: The Life and Work of a Victorian Genius.* New York: Taplinger, 1974.

Franchot, Jenny. "The Punishment of Esther: Frederick Douglass and the Construction of the Feminine." Sundquist 141–65.

Fraser, Nancy. "False Antitheses." Benhabib et al. 59–74.

———. "Pragmatism, Feminism, and the Linguistic Turn." Benhabib, et al. 157–72.

Fraser, Nancy, and Linda J. Nicholson. "Social Criticism without Philosophy: An Encounter between Feminism and Postmodernism." Nicholson 19–38.

Freud, Sigmund. "Female Sexuality." *Sexuality and the Psychology of Love.* New York: Collier-Macmillan, 1963. 194–211.

———. *Leonardo da Vinci: A Psychosexual Study of Infantile Reminiscence.* Trans. A. A. Brill. London: Kegan, Trench Trubner, 1922.

———. *On Dreams.* Trans. and ed. James Strachey. New York: Norton, 1952.

Fuss, Diana. *Identification Papers.* New York: Routledge, 1995.

Galton, Francis. *Hereditary Genius: An Inquiry into Its Laws and Consequences.* London: Macmillan, 1869.

———. "Generic Images." *Nineteenth Century* 6 (1879): 157–69.

———. *Inquiries into Human Faculty and Its Development.* London: Macmillan, 1883.

Gates, Henry Louis, Jr. "'Dis and Dat': Dialect and the Descent." *Figures in Black: Words, Signs, and the "Racial" Self.* New York: Oxford UP, 1987. 167–95.

———, ed. *"Race," Writing, and Difference.* Chicago: U of Chicago P, 1987.

———, ed. *Reading Black, Reading Feminist: A Critical Anthology.* New York: Meridian-Penguin, 1990.

——. *The Signifying Monkey: A Theory of African-American Literary Criticism.* New York: Oxford UP, 1988.

——. "A Tragedy of Negro Life." Hughes and Hurston 5–24.

Gates, Henry Louis, and K. A. Appiah, eds. *Zora Neale Hurston: Critical Perspectives, Past and Present.* New York: Amistad, 1993.

Giddings, Paula. "The Last Taboo." Morrison 441–65.

Gilbert, Sandra, and Susan Gubar. *Madwoman in the Attic: The Woman Writer and the Nineteenth-Century Imagination.* New Haven: Yale UP, 1979.

Glasgow, Ellen. *Barren Ground.* 1925. San Diego: Harvest/Harcourt Brace Jovanovich, 1985.

——. "Feminism." 1913. J. R. Raper 26–36.

——. " 'My Fellow Virginians.' " J. R. Raper 53–67.

——. "No Valid Reason against Giving Votes to Women: An Interview." 1913. J. R. Raper 19–26.

——. "A Reasonable Doubt: What I Believe." J. R. Raper 219–27.

——. "Some Literary Woman Myths." J. R. Raper. 36–45.

——. *Virginia.* New York: Doubleday, Page, 1913.

——. *The Voice of the People.* New York: Doubleday, Page, 1900.

——. *The Voice of the People.* Ed. W. L. Godshalk. New Haven: College and University P, 1972.

——. *The Woman Within.* New York: Harcourt, Brace, 1954.

Glassman, Steven, and Kathryn Lee Seidel, eds. *Zora in Florida.* Orlando: U of Central Florida P, 1991.

Goldensohn, Lorrie. *Elizabeth Bishop: The Biography of a Poetry.* New York: Columbia UP, 1992.

Goodman, James E. *Stories of Scottsboro.* New York: Pantheon, 1994.

Grant, Alice Morgan, ed. *All about Zora: Views and Reviews by Colleagues and Scholars.* Winter Park, Fl.: Four-G, 1990.

Grewal, Inderpal. "Autobiographic Subjects and Diasporic Locations: *Meatless Days* and *Borderlands.*" Grewel and Kaplan 231–54.

Grewel, Inderpal, and Caren Kaplan, eds. *Scattered Hegemonies: Postmodernity and Transnational Feminist Practices.* Minneapolis: U of Minnesota P, 1994.

Hall, Jacquelyn Dowd. *Revolt against Chivalry: Jessie Daniel Ames and the Women's Campaign against Lynching.* New York: Columbia UP, 1979.

Haller, Mark H. *Eugenics: Hereditarian Attitudes in American Thought.* New Brunswick, N.J.: Rutgers UP, 1963.

Harrison, Victoria. *Elizabeth Bishop's Poetics of Intimacy.* Cambridge: Cambridge UP, 1993.

Hartsock, Nancy. "Foucault on Power: A Theory for Women?" Nicholson 157–75.

——. "Rethinking Modernism." *Cultural Critique* 7 (Fall 1987): 187–206.

Hemenway, Robert. "Account from His Biography of Zora Neale Hurston." Hughes and Hurston 161–88.

Hirsch, Marianne, and Evelyn Fox Keller, eds. *Conflicts in Feminism.* New York: Routledge, 1990.

Hofstadter, Richard. *Social Darwinism in American Thought.* Rev. ed. New York: Braziller, 1959.

hooks, bell. "Critical Interrogation: Talking Race, Resisting Racism." *Yearning* 51–56.

———. "Postmodern Blackness." *Yearning* 23–32.

———. "Representations: Feminism and Black Masculinity." *Yearning* 65–78.

———. *Yearning: Race Gender and Cultural Politics*. Boston: South End, 1990.

Hughes, Langston. *The Big Sea*. New York: Knopf, 1940.

———. "Letter to Arthur Spingarn." 21 Jan. 1931. Hughes and Hurston 229–39.

Hughes, Langston, and Zora Neale Hurston. *Mule Bone*. Ed. George Houston Bass and Henry Louis Gates Jr. New York: Harper Collins, 1991.

Huie, William Bradford. *Ruby McCollum: Woman in the Suwanee Jail*. New York: Dutton, 1956.

Hurston, Zora Neale. "The Bone of Contention." Hughes and Hurston 25–39.

———. "1st Day in Court." *Pittsburgh Courier* 11 Oct. 1952: 1+.

———. "Folds of Fate Were Closing In." *Pittsburgh Courier* 18 Apr. 1953: 2.

———. *Jonah's Gourd Vine*. 1934. New York: Harper Collins, 1990.

———. "The Life of Mrs. Ruby J. McCollum! (Third Installment)" *Pittsburgh Courier* 14 Mar. 1953: 2.

———. "The Life of Mrs. Ruby J. McCollum! (Sixth Installment)" *Pittsburgh Courier* 4 Apr. 1953: 4.

———. "The Life of Mrs. Ruby J. McCollum! (Ninth Installment)" *Pittsburgh Courier* 25 Apr. 1953: 3.

———. *Mules and Men*. 1935. New York: Harper Collins, 1990.

———. *Seraph on the Suwanee*. New York: Harper Collins, 1991.

———. *Their Eyes Were Watching God*. Chicago: U of Illinois P, 1978.

James, William. *The Principles of Psychology*. Chicago: Encyclopaedia Britannica, 1952.

Johnson, Barbara. "Metaphor, Metonymy, and Voice in *Their Eyes Were Watching God*." *Black Literature and Literary Theory*. Ed. Henry Louis Gates Jr. New York: Routledge, 1984.

———. "Thresholds of Difference: Structures of Address in Zora Neale Hurston." *"Race," Writing, and Difference*. Gates 317–28.

Johnson, Osa. *I Married Adventure*. New York: Lippincott, 1940.

Kalstone, David. "Elizabeth Bishop: Questions of Memory, Questions of Travel." Schwartz and Estees 3–31.

Kaplan, Carla. "The Erotics of Talk: 'That Oldest Human Longing' in *Their Eyes Were Watching God*." *American Literature* 67.1 (1995): 115–42.

Klein, Melanie. *Contributions to Psycho-Analysis, 1921–1945*. London: Hogarth, 1950.

———. "A Contribution to the Psychogenesis of Manic-Depressive States." 1935. *Contributions* 282–310.

———. "Infantile Anxiety-Situations Reflected in a Work of Art and in the Creative Impulse." 1929. *Contributions* 227–35.

———. *Love, Guilt and Reparation and Other Works, 1921–1945*. Vol. 1. New York: Free Press, 1975.

———. "The Oedipus Complex in the Light of Early Anxieties." 1945. *Contributions* 339–90.

———. *The Psychoanalysis of Children*. Trans. Alix Strachey. New York: Grove, 1960.

———. "Weaning." 1936. *Love, Guilt and Reparation* 290–305.

Leacock, Ruth. *Requiem for Revolution: The United States and Brazil, 1961–1969.* Kent, Ohio: Kent State UP, 1990.

Lombardi, Marilyn May. *The Body and the Song: Elizabeth Bishop's Poetics.* Carbondale: Southern Illinois UP, 1995.

Lubiano, Wahneema. "Black Ladies, Welfare Queens, and State Minstrels: Ideological War by Narrative Means." Morrison 323–63.

McCabe, Susan. *Elizabeth Bishop: Her Poetics of Loss.* University Park: Pennsylvania State UP, 1994.

McCarthy, Kevin M. "Three Legal Entanglements of Zora Neale Hurston." *Zora in Florida.* Ed. Steve Glassman and Kathryn Lee Seidel. Orlando: U of Central Florida P, 1991. 174–182.

McDowell, Deborah E. "Reading Family Matters." Wall 73–97.

McDowell, Frederick P. W. "Ellen Glasgow and the Art of the Novel." *Philological Quarterly* 30 (1951): 328–47.

McKay, Nellie Y. " 'Crayon Enlargements of Life': Zora Neale Hurston's *Their Eyes Were Watching God* as Autobiography." Awkward 51–70.

———. "Remembering Anita Hill and Clarence Thomas: What Really Happened When One Black Woman Spoke Out." Morrison 269–89.

MacMahon, Candace. W. *Elizabeth Bishop: A Bibliography, 1927–1979.* Charlottesville: U of Virginia P, 1980.

Martin, Biddy. "Feminism, Criticism, and Foucault." *Feminism and Foucault: Reflections on Resistance.* Ed. Irene Diamond and Lee Quinby. Boston: Northeastern UP, 1988. 3–20.

———. "Sexual Practice and Changing Lesbian Identities." *Destabilizing Theory: Contemporary Feminist Debates.* Ed. Michelle Barrett and Anne Phillips. Stanford: Stanford UP, 1992. 93–119.

Martin, Biddy, and Chandra Talpade Mohanty. "Feminist Politics: What's Home Got to Do with It?" De Lauretis 191–212.

Mazzaro, Jerome. *Postmodern American Poetry.* Urbana: U of Illinois P, 1980.

Michaels, Walter Benn. *Our America: Nativism, Modernism and Pluralism.* Durham, N.C.: Duke UP, 1995.

Miller, Nancy K. "Changing the Subject: Authorship, Writing, and the Reader." De Lauretis 102–20.

Millier, Brett C. *Elizabeth Bishop: Life and the Memory of It.* Berkeley: U of California P, 1993.

Modleski, Tania. *Feminism without Women.* New York: Routledge, 1991.

Mohanty, Chandra Talpade. "Under Western Eyes: Feminist Scholarship and Colonial Discourses." Mohanty, Russo, and Torres 51–80.

Mohanty, Chandra Talpade, Ann Russo, and Lourdes Torres, eds. *Third World Women and the Politics of Feminism.* Bloomington: Indiana UP, 1991.

Moore, James T. "Black Militancy in Readjuster Virginia, 1879–1883." *Journal of Southern History* 41.2 (1975): 167–86.

Moraga, Cherrie. "From a Long Line of Vendidas: Chicanas and Feminism." De Lauretis 173–90.

Morrison, Toni. "Introduction: Friday on the Potomac." Morrison vii–xxx.

———, ed. *Race-ing Justice, En-gendering Power.* New York: Pantheon, 1992.

Mouffe, Chantal. "Feminism, Citizenship, and Radical Democratic Politics." Butler and Scott 369–84.

Newton, Judith Lowder. "History as Usual? Feminism and the 'New Historicism.'" Veeser 152–67.

Nicholson, Linda, ed. *Feminism/Postmodernism*. New York: Routledge, 1990.

———. Introduction. Nicholson 1–16.

Painter, Nell Irvin. "Hill, Thomas, and the Use of Racial Stereotype." Morrison 200–214.

Parker, Robert Dale. *The Unbeliever: The Poetry of Elizabeth Bishop*. Chicago: U of Illinois P, 1988.

Paxton, Nancy L. *George Eliot and Herbert Spencer: Feminism, Evolutionism, and the Reconstruction of Gender*. Princeton: Princeton UP, 1991.

Pearson, Charles Chilton. "The Readjuster Movement in Virginia." New Haven: Yale UP, 1917.

Pinsky, Robert. "The Idiom of a Self: Elizabeth Bishop and Wordsworth." Schwartz and Estess 49–60.

Porter, Carolyn. "What We Know That We Don't Know: Remapping American Literary Studies." *American Literary History* 6 (1994): 467–526.

Radford-Hall, Sheila. "Considering Feminism as a Model for Social Change." De Lauretis 157–72.

Rampersand, Arnold. "Account from His Biography of Langston Hughes." Hughes and Hurston 189–211.

Raper, Arthur F. *The Tragedy of Lynching*. New York: Negro Universities P, 1933.

Raper, Julius Rowan, ed. *Ellen Glasgow's Reasonable Doubts: A Collection of Her Writings*. Baton Rouge: Louisiana State UP, 1988.

———. *From the Sunken Garden: The Fiction of Ellen Glasgow, 1916–1945*. Baton Rouge: Louisiana State UP, 1980.

———. *Without Shelter: The Early Career of Ellen Glasgow*. Baton Rouge: Louisiana State UP, 1971.

Roberts, John W. *From Trickster to Badman: The Black Folk Hero in Slavery and Freedom*. Philadelphia: U of Pennsylvania P, 1989.

Romero, Lora. "Vanishing Americans: Gender, Empire, and New Historicism." *American Literature* 63 (1991): 386–404.

Sanchez-Eppler, Karen. "Bodily Bonds: The Intersecting Rhetoric of Feminism and Abolition." Fisher 228–59.

———. *Touching Liberty: Abolition, Feminism and the Politics of the Body*. Berkeley: U of California P, 1993.

Sandoval, Chela. "U.S. Third World Feminism: The Theory and Method of Oppositional Consciousness in the Postmodern World." *Genders* 10 (Spring 1991): 1–24.

Sanger, Margaret. "Is Race Suicide Probable?" *Collier's* 15 Aug. 1925: 25.

———. *Women and the New Race*. New York: Brentano's, 1920.

Santas, Joan Foster. *Ellen Glasgow's American Dream*. Charlottesville: UP of Virginia, 1965.

Saunders, Catherine. *Writing the Margins: Edith Wharton, Ellen Glasgow, and the Literary Tradition of the Ruined Woman*. Cambridge, Mass.: Harvard UP, 1987.

Sawicki, Jana. *Disciplining Foucault*. New York: Routledge, 1991.

Schwartz, Lloyd, and Sybill P. Estess, eds. *Elizabeth Bishop and Her Art*. Ann Arbor: U of Michigan P, 1983.

Scura, Dorothy. "A Knowledge of the Heart: Ellen Glasgow, the Woman's Movement, and Virginia." *American Literary Realism* 22.2 (1990): 30–43.

Sedgwick, Eve Kosofsky. *Epistemology of the Closet*. Berkeley: U of California P, 1990.

Showalter, Elaine, ed. *The New Feminist Criticism: Essays on Women, Literature, and Theory*. New York: Pantheon, 1985.

Silverman, Kaja. *The Acoustic Mirror: The Female Voice in Psychoanalysis and Cinema*. Bloomington: Indiana UP, 1988.

——. *Male Subjectivity at the Margins*. New York: Routledge, 1992.

——. *The Threshold of the Visible World*. New York: Routledge, 1996.

Smith, Barbara. "Toward a Black Feminist Criticism." Showalter 168–85.

Smith, J. David, and K. Ray Nelson. *The Sterilization of Carrie Buck*. Far Hills, N.J.: New Horizon, 1989.

Smith, Paul. *Discerning the Subject*. Minneapolis: U of Minnesota P, 1988.

Smith, Valerie. "Black Feminist Theory and the Representation of the 'Other.' " Wall 38–57.

——. " 'Loopholes of Retreat': Architecture and Ideology in Harriet Jacobs's *Incidents in the Life of a Slave Girl*." Gates, *Reading Black, Reading Feminist* 212–26.

Spencer, Herbert. "Physical Training." *British Quarterly Review* (April 1859): 362–97.

Spivak, Gayatri Chakravorty. "French Feminism Revisited: Ethics and Politics." Butler and Scott 54–85.

——. "Three Women's Texts and a Critique of Imperialism." *Critical Inquiry* 12.1 (Autumn 1985): 243–61.

Stansell, Christine. "White Feminists and Black Realities: The Politics of Authenticity." Morrison 251–68.

Starbuck, George. " 'The Work!': A Conversation with Elizabeth Bishop." Schwartz and Estess 312–30.

Sundquist, Eric J., ed. *Frederick Douglass: New Literary and Historical Essays*. Cambridge: Cambridge UP, 1990.

Todorov, Tzvetan. " 'Race,' Writing, and Culture." Gates, *"Race," Writing, and Difference* 370–80.

Veeser, H. Aram, ed. *The New Historicism*. New York: Routledge, 1989.

Vendler, Helen. "Domestication, Domesticity, and the Otherworldly." Schwartz and Estess 32–48.

Wagner, Linda W. *Ellen Glasgow: Beyond Convention*. Austin: U of Texas P, 1982.

Wald, Priscilla. "Becoming 'Colored': The Self-Authorized Language of Difference in Zora Neale Hurston." *American Literary History* 2 (1990): 79–100.

Wall, Cheryl A. "Zora Neale Hurston: Changing Her Own Words." Gates and Appiah 76–97.

——, ed. *Changing Our Worlds: Essays on Criticism, Theory, and Writing by Black Women*. New Brunswick: Rutgers UP, 1989.

Wardley, Lynn. "Reassembling Daisy Miller." *American Literary History* 3.2 (1991): 232–54.

Washington, Mary Helen. "Zora Neale Hurston: A Woman Half in Shadow." *I Love Myself When I am Laughing*. Ed. Alice Walker. New York: Feminist, 1979. 7–25.

Wells, Ida B. *Crusade for Justice: The Autobiography of Ida B. Wells*. Ed. Alfreda M. Duster. Chicago: U of Chicago P, 1970.

Wexler, Laura. "Tender Violence: Literary Eavesdropping, Domestic Fiction, and Educational Reform." *The Culture of Sentiment,* Ed. Shirley Samuels. New York: Oxford UP, 1992. 9–39.

Wiegman, Robyn. *American Anatomies: Theorizing Race and Gender*. Durham, N.C.: Duke UP, 1995.

Willis, Susan. *Specifying: Black Women Writing the American Experience*. Madison: U of Wisconsin P, 1987.

Woodward, C. Vann. *Origins of the New South, 1877–1913*. Baton Rouge: Louisiana State UP, 1951.

Yaeger, Patricia. *Honey-Mad Women*. New York: Columbia UP, 1988.

Yarborough, Richard. "Race, Violence, and Manhood: The Masculine Ideal in Frederick Douglass's 'The Heroic Slave.' " Sundquist 166–88.

Zangrando, Robert L. *The NAACP Crusade against Lynching, 1909–1950*. Philadelphia: Temple UP, 1980.

INDEX

Mouffe, Chantal: "Feminism, Citizenship, and Radical Democratic Politics," 162n.3

NAACP (National Association for the Advancement of Colored People), 58–59, 65, 166n.14
National Geographic, 146–48, 150–52
New historicism: and feminist critique of, 6–7, 162n.7; and Glasgow criticism, 79, 84
Newton, Judith Lowder: "History as Usual," 162n.7

Painter, Nell Irvin: "Hill, Thomas, and the Use of Racial Stereotype," 57
Parker, Robert Dale: *The Unbeliever,* 173nn.9 and 10
Patriarchal ideology: and discourses of race and class privilege, 6, 9–12, 78, 81–85, 90–94, 106, 109–114, 119–20, 127–28, 132–33, 137–44, 145–54; and oedipal subjectivity, 10, 103–104, 115–18; and oppositional discourses, 4–5, 8–9, 13–15, 21–22, 28–30, 40–43, 44–48, 62–65; and the regulation of female self-difference, 2–12, 13–14, 16, 21–22, 25–30, 30–32, 37–38, 41–43, 47–51, 78, 80–81, 85–94, 106, 109–114, 116–18, 119–21, 128, 132–34, 143–44, 153, 154–59. *See also* Female subjectivity
Patterson, Haywood, 59–60, 69
Pinsky, Robert: "The Idiom of the Self," 174n.17
Pittsburgh Courier: Hurston's coverage of McCollum trial in, 46, 71–77
Porter, Carolyn: "What We Know That We Don't Know: Remapping American Literary Studies," 162n.8
Poststructuralist feminism: and feminism across social boundaries, 4, 43, 156–57; and a feminist counterhegemony, 155–59; and feminist theories of the subject, 3–6, 13–15, 15–22, 25–30, 30–34, 40–44, 96; and impasses in, 2–6, 13–14, 22–23, 25, 30–33, 35, 40–44, 78, 154, 159
Poststructuralist feminist critics: patriarchal regulation of, 4–6, 14–15,

21–22, 24, 28–30, 40–43; and resistance to patriarchal regulation, 5–6, 12, 14, 22–25, 29–30, 42–43
Price, Victoria, 58–59
Psychoanalysis. *See* Bishop; Freud; Glasgow; Klein

Queer theory: and theories of self-difference, 3

Racial Integrity Act (1924), 105–106, 116
Racism: as authorizing white feminism, 109–118, 148–49; and nonelite white men, 9–10, 79, 94–103; and the Readjustor movement, 98–99, 102; as undermining white feminism, 109–113, 118, 148–49; and white courts, 61–70; white feminist, 24, 26–27, 154, 156–57
Raper, Arthur: *The Tragedy of Lynching,* 166n.12
Raper, J. R.: *Without Shelter,* 79, 83–84, 169nn.6 and 7, 170n.20
Readjustor movement, 10, 81, 97–102, 170n.17
Resignification: and discursive regulation, 3–4; as enabled by dominant discourses, 120, 136–37, 142, 145; valorization of in poststructuralist feminism, 2–3, 13, 15, 155, 162n.2
Roberts, John: *From Trickster to Badman,* 54, 164n.13
Romero, Lora: "Vanishing Americans," 162n.7

Sanchez-Eppler, Karen: *Touching Liberty,* 82, 169n.5
Sandoval, Chela: "U.S. Third World Feminism," 161n.3, 163n.4
Sanger, Margaret: "Race Suicide," 171n.24; *Women and the New Race,* 171n.24
Sawicki, Jana: *Disciplining Foucault,* 161n.1
Scottsboro trials, 8, 45–46, 50, 57–64, 68–72, 74, 76–77, 166–67n.14; antiracist discourses forged by, 58–64; and challenges to racist stereotypes, 57, 72. *See also* Antilynching discourses

Susan Lurie is Associate Professor in the Department of English
at Rice University.

Library of Congress Cataloging-in-Publication Data
Lurie, Susan.
Unsettled subjects : restoring feminist politics to
poststructuralist critique / by Susan Lurie.
p. cm.
Includes bibliographical references and index.
ISBN 0-8223-2003-7 (cloth : alk. paper). —
ISBN 0-8223-1999-3 (pbk. : alk. paper)
1. Feminist literary criticism.   2. Feminism and literature.
3. Women in literature.   4. Minority women in literature.
5. Literature, Modern — Women authors — History and
criticism.   I. Title.
PN98.W64L87   1997
810.9'9287 — dc21   97-3845   CIP